THE
LIFE AND TIMES
OF
Rev. Samuel Patton, D. D.

AND
ANNALS OF THE
HOLSTON CONFERENCE

D. R. M'Anally

HERITAGE BOOKS
2024

HERITAGE BOOKS

AN IMPRINT OF HERITAGE BOOKS, INC.

Books, CDs, and more—Worldwide

For our listing of thousands of titles see our website
at
www.HeritageBooks.com

A Facsimile Reprint
Published 2024 by
HERITAGE BOOKS, INC.
Publishing Division
5810 Ruatan Street
Berwyn Heights, MD 20740

St. Louis:
Printed at the Methodist Book Depository.
1859

— Publisher's Notice —
In reprints such as this, it is often not possible to remove
blemishes from the original. We feel the contents of this
book warrant its reissue despite these blemishes and
hope you will agree and read it with pleasure.

International Standard Book Number
Paperbound: 978-0-7884-7736-2

PREFACE.

To write a Preface, and do it properly, is often the most difficult task pertaining to the work of book-making; and yet custom,
if nothing else, requires a Preface should be written. Once it
was common to find in every book a Dedication, Preface and
Introduction; and, although it is not as uniform now as heretofore, the custom still prevails to some extent, and at least a
Preface or Introduction accompanies almost every volume sent
forth. Something more than custom, however, requires that
the volume now introduced to the public be prefaced by a few
remarks.

Soon after the death of the late Dr. PATTON, a number of
his personal friends, together with the members of his surviv-
ing family, earnestly solicited the present writer to prepare
such sketches of the life and times of the deceased as his means
and ability would allow; and, though the proposition was favorably entertained, the work was not fully resolved on, until after
the Holston Annual Conference had, by a formal vote unani-
mously passed, urged a similar request. Under these circumstances, he did not feel at liberty to decline the effort, however greatly he mistrusted his ability to do full justice to the

subject. A high regard both for the memory of the deceased
and for the friends, and especially the Conference making the
request, left him no alternative but to undertake the work, and
do tho best he could.

The private papers of Dr. PATTON which came into the
writer's hands were very few, and these few had, for the most
part, little or no direct reference to himself; and the following
pages have been prepared mainly with such aids as the personal
recollections of the writer and other friends of the deceased
could afford.

To a brother of Dr. PATTON's—Rev. E. Patton, of Alabama—is the writer indebted for almost all his information
concerning the earlier history of the subject of his sketches.

A singular delay in the transportation of the papers from
Tennessee to Missouri, caused a corresponding delay in the appearance of this volume. Those papers did not reach the
writer for nearly twelve months after they had been started on
their way ; consequently the volume is sent out full twelve
months later than otherwise would have been the case.

In giving some account of the life and labors of Dr. PATTON,
special care has been given to secure accuracy ; and, although
much has been omitted which might have been said, it is believed that what is stated may be regarded as entirely reliable.

In preparing the Annals of the Holston Conference, the
writer was also particular to have all the names and dates as
correctly given as it was possible ; but, with all his care, one
or two slight errors escaped attention, until too late to correct
them. These will hereafter be corrected, and some blanks,
where statistics should have appeared, will also be filled, as the

data from which to fill them came to hand too late for the present edition.

In referring to the circumstances connected with the labors of the subject of the following sketches, honest efforts were made to do full justice to all parties, and especially not to express aught, even of truth, in a manner that might wound the feelings of Christian people, or be construed in any way contrary to the spirit of true Christian charity.

In reference to the introduction and early history of Methodism in the Holston country, the reader will here find many facts and suggestions not likely to be met with elsewhere; and the entire volume, as it is, is now sent out with a hope it may prove acceptable to those at whose suggestion, and by whose request, it was written, and be of some service, also, to the general reader.

D. R. M.

St. Louis, Mo., *April*, 1859.

CONTENTS

CHAPTER I.

CHAPTER II.

CHAPTER III.

CHAPTER IV.

CHAPTER V.

CHAPTER VI.

CHAPTER VII.

CHAPTER VIII.

CHAPTER IX.

CHAPTER X.

CHAPTER XI.

CHAPTER XII.

viii

 CONTENTS.

CHAPTER XIII.

CHAPTER XIV.

APPENDIX.

LIFE AND TIMES

OF

SAMUEL PATTON, D. D.

CHAPTER I.

INTRODUCTORY.

SEC. 1—*South Carolina and South Carolinians.*

THE first settlers of any country mould the character
and shape the manners of the people through many
subsequent generations. The hardy, iron-nerved and
iron-willed Puritans left the impress of their character
on the people of New England. The descendants of
the old Cavaliers, through the training their fathers
gave them, gained for Virginia the *sobriquet* of Old
Dominion — the Mother of Presidents ; and the people
of South Carolina still retain the lessons of patriotism,
urbanity, hospitality and refinement taught them by
the old French Huguenots, who, rather than submit to
the injustice and cruelties an arrogant priesthood and
a persecuting Church threatened to inflict upon them,
left home and friends, and all the worldly man holds

dear, and planted themselves in that inviting country, where they might enjoy religious liberty, worship their Maker agreeably to their own sense of propriety and dictates of conscience, and train their families in a purer and more scriptural form of religion.

The Huguenots of France, and the Seceders and Covenanters of Scotland, Ireland and England, were the leaders and the majority in the settlement of the colony of South Carolina; and never was there collected together a better material of which to make a prosperous community and an independent and noble State. Scorning oppression, and seeing no prospect of being relieved from it where they were, they fled to another, a far-off and untried country, to enjoy what was denied them in the land of their fathers; and from the early settlement of the colony to the present day, the country there has borne the impress of their daring spirits, cultivated minds, and refined manners.

The calm, unprejudiced reader of American history may well wonder why so much has been said and written of the noble spirit and daring deeds of the pilgrim fathers, and so little notice taken of those early settlers in the South, who fled from persecutions far more bitter and cruel than ever followed the Puritans, and endured hardships more severe than they. No such persecutions as were poured upon the French Huguenots ever followed the Puritans; nor did they ever experience such injustice, cruelty and hardships. Did they come to the wilds of America for the sake of civil and religious liberty? So it has been affirmed, thousands of times, though it is somewhat difficult for the reader of history to ascertain what liberty or what religious privileges they desired beyond what they enjoyed in Holland previously to their emigration to America. In England they had been engaged in a fierce and bitter contest for civil power — had been defeated — were not willing to submit to their opponents, who were superior in numbers; consequently they left, first for Holland, and then for America. The expatriation of the Huguenots was under very different circumstances. Their persecutions were of a different and a severer kind; and they left the land of their birth, not that they disliked it, nor that they sought to control the affairs of civil government, nor yet because they desired to form a new government, modeled agreeably to their own peculiar and strange notions, but left for "conscience' sake." They were compelled either to leave, abandon their religion, or suffer all the cruelties the Romish Church could inflict upon them. The two latter alternatives they did not choose, so the first was all that remained. And when they reached this country, they were, from the first, quiet, law-abiding citizens. The restless spirit of innovation, always characteristic of the Puritans, never pervaded them. They sought only their rights, and with these they were content. Indifferent as to whether they were or were not lauded by the historian, poet and orator, they pursued calmly the even tenor of their way, content to be right and do right, whether praise or blame should follow. Hence, in the revolutionary struggle, they were true Whigs, ready to suffer and die for their country's rights and their country's good. The Tories of South Carolina — and there were many of them — belonged to that class whom large land-holders had induced to immigrate to this country, under promise of pecuniary reward — men who belonged to the unsettled, floating class of the population at home, had but little to lose, and were ready to catch at any prospect of gain — men, unsettled in mind and habits, who acted more from impulse, whim, caprice or outward circumstances, than from settled convictions of right and duty. Such are to be found everywhere, and, though they may claim the right of private judgment, they seldom exercise what they claim ; and, being long accustomed to be guided by those to whom they look for example, find it difficult to break off old associations of thought and feeling, and are, consequently, slow to adopt or enter upon new plans or new modes of action. Such were the Tories of the South, in the American Revolution. They were the parasites of others ; and their long habits of obedience, accompanied, of course, with a corresponding feeling, caused them to shudder at the idea of revolting against their king. They had depended upon others—lived to serve and obey others— and rebellion against the king was, in their estimation, the greatest of crimes, justly exposing the perpetrators to the greatest of punishments. But with the Huguenots, the Covenanters and Seceders, it was otherwise. They had trained themselves to think ; and though their heads were often wrong, their hearts were right. They desired the right, and, as far as they could judge of it, sought, maintained and defended it with all their powers ; consequently their names and deeds form so bright a page in American history ; and, if the time ever come when their full meed of praise is given, and they occupy the place in the written history of this country their excellencies, merits and deeds deserve, they will far outshine their Puritan brethren. Compared with the latter, they had as many virtues, and fewer faults. There was in them as much to admire, as much to imitate, and far less of which their posterity may justly be ashamed, or over which good men may grieve. As they were less ambitious of temporal power, so they were less ambitious of fame; and neither they or their descendants took the pains to have their deeds proclaimed and their praises sung, that seem to have been taken by their more northerly brethren. The relation of the two classes may be illustrated — not inaptly, either — by the fable of the huntsman and the lion. These contended, each for the superiority of his race over the other — the man over the lion, and the lion over the man. At length the huntsman proposed to decide the controversy by reference to a work of art which he knew, and accordingly conducted the lion to where a sculptor had represented a contest between a hunter and one of the kings of the forest. The lion was down, and the hunter astride him. "There," exclaimed the huntsman, "there is proof that man is the superior of the lion." "Aye," said the lion; "let us be the sculptors, and we will represent it the other way. We will show the lion astride the man." In the case under notice, the Puritans and their descendants have been the sculptors, and have shown things according to their own notions — represented them in a light of their own creation; but were the others to speak, or rather were what they have spoken listened to, the aspect of affairs would be changed. Few names that adorn the pages of American history deserve higher consideration than those of the Laurenses, Pinckneys, Lees, Rutledges, and others of the same State, associated with them in founding, defending and sustaining this Republic. And, in later days, South Carolina has sent forth many men, in all the departments of mental labor, of whom any country and any people might justly be proud.

It was, perhaps, the misfortune — certainly not the fault — of some of them, that they were half a century in advance of the age in which they lived, consequently were not appreciated as they deserved, nor as they will be when time shall have carried away the prejudice that was excited against them personally, and shall also have mellowed that acerbity of feeling produced by partisan strife, and for partisan purposes; and, notwithstanding all the reproaches, obloquy and abuse heaped on South Carolinians, the future candid historian will award to them the credit of being among the very first of all this nation, in all those qualities that constitute the true, dignified gentleman and genuine patriot.

Sec. 2—*Parentage and Family Connections.*

It has been said of Napoleon Bonaparte, that, when sadly viewing the consequences of the infidelity which for years had reigned in France — when he contemplated the individual licentiousness, the social wretchedness, and the political ruin it had brought upon that people — he asked one of his wisest counselors, " What can be done for France ? The present generation seems hopelessly gone. What can be done for the next? What is wanted to train them to a better state of things, and bring them back from this wretched condition?" The short, but significant, reply was "*Mothers*." The right sort of mothers will usually train sons in the right way. The cause of truth and righteousness — the welfare of the country and the prosperity of the Church of God — will be secured and advanced in every place where mothers are well informed, intelligent and pious. A good man once said, " When I was a child, my mother used to bid me kneel beside her, and placed her hand on my head while she prayed. Ere I was old enough to know her worth, she died, and I was left to my own guidance. Like others, I was inclined to evil passions, but often felt myself checked, and, as it were, drawn back by the soft hand upon my head. When I was a young man, I traveled in foreign lands, and was exposed to many temptations; but when I would have yielded, that *same hand was upon my head*, and I was saved. I seemed to feel its pressure, as in the days of my happy infancy, and sometimes there came with it a voice in my heart — a voice that must be obeyed — ' O, do not this wickedness, my son, nor sin against thy God.' "

An elegant writer has said, " I believe that if Christianity should be compelled to flee from the mansions of the great, the academies of the philosophers, the halls of legislators, or the throng of busy men, we should find her last and purest retreat with woman at the fireside. Her last altar would be the female heart ; her last audience would be the children gathered around the knees of a mother ; her last sacrifice, the secret prayer escaping in silence from her lips, and heard, perhaps, only at the throne of God."

Happy the country where pious mothers train the youth, and happy the youth who are blessed with mothers that fear God, work righteousness, and train them aright.

Like those of young Timothy, the mother and the grandmother of the subject of these sketches may be referred to as having taught him the fear of God and the ways of truth ; and to them he was mainly indebted for those sound principles of moral and Christian conduct that guided him through life, and enabled him to wield so great a moral influence over his fellow-men. He received, as will hereafter be seen, the right kind of instruction, at the right time ; and, once started right, it was comparatively easy for him to continue, and gather fresh strength at every step, for now and more arduous conflicts. His mother and his paternal and maternal grandmothers, who, for a long time, all lived in the same house, and contributed their joint efforts to mould his mind aright, were all God-fearing, pious women, who deemed it both a duty and a privilege to do what they could to bring up their children in the nurture and admonition of the Lord, and train them for future usefulness and everlasting happiness. The grandmother, on the father's side, and mother were Old Side Presbyterians, and the grandmother, on the mother's side, was a Scotch Seceder — all strict in their adherence to the doctrines and discipline of their Church, and all much given to that excellent practice, too much neglected in later days, of regularly and systematically catechising the children, and thus indoctrinating them in the great truths and fundamental principles of the Christian religion. And this catechising was more than a mere form—more than merely repeating and answering the questions found in the "Shorter Catechism;" but these were accompanied with such explanations, illustrations and applications as the parents were able to give, and the children able to receive. It may be true that, in the great multiplicity of books, and other facilities for communicating knowledge, which characterize the present day, Christians are better informed on general subjects than they were fifty years ago ; but whether they are closer biblical students, and are better acquainted with the doctrines of Christianity, now than then, is very questionable. The preaching of that day was more doctrinal in its character than that of the present day. Private and public discussions on doctrinal points were common. The public mind, having less of other matters to interest and excite it, was more generally turned in this direction, and all who were professedly Christian at all had some well-defined creed. They knew *what* they believed, whether they could or could not give reasons why they believed it.

Grandma Patton, as the children called her, seems to have been quite liberal in her views, considering the period in which she lived, and the influences which had been brought to bear upon her religious training ; while grandma Nichols was as rigid and exclusive as the creed under which she had been brought up. If foiled in argument in reference to any point bearing upon the experience or practice of a Christian, she invariably fell back on her cherished dogma, and announced, in good, broad Scotch, "Weel, if I'm elected, I'll be saved; an if I'm na elected, I'll na be saved." She was none the less diligent, however, in efforts to teach her grandchildren the good and the right way, and have them to walk therein. The other grandmother, entertaining, as intimated, more liberal views, strove diligently to impress the minds of the children with correct views, not only as to the doctrines, but also the experience and practice, of religion. How well she succeeded in this, will be seen as the history progresses.

The Pattons of this country are mostly of Irish descent. So it was with the family to which the subject of these sketches belonged. His grandfather, John Patton, was a Pennsylvanian by birth, twice married, and raised eighteen children. His father, who was also named John, was the youngest of the family born in Pennsylvania; but how long he resided there, or at what time he settled in South Carolina, is unknown to the present writer. His removal, and that of the family, was early enough for them to participate in the struggles, and experience the sufferings, attendant upon the American Revolution. During these times they lost much, as well as suffered and endured much. Both the grandfather and the father were farmers by occupation, and depended on their own labor, under the blessing of Providence, for the means of support for themselves and families. John Patton, Jr., father of the subject of these remarks, was early married to a Miss Nichols, the daughter of a Scotch Seceder, who had immigrated to this country previously to her birth. The parents of both these were strictly pious, particu-

..larly the mother of Mr. Patton, who, as she had long been in widowhood, lived with her son, whom she had carefully trained to the ways of religion. The mother of Mrs. Patton also, after the death of her husband, lived with, or near, the family for many years. Thus the children of John Patton had the advantage of the pious precepts and examples of their own parents and of their grandmothers, on both sides of the house. Of these children there were twelve, two of whom died in infancy. The other ten — eight sons and two daughters — grew up to mature age; but a majority of them passed away previously to the death of Samuel. He was the third son, and was born in Lancaster District, South Carolina, on the 27th of January, 1797.

CHAPTER II.

EARLY TRAINING, PHYSICAL, MENTAL AND MORAL.

To say that children, as well as men, differ, is but to utter a truism which none deny ; and that difference is no greater in configuration of face than in the peculiar traits, aptitudes and susceptibilities of mind. Original genius, though its existence be doubted by some, and denied by others, still exhibits itself in the history of man. An aptness for one branch of learning over others, or a capacity to excel in some particular study, some special branch of mechanism or handicraft work, is by no means uncommon, if indeed such a thing, properly inquired into and properly brought out, would not be found universal. That is to say : Every man is, by nature, better adapted to some one special kind of mental or physical labor than to all other kinds ; and, if rightly trained and applied, his talent for this would always lead him to a greater or less degree of success, and in this particular pursuit he would both serve himself and others better than in any other.

These differences and aptitudes extend to sensitive as well as purely intellective nature, and affect the sensibilities of the heart, as well as the operations of the mind. One is light and cheerful ; another, perhaps equally healthy and vigorous, is sedate, or, it may be, melancholy. One is open and confiding; another, shy and mistrustful. The feelings of one are warm and ardent; those of another, cold and retiring. Then, again, there is a difference in the moral feelings. Though all have suffered by the fall of man, and all inherit a depraved nature, some children are naturally worse than others. Moral qualities, like those of mind and body, are entailed and inherited; and sometimes, like a subterranean stream, moral qualities for good or evil seem to lie dormant for a generation or two, and only break out here and there, as if to prove they still existed, though unseen. Hence, in some very bad families, there is occasionally found along the line of its history one whose virtuous traits and moral excellencies are worthy of all imitation. So, also, of very good families. From them sometimes springs a very prodigy of wickedness and crime.

The ancestral line of the subject of this biography is briefly alluded to in the introductory chapter. So far as is now known, they were a sober, industrious people, who, under the wholesome training of the Churches with which they were connected, cherished great reverence for sacred things, and how much they may or may not have known of the power, they constantly and solemnly maintained much of the forms of a pure, life-giving religion. If any, since the time of the forerunner of our blessed Savior, have, from very infancy, been called to the holy work and office of the ministry, there are reasons to believe Samuel Patton was of the number. The earliest accounts of him refer to his religious impressions and convictions, while

the idea of being a preacher, feeling the responsibilities
and performing the work of the holy office, possessed
and filled his mind from the cradle to the grave. At
three years of age he announced to the parish minister
who was catechising him, that he would be a preacher,
and his shrewd, yet respectful, replies to the questions
of the good man — Rev. John Brown, afterwards Professor in the University at Athens, Georgia — so interested and pleased him that he gave little Sam. a seven-
pence, with which to buy him a book, in order that he
might learn how to preach. At least this was the reason
the minister assigned for the bestowment of the gift.
The book was soon procured, and forthwith the owner
insisted the other children should arrange themselves,
and observe due silence and propriety while he preached.
This he was wont to do frequently. The idea of being
a preacher so thoroughly imbued his mind, that it
seemed to make a part of all his thoughts and feelings,
and interweave itself with all his aspirations and
hopes. When about six years old, after he had learned
to read, during the week he prepared him a house of
clap-boards, arranging it internally somewhat after the
manner of a dwelling, containing his bed, or something to imitate a bed, a table, and a book-case, in
which he put some books, fixed it all up as his study,
and on Sabbath morning, after family prayers and
breakfast, he invited his little brothers to visit him.
They did so. On their arrival they were kindly met
at the door, fraternally saluted, and invited in. They
entered, were seated, and, after a few common-place
questions and answers, such as were usual among
neighbors when they met, little Sammy introduced the

subject of religion, earnestly inquired after their spiritual prosperity, manner of life, and prospects for a better world, and proposed prayers; laid down some books, which he called the Bible and Hymn Book, addressed his brothers, reminding them it was the Lord's day, on which they should be more than ordinarily serious and devout, and asked them, one by one, to lead in prayer. They all respectfully declined. He then inquired if it would be agreeable to them to join him. They assented, and he proceeded, agreeably to the old fashion among Presbyterians, first to sing, then read a chapter, then pray. He sang, then read, after which they all kneeled, and he solemnly repeated the Lord's Prayer. At the close of the services, some other boys came up, ascertained what had been going on, and began to laugh and make sport of him. This conduct drew from him a most indignant rebuke. He told them it was shameful to treat the Lord's day, that had been given them for rest and religious improvement, in such a manner, pointed them to the consequences of sin, and brought truth home to their feelings so forcibly that they were glad to withdraw, and leave him and his brothers alone. Such fraternal meetings and such exercises were common with them.

Soon after this, he got hold of a little book, entitled "History of Cain and Abel," which, as those who have seen it know, contains some very good things. Its accounts of the fall of man, the trouble and sorrows of Adam and Eve, their bitter self-reproaches, the sad wailings and piteous lamentations, the death of Abel, Adam's fleeing to Christ, and his subsequent death, are very touching, and well calculated to affect so sensitive a mind as was that of young Patton. This book was a great favorite. Many of the more touching parts he committed to memory, and, at the meetings just alluded to, or in the fields while at work, he would rehearse them with a heart so full of tenderness—in tones so soft and plaintive, and with tears literally streaming from his eyes—that his little auditors, unable to repress their feelings, would cry most heartily. Everywhere—all the time—the one idea of being a preacher and preparing for that work, clung to him, and shaped and colored almost all he did. Let the reader call this mock seriousness, or attribute it to boyish freaks, if he will; but boyish freaks show the bent of boyish minds and feelings; and, though there may have been much of mock seriousness in such matters, there is no evidence of bad intention. The regard for religion was deep and strong; and there is no doubt, at least in the mind of the writer, but that these services were every whit as acceptable to the great Searcher of hearts as is much of that performed in some modern Churches, where choirs and organs, and readers of dull, dry sermons officiate.

When such impressions as those now alluded to have been once made, and such notions once formed, it is easy to understand how they may be cherished, be strengthened, and become more deep and abiding; but it is sometimes difficult to account for their origin. It is so in this case. What led young Patton to imbibe these feelings at so very early an age, and cherish them through all his life? Was it a mere whim at first? Whims do not usually impress so deeply, or last so long. But, suppose it were but a whim, why should it have taken this particular direction? There is not, in the solemn office and fearful responsibilities of the Christian ministry, that which is likely to captivate the joyous buoyancy of youth; and yet, though he afterwards, agreeably to his own statement, became more worldly in his feelings, fell into sin, and did many things that were wrong, these convictions never left him but temporarily. They would come back. Sometimes, in the midst of mirth and gayety, they would suddenly return with a force that damped his earthly joys, and quite disqualified him for further enjoying the sports and pleasures in which he was engaged. And let it be remembered, it was not so much *a desire* to be a preacher as an abiding conviction that he *ought to be* one. These convictions of duty followed him all the time and everywhere; and, unless they be referred to the Spirit and providence of God, as their direct cause, it must be admitted his was a mind extremely susceptible to the force and power of Divine truth, and on which that truth had taken an unusually deep and firm hold. In some memoranda of his early history, written by himself, he remarks that his earliest impressions were connected with the services of religion at the family altar. It was fortunate for him there was such an altar, and that the services thereof were of that reverent and solemn character thus to impress his mind and, doubtless, to influence his life. It is fortunate for any child thus to be raised; and it is a blessed privilege, in manhood or old age, to look back to the hearthstone scenes of childhood's joyous hours, and associate them with the sweet, solemn worship of Almighty God. Such a blessing is beyond all price.

The longer one lives — the more he sees, and feels, and suffers — the more he prizes such fond recollections. They are oases in the desert of life, or like springs of water welling up in dry and thirsty lands.

. That the convictions alluded to affected the conduct and conversation of young Patton, the reader will not be slow to admit; but their effect was beyond what might, at first view, be supposed. An incident or two will illustrate this: When only seven, or at most eight, years old, he and his brother Edward were passing by the door of the room in which the two grandmothers were sitting, and earnestly discussing the question, whether it be possible for us to know for ourselves that our sins are pardoned and our hearts renewed. Mrs. Patton favored the idea, but Mrs. Nichols denied. The boys paused to listen. The discussion went on for some time, until Mrs. Nichols, foiled in argument, fell back upon her favorite dogma, and exclaimed, " Weel, if I'm elected I'll be saved, and if I'm na elected I'll na be saved." The conversation ceased, and the boys walked on. Soon Samuel remarked, " Brother Ed., grandma ought to know ; but I can't believe that doctrine. Can it be that God would choose to save one, and not another, when neither had done good or evil ? The Book says God is good ; but that doctrine would make him some good and some bad. I can't believe it, and, if ever I preach, I'll never preach that doctrine." That he kept his word in this respect, and did not preach that doctrine, thousands can testify.

Soon after this, he and the same brother Edward — to whom the present writer acknowledges himself indebted for the greater portion of his information in reference to the early history of Samuel — were one evening at the barn, feeding cattle — which formed a part of their evening's work, generally — and, after performing that duty, they fell into conversation in reference to what they had previously heard from their grandmother Nichols, in regard to election. They talked long and earnestly, until at length they began to rehearse to each other what grandmother Patton had taught and tried to impress upon them — how she had taught them to pray, put words in their mouths, urged them to pray in secret, and to have their minds in proper frame, recommended them to look at the moon and stars, think of the heaven they could not see, and the awful punishment awaiting those who lived and died in sin, and to remember God had prepared a heaven for those who loved and served Him, that all must die and go to judgment — and how she had taught them that God would hear and answer their prayers, if they were sincere, and were asked agreeably to His will; that he would pardon their sins, shed abroad His love in their hearts, so they would not be afraid to die, but feel that God was their best friend, and loved them more than all earthly friends could love. These things they talked over, until they became much impressed and greatly moved, and resolved they would henceforth do the best they could to carry out these instructions, particularly in reference to seeking pardon for their sins and peace with God. Accordingly they selected a spot in a thick growth of underbrush, amid a clump of tall pines that stood near the barn, to which they might retire for secret prayer. Thither they went, evening after evening, when the work of the day was over, and, as best they ·could, called upon God, in the name of Him who said, "Suffer little children to come unto me, and forbid them not, for of such is the kingdom of heaven." Happy boys! Mere formalism might have looked coldly — or even sneeringly — on ; rationalism might have ridiculed, and infidelity scoffed ; but ye were blunting the point of many a thorn, and strewing many a flower in the future pathway of life. Ye were then, through grace, spinning cords that should afterwards bind your hearts to the skies, and hold your hopes and affections there, amid many a threatening storm that blew against you. Ye were fortifying yourselves against many bitter adversities ye were subsequently called to pass through, and gathering nourishment that should enable you, in after days, to pass o'er many a desert waste and barren plain.

They continued this practice until, in the language of Edward, in a letter to the present writer, "One evening we grew more earnest. We desired the things we asked for. We wept, confessed our sins, and, in words that seemed to come readily to us, after we had repeated the prayers we had learned by heart, we prayed on earnestly, fervently, importunately. Suddenly a change came o'er us. A strange joy filled our hearts. We were glad. We embraced each other, and thanked the Lord. We thought the moon and stars never before looked so beautiful. The very pine trees looked glad, and seemed to praise the Lord. We felt as though we could never be cross to each other again, disobedient to our parents, or otherwise than good and kind to our little brothers and sisters."

Reader, art thou a Christian? Hast thou passed
from death unto life, and felt the power of redeeming,
saving grace? Then thou understandest all these
little boys felt and expressed. But the narrative continues:

"We greatly desired to tell these things to our
father and mother, but feared they would be displeased.
Our people spoke hardly of the Methodists, for encouraging things like these — especially encouraging them
in children, as they supposed it would lead children to
mock at true religion. Though conscientious, and desirous of being and doing good, they did not then understand these feelings; so we kept them to ourselves,
and continued our prayers. At length, one day, we
got off our guard, while playing with some other boys,
and participated in some mischievous tricks, and indulged in some improper words. When night came,
Samuel said, "Brother Ed., we must not pray to-night.
I would be ashamed to ask the Lord to bless us, after
we have acted so badly. So we gradually left off regular prayers in secret, and prayed only when in sick-
ness or distress."

How much of human nature is here displayed! and
how much, too, of the strategy of the wicked one!
How like the course of many an older person and more
experienced Christian was theirs! What a pity but
that these simple-hearted, sincere, and, no doubt, really
converted little boys had been with some one who
understood their case, and appreciated their feelings,
and could have taken them by the hand, and guarded
them affectionately against this danger and that difficulty or temptation, and when, in a moment of inad-

vertence, they were overcome, to have taken them tenderly under council, and quietly whispered to them, " If any man sin, we have an advocate with the Father." What an incalculable blessing it would have been! Very likely grandma Patton could have done this ; but she, like the father and mother, was, perhaps, kept in ignorance of the true state of their feelings. Alas! these were not all who have suffered spiritual declension and dearth, because they were afraid or ashamed to tell what the Lord had done for them. To conceal religious feeling is a dangerous experiment, try it who will.

Though, for a time, Samuel thus lost his religious enjóyment, he did not lose his religious convictions, or entirely forfeit his religious principles. His subsequent history in respect to these will be traced hereafter. It is proper now to turn aside and consider his boyhood in other aspects in which it presented itself, that the reader may learn as much as possible of him whose biography he is asked to peruse, and whose excellencies of character are presented for his imitation.

Until eighteen years old, young Patton, though small of stature, was remarkably active and sprightly, willing and ready to bear his full part as a laborer in the fields, fond of those athletic exercises in which country boys so frequently and so properly engage, and a good deal given to feats of daring. While in the nineteenth year of his age, he was attacked violently with measles, and, though he pretty safely passed through the attack in the ordinary forms of the disease, yet, by venturing out too soon, he took a cold, which fell upon his lungs, and so affected him that for a long time it was thought he could not recover; nor did he ever entirely recover from the effects. His lungs were weak through all his life subsequently, and he often suffered severely from what was, no doubt, the legitimate effects of this serious attack. But previously to this, his health was good, and he possessed a large share of muscular action and strength. In all his sports and pastimes — in all his boyish tricks and feats of boyish daring — he seems never to have lost sight of his obligations to his Maker and to his parents; and this feeling of obligation influenced him, more or less, in all he did; and he was sometimes wont to refer the mishaps and accidents which befel him to an interposition of Providence, as punishment for his disobedience and misconduct. An instance of this occurred as follows: He was remarkably expert at climbing, and passionately fond of the exercise. A squirrel, or even a bunch of hickory nuts, though at the tops of the tallest trees. was enough to call forth at once his strong propensities to climb. Even were these wanting, he would not unfrequently climb high and difficult trees, and perch himself among the branches, merely through love of the sport. These freaks having been reported to his mother, she, much alarmed for his safety, peremptorily forbid his doing so any more. For a time he was restrained; but one day, discovering some nuts near the top of a tall hickory tree, his propensity to climb overcame his sense of filial obligation, and he started up after the prize. The tree was not only tall, but also difficult to be climbed; but he was expert, resolute and strong, for one of his age (not then more than ten years old), and he pulled and tugged, and tugged and pulled, until

at last he reached the branches. Now his work was
easier, and on he went, until presently he was high up
among the topmost limbs of the tree. Still the nuts
were not in reach. To get them he must go out on one
of the frail branches. So out he crept, until he was
almost in reach of them, when the limb broke short off
at the trunk, and down it and he came together. He
fell ten or twelve feet, when, as he was falling, he suddenly let go the broken limb, and seized another as he
was about to pass it. But he caught this so far from
the trunk of the tree that it bent downwards, and
seemed to promise him but little relief. With wonderful agility, as well as presence of mind, he threw up
his feet, and with them caught the limb nearer to the
trunk of the tree, and then worked himself along,
feet foremost, until the trunk was reached, and he enabled to descend in safety. This narrow escape made
a deep impression upon him. He regarded it as a
warning. It called up to his mind the sin of disobedience of which he was guilty, and led him to resolve
that he would be guilty of the like no more, and, it is
believed, he kept the resolution.

The following incident, which occurred when he was
but a child, illustrates the naturally thoughtful and
contemplative cast of his mind : He did something
which his mother had forbidden, and she corrected
him. He complained that the whipping hurt terribly,
and some time afterwards, when he thought he might
safely expostulate with his mother, he did so, by telling
her that if he were a man, and had a little son, he
would not whip him so hard for so little a thing. On
being asked why, he replied that he would desire his

little son to love him, and feared he could not do so, if he were to whip him so severely. His mother then explained more fully why she had corrected him — not so much because of the value of the things he had destroyed as for his disobedience to her orders — and strove to impress him with the fact that disobedience against the lawful commands of parents was disobedience also against God, and finally told him it was because she loved him, and desired he should be a good and obedient boy, that he had been corrected. This seemed to satisfy him fully, and he promised to be a good boy in future, and declared he loved her the more for her efforts to make him what he ought to be. In this incident was evinced a trait that characterized him all through life. Convince him a thing was right, and, no matter how great the toil or the suffering, he was ready to perform the one, or endure the other. Those who knew him, as did the writer of this, will appreciate this remark. No one trait in his character was more prominent or uniform in its manifestations than this. What is right? was the question of his life, and that influenced his private no less than his public conduct.

In the days of his boyhood, and in the section of country where he was raised, schools were few, and of very imperfect character. Many of those in the country were superintended — if superintendence it may be called — by a class of men as little qualified for this as almost any other pursuit in which they could have engaged. They only professed to teach "reading, writing and ciphering" — the latter as far, it may have been, as the Rule of Three — while a few — not all —

would offer to teach even farther than that.   The
usual text-books were a Primer, or Dilworth's or
Webster's Spelling Book, and a copy of the New Testament ; while those who were sufficiently advanced to
use the Columbian Orator, English Reader, or Scott's
Lessons, were looked upon as having already ranged
pretty widely in the fields of science.   As to Arithmetics, it not unfrequently happened there was not one
in the school, and, if but one, it and the Key thereto
were in the possession of the teacher, who, when he
was not using them himself, kept them carefully locked
away, as though he feared others might chance to become as wise as himself.   The manner of teaching
arithmetic was as follows : The teacher gave the rule—
say for addition, subtraction or multiplication — the
scholars wrote it in their ciphering books, as they were
called ; then the examples to be performed under that
rule were stated by the teacher on the slate of each
pupil, and, without further instructions, the pupils had
to go and perform those examples as best they could,
and as soon as they could.   If they did their work
quickly, unfair play was at once suspected, and the
teacher looked carefully after the Key to his Arithmetic — sometimes plainly intimating that he suspected
the scholars for having got hold of it, and from it
copied the solution to the question stated.   If their
questions were solved in half a day — if they toiled
and fretted over them the entire day, or during two or
three days — no matter ; they must work at them until
they were finished and proven.   If they ventured to
ask for an explanation of this or that, or for instruction as to how this or that was to be done, they were

simply answered with, "*Look at the rule.* What does the rule say?" This was the end. There was no appeal from it; and the puzzled pupil — thus puzzled still the more — had no alternative but to go to his seat *and look at the rule.* The present writer remembers a case which, though it occurred long after the period above referred to, and at a time when it was thought schools had greatly improved, and had teachers much more competent, will, nevertheless, throw some light on the practice of teaching, as pursued in other days. Arithmetics were abundant. Pike, Smiley and others had blessed the world by their labors, and the world enjoyed the blessing. Adams' Geography and Murray's Grammar were even talked of; and yet, with all these facilities and advancements, a timid little girl inquired of her teacher — a man, too, of no mean repute in his profession — why, in the addition of whole numbers, she was required to carry as many units to the next left-hand column as there were tens in the column added. "Why," said old Pedagogus, his eyes staring with wonder, "why! Don't you see *the rule says so?* There it is, as plain as can be. The rule says so — that's why." The pupil was silenced, but not satisfied. The teacher had known no other reason. He had heard or thought of none other. This had satisfied him; and he, doubtless, wondered how any child could be so stupid as to inquire for anything further.

When young Patton was first sent to school, the old *a betsel fa* system of spelling, or rather learning to spell, had not been entirely abandoned, and it is more than likely his first lessons were taught and learned under that system. As every reader may not under-

stand this allusion, a word or two, by way of explanation, may not be out of place. In words of two
syllables, where the first was composed of a single
vowel, the learner was taught to repeat them thus:
a, by itself—a-ble, *bel*, able ; o, by itself—o-ver, *ver*, over ;
and so of others. These, in a hurried articulation, were
soon contracted into—a, *betsel fa*, b-l-e, ble, able ; o, *betsel
fo*, v-e-r, ver, over, and so of the rest. How such a system
was ever introduced, or why it was ever practised, is
difficult, at this time, to determine ; but that the practice did once generally prevail in the common schools
of this country, there can be no reasonable doubt.

In all that is said above, there is no design towards
an intimation that there were no good schools in the
periods referred to, or that scholars were not trained
as thoroughly then as now. There were good schools
then, that trained and turned out good scholars. The
process of attaining to scholarship was slower and
more difficult, the labor more arduous and severe ; but
the rank of good scholarship was then as high, if not
higher, than in more recent times. But it is maintained
that, as the country was but sparsely settled, school-
houses and school-teachers few, the great mass of the
people, particularly those with small or but very moderate means, were favored with very few advantages
for the education of their children. Besides the disadvantages growing out of the want of good teachers
and suitable houses, books were very scarce and high-
priced — so much so that it not unfrequently happened
that the same books had to serve all the children of
the family, if, indeed, they were not then afterwards
loaned to, and used by, children of other families. In

thinly-settled neighborhoods, schools could be had only two or three months in the year. The people, in many places, were not able to have them continue longer, nor were they able to pay an amount sufficient to engage the services of the best teachers, even for that short time. Hence they were compelled to take such as they could employ at a small cost, and for such periods, only, as their limited means would allow. And as many of them were not able to spare the time of their boys after they had grown sufficiently to be useful on the farms, they could only send them to school at intervals, from the age of five to that of ten or twelve years. This is believed to have been the case with Mr. Patton. Samuel, the subject of these sketches, was started to school by himself when about five years of age; his two older brothers being kept at home to work on the farm; and the presumption is, that when he became able to be serviceable on the farm, he was placed there, and the children younger than he took their turn at school. Very little as to his educational advantages has come to the knowledge of the present writer, but all that has been gathered on this point favors the idea that whatever attainments of a scientific or literary character may have been made by him, were made after he had passed the scenes of his school-days. At school he was only enabled to receive instruction in the mere rudiments of learning— only taught how to begin to acquire knowledge; but that he made a most excellent use of these beginnings, and carried them out to most profitable results, will appear as the reader proceeds with his subsequent history.

As he was sent to school when but five years old —
had to go by himself, and the school-house a mile distant from his father's — it is not strange that he should
have manifested some reluctance toward the undertaking. This, however, was easily overcome by his father
telling him that he could not possibly be a preacher,
unless he went to school and learned. Another difficulty in his way was, the teacher was known to belong
to that class who seem to have entertained the idea,
that the quickest and easiest way to get learning into
a boy's head is by a counter irritation produced by
the rod or ferule ; and little Samuel feared he might
incur his displeasure, and suffer the usual penalty.
This difficulty was overcome by his father charging
him to tell the teacher, or master, as it was then usual
to call such, that he must not whip him, for he was
daddy's own little son. This was satisfactory to the
little fellow, and away he tripped to school. Things
went on very well for some time ; but after a few
weeks, when he had become somewhat familiar with
the place and people, or, as another little fellow once
expressed it, got the hang of the school-house and the
things therein contained, he was more at ease — more
free and less watchful. So one day, when he had given
way to a passion for some childish pranks, the teacher
struck him keenly across the legs with a limber rod.
Immediately he sprang up on a bench, and exclaimed,
in his usual manner—for then he lisped prodigiously—
" O grathuth, mathy, it duth hurt too bad. Mither
Lethley, I can't sthand it. You muth not whip me, for
I'm daddeth thun !" This threw the whole school —
teacher and all — into a most uncontrollable fit of

laughter, which continued for some time. Soon after this, Mr. Lesley, the teacher, who, it seems, boarded round with the scholars, went home with his lisping pupil to spend the night. As the evening wore away, something was said about family prayers, when Mr. Lesley remarked, "Sam. ought to pray, for he is a sinner, and made all the school laugh." Upon this, Sammy turned to his father, with — "Daddy, mather ought to pray, too, for he ith the bigeth thinner of any of uth. He laughed the loudeth!" "O, then," said the teacher, "I will have to employ you to pray for me, as you are to be a preacher; but you are so tongue-tied, I am afraid it will be a poor prayer." Sam. paused a moment, and then replied, "Thumtime my tongue will get looth, and then I'll pray for thinnerth, and preach, too."

Though his educational advantages were very limited, he early contracted a taste for reading, which was so cultivated, even in boyhood, that he eagerly devoured whatever he could lay hands on, in the way of books; and, from comparative infancy, he would, almost at any time, deny himself the pleasure of the company and sports of other boys, for the sake of reading some new or interesting book. Among his favorites were such as "Valentine and Orson," "Fairy Tales," "Charlotte Temple," and "Robinson Crusoe." But that which most interested and pleased his childish fancy was the "Pilgrim's Progress" — a work that has charmed and instructed thousands and millions, of all ages, and of both sexes. This he read, and re-read, with a thrilling interest he felt in reference to no other book; and from it he seems, at a very early age, to

have drawn lessons of wholesome instruction, that were
useful to him throughout the whole of his subsequent
life. This kind of writing, more, than any other,
always interested and delighted him. It may be said
he was passionately fond of the allegorical, especially
when it illustrated the experience or practice of the
Christian. There was in his natural cast and temperament of feeling something which well accorded with
productions of this character. Montgomery's " Wan-
derer of Switzerland " was always a great favorite
with him. His nature was sensitive, and well attuned
to the pathetic, especially when expressed in numbers.
Elegiac and lyric poetry were his delight. Of a mild
and gentle nature himself, he loved whatever was mild
and gentle, and delighted greatly in those productions
that touched the sympathies, and awoke in the human
breast those sacred and mellowing emotions that no
only tend to ennoble the nature, but also to lead man
to feel for, and suffer with, his fellow-man everywhere.
This peculiarity of his nature he cherished all through
life ; and, while it was evident to all who knew him
that he had a head that could think clearly and
forcibly, he had also a heart that could feel deeply and
tenderly ; so that while, in after life, he was a safe
counselor, he was, at the same time, a true friend—one
who might be trusted, and in whom reliance could
always be placed. He was not fickle, but pitied and
prayed for the erring and the wrong-doer, and loved
the pious and the good, because of the qualities of mind
and heart which they possessed, and in which he saw
reflected the image of the blessed Savior, whom he
loved more than all.

CHAPTER. III.

METHODISM IN THE COUNTRY WHERE MR. PATTON WAS RAISED — HIS CONVERSION, AND CONNECTION WITH THE CHURCH.

As was the case in almost every other place, Methodism was regarded with a jealous eye, and Methodists were looked upon as deluded fanatics, by a portion of the people in the section of country where Dr. Patton was brought up; and he who ventured to hear them, or speak favorably of them, was in imminent danger of being ridiculed and persecuted to an extent that none like, and few can quietly endure. When he was quite a boy, the Methodists established a preaching-place and formed a small society, near to his father's; but though their own Church was ten miles off, and they could attend it but at irregular periods, the family did not dare to visit the place where the Methodists preached and held their prayer and class-meetings. This, to their minds, would have been wrong. The Methodists they regarded as the false prophets, the deceivers, and the blasphemers of whom the Scriptures speak as appearing in the last days; and to have encouraged them in any way would, in their estimation, have been a most heinous offense, both against God and His Church. In this feeling they were sincere; and as

Saul of Tarsus verily thought he ought to do things contrary to the name of Jesus of Nazareth, so these thought it a matter of religious duty to oppose Methodists and Methodism. What Methodism was, in itself, or in its relations to the Word of God, or the true interests of man, they, most likely, did not know, had never inquired, nor thought it worthy of investigation. The preacher had opposed it, and, from the pulpit, warned the people against it, and this was enough. They had been accustomed to look to him for religious instruction; and opposition on his part was almost sure to be followed by a like opposition from them. Thus it was with the people of that part of Lancaster District in which the Pattons lived; and thus it was with them and their neighbors, when the Methodists formed their first society among them. These good people, however, were, perhaps, not aware that when children are taught to regard, and allowed to speak of, one body of evangelical Christians with lightness and disrespect, the natural tendency is to lead them to a disregard of all religion. But such is the fact, and it has had melancholy illustrations in the history of thousands. Look anywhere and everywhere at the conduct of those children whose parents, though great sticklers, it may be, for their own peculiar forms of religion, are ever deriding and sneering at the forms of others. They are illustrations of the fact. When are they seen to conduct themselves with decorum and propriety at a religious assemblage that happens not to be of the sect to which their parents belong? At meetings conducted by the sect or sects their preachers and parents oppose, they are often ir-

reverent, disrespectful and disorderly ; and very soon
the feeling thus cherished extends to all religious as-
semblages and all religious services.

It was fortunate for young Patton, as well as for the
other children of the family, that these things affected
them no more seriously than they did. The little society of Methodists worshiped in an old house which
stood near the middle of an old waste field, because
they had no better, and could afford no better. This
house was derisively called the " Scream House," the
" Place of Delusion," the " Black Lodge," etc., and all
manner of opprobrious epithets were applied to those
who worshiped there. Such things are readily caught
up by children. Scoffing and derision come much
more naturally than respect and reverence, and of
them the depraved heart is much more fond. The same
children who were accustomed to hear these things,
and who were kept away from Methodist meetings, lest
they should sin against God by going, were allowed to
assemble together at their corn-shuckings, cotton-pick-
ings, quiltings, and the like, hasten through the work
they had assembled to do, then dance, with occasional
drinks, for some hours, when the older people would
call them to order and to prayers. But this course,
though by no means justifiable in all its aspects, was
still less likely to affect them injuriously than were the
prejudices they formed and cherished against the Methodists. The former would, in its natural tendencies,
lead to frivolity of feeling, dissipation of thought, and
neglect of things serious ; while the latter, from disrespect and disregard of religion, as maintained and
practised by one sect, would proceed, little by little,

until it resulted in disrespect for all sects, and a disregard of all religion. It is very difficult for men to retain their respect for religion itself, or things sacred, after they lose their respect for the ministers and ministrations of religion, and those who profess to yield to its claims and practise its precepts. Great care should, therefore, be taken to cherish everywhere in the public mind a deep and solemn regard for all things sacred ; and great care should everywhere be taken by the ministers and professors of the Christian religion to conduct themselves in such a manner as that the closest scrutiny may not detect in them extravagancies or inconsistencies.

The little society to which reference has been made, for a long time, consisted of not more than ten or twelve members ; but of these there were two plain, simple-hearted, pious and exemplary local preachers — John Horton and Oliver McHaffey — who, with the rest, amid all the jeers, and taunts, and bitter persecutions heaped upon them, maintained the even tenor of their way, and served God in humility and singleness of heart. Rev. James Jenkins, who, only a few years since, went to his reward on high, frequently preached to the people at that place, and he was specially the butt of ridicule for the opposing part of the neighborhood. In the "gude, bra Scotch" of the people, he was called "auld Jamie Jenkins," or "Thundering Jenkins, the hell and damnation preacher." *Little Jamie Russell*, old Father Gassaway, and a man named Cannon also preached there occasionally. This last named preacher they were accustomed to call the "Distracted Man," because, perhaps, of his earnest, zealous manner of preaching. The members of this society continued of one heart and one mind, going forward in their work of faith and labor of love, until, in a few years, another society was formed, about nine miles distant, on Lynch's Creek, and the preaching-place was called Hopewell. In the mean time, the Pattons had removed a short distance ; so that, while they were still ten miles from their own meeting-house, they were between two preaching-places of the Methodists — one at Hanging Rock, three miles distant, on one side ; the other at Hopewell, six miles distant, in the opposite direction. Still they did not attend preaching by the Methodists. The prejudice was deep, and the opposition strong, in the minds of all, except Samuel, and, strange to say, he, from the first, contended they were good people, and sought to learn of them all he could, without being allowed to hear for himself. He engaged in the sports and pastimes of the day less than other boys of the neighborhood, and much less than his own brothers were accustomed to do ; and more than once, when thus engaged, he would suddenly stop, and turn away from the dance, with a sad countenance and heavy heart, and afterwards tell his brother Edward that, amid all his attempts to appear cheerful and gay, he could not forget the scenes of the pine grove—the prayers there offered, the vows there made, and the peace he there experienced. The recollection of these dampened all his earthly joys, and caused his sickened heart to turn sadly away from earth's pleasures, painfully realizing the loss it had sustained, and the aching void it then experienced, which the world could never fill.

When Samuel Patton was about fifteen years old, the neighborhood in which he lived sustained a serious loss in the death of old Father Horton, who had been among them as a light in a dark place, and whose patient endurance of the persecutions heaped on him and the other members of the little society to which he belonged, had won the respect and confidence of all around. Though many still regarded the Methodists in the same light as formerly, they had come to look upon old Father Horton as an exception. "The Methodists," said they, "are a deluded people; but Father Horton must be a good man, if there's one on earth." Well, Father Horton sickened, and report said he was about to die. Many of the neighbors called to see him, and found him happy in the love of God, and rejoicing in hope of a blessed immortality. Among others who called to see him, was James Patton — Samuel's oldest brother. Father Horton received him kindly, and exhorted him faithfully. James received the exhortation meekly, and with much deep feeling; and, while he listened to the admonitions and exhortations, and heard the shouts and praises of the dying saint, conviction fastened in his heart, and he then and there resolved that, by the grace of God, he would seek the pardon of his sins, and live henceforth in the service of the Most High, that he also might die the death of the righteous. These convictions never wore off, and these resolutions were kept and acted out. For a time he mourned in secret, and sighed for counsel he did not receive. Not long afterwards he learned the Methodists would soon hold a camp-meeting at a place some twenty miles distant. He obtained his father's consent to attend it. He did so, and the scenes which occurred upon his return home are thus described by a member of the family: "There had been a change. It was not the former James exactly. All eyes were upon him; and though but little was said for some days, we eyed him closely. A strange smile was upon his countenance, while the soft, bright tear would gently trickle from his eye. At length, one day, while we were all together in the cotton-field, he began to tell what the Lord had done for his soul — how that his sins were forgiven — his soul filled with joy and peace in the Holy Ghost — and how he was grieved to think the rest of us were unforgiven, and in danger of being lost forever. Then, with streaming eyes, he exhorted us to flee the wrath to come, and prayed with and for us, in a manner that affected us deeply.

"James had learned the time for circuit preaching, and when the day came and the time arrived to start to the meeting-house, having previously obtained permission to attend, he approached his father, who at that moment was leaning against a tree in the yard, apparently in deep thought, and remarked, 'Father, the Lord has forgiven my sins and converted my soul. I know it, and desire to join the Methodist Church, and I want your consent for me to do so.' A flood of tears gushed from the old man's eyes, and, in broken accents, with many sobs, he replied, 'My son, I know not what to do with myself. Do what you think is right.' James went and joined the Church; and from that time," continues the writer, "father, mother, James, myself, Samuel, Thomas, John, and our sister Prudence were

all praying, almost day and night. Little else was
done for some time. Scarcely a word else was spoken,
if not strictly necessary."

The reader will observe, those named above constituted the family. And what a touching picture is given
of a soul deeply convinced of sin, and earnestly groaning for redemption! How like the feelings of all who
earnestly seek after God! Truth is everywhere and
all the time the same. Its legitimate effects on honest
hearts are substantially the same. Hence the inward
experience of one good man is at least an epitome of
the inward experience of all good men; and it were
well if ministers and private Christians would remember this in their ministrations and intercourse one with
another. The good Christian man, who studies his
own heart, and preaches from the heart — telling of
the heart's trials, struggles and conquests, through the
grace of God, in Christ Jesus — will be sure to reach
the hearts of others. Other good men will find in
themselves that which corresponds with what is thus
preached; while the unconverted will be sure to contrast these feelings with their own, feel their lack, and,
through grace accompanying the power of truth, may
be brought to repentance.

Samuel Patton set out anew to seek the salvation of
his soul, at the time of the interview with his brother
James in the cotton-field, as referred to above. The
conversion of James, and his subsequent connection
with the Methodist Church, broke down all the opposition the family had previously felt towards that
people, and soon they began to attend Methodist
meetings with some regularity, and great seriousness.

The more they learned of this people, the more they were pleased with their doctrines, discipline and usages. But none were more interested than Samuel, who, ere long, took occasion to ask his father's consent to join the Methodist Church as a seeker, in hope that thus, having superior advantages, and increased facilities for being more perfectly taught, he might the more certainly work out his salvation, while the Spirit of the Holy One was evidently working in and with him. Consent was given, and in November, 1813, he was received into the Church as a probationer, earnestly seeking the salvation of his soul; and soon after this, he was followed into the Church by father, mother, all his brothers (except James, who had preceded him), and his sister; and thus the entire family were unitedly endeavoring to make their calling and election sure, and lay up treasures where moth and rust do not corrupt. Happy family! How much better to have been thus, than to have been toiling, worrying and fretting away the strength of life in vain and fruitless efforts to satiate the cravings of immortal minds, by the accumulation of the things of earth, or to ease the pains of throbbing hearts by the delights of the eye or the pleasures of sense! Ye were poor in this world's goods, but likely to become rich in faith. Ye were, in the world's estimation, little and unknown; but ye were preparing to become joint heirs with Christ, and to be kings and priests unto God. While clad in humble habiliments — the workmanship of your own hands — ye were preparing to wash your robes, and make them white in the blood of the Lamb, and were looking forward to the period when you should be clothed with garments white and clean, and be forever with the Lord.

From the facts stated, and the intimations already given, the reflective reader will now be prepared to appreciate the following statements: I. The family in which Samuel Patton was raised was a well-ordered family. They were well governed, and, in things pertaining to their moral interests, well trained. This is shown, most of all, in the respect paid to parental authority, and the sacred regard manifested for parental feelings. When the sons — one of whom was grown at the time — desired to connect themselves with the Church, they respectfully applied to their father, that they might first gain his approval. This respect for parents and parental authority lies deep among the foundations of all good governments, and is essential to that domestic happiness that makes home so pleasant, and causes man, in all after life, to look back on the scenes of childhood and youth with emotions at once so dear and thrilling.

II. It was a united family. Each considered, and sought to promote, the interests of the others, as well as his own. This is another fruitful source of domestic quietude and bliss. Selfishness is no less destructive of domestic than of social happiness; and as are the children, so, in all probability, will be the men and women. The character of the child is usually the character of the man or woman, with the difference, only, of greater development.

. III. It was a confiding family. Each confided in the others; hence the sorrows and joys of one were, to some extent, the sorrows and joys of all. They bore each other's burdens, and thus the burdens became comparatively light. Witness the interest manifested in each other's spiritual welfare, and the free, confiding manner in which the hopes and fears, or joys and griefs, of one were communicated to the other; and this will yet be more clearly seen as the history proceeds.

To these particulars, together with others of kindred character, which will, no doubt, be suggested to the mind, the reader's attention is specially invited. These are the family traits and characteristics on which the blessings of God may be expected to rest, and these are the kinds of families whence usually come the most pious, faithful and reliable men for the ministry, as well as for other departments of mental and moral labor. That family which desires the blessings of God upon it, and desires its members to become useful citizens, worthy Church members, and happy men and women, must look well to its internal arrangements — look well to the tempers, tones of mind, habits of thought, and class of feelings indulged and cherished among them. Train man everywhere, from early youth, to love home — imbue his mind and heart with a proper sense of parental authority and filial obligation — interweave with every filament of his nature the proper love of father, mother, brother and sister — and not one in a thousand — if one in ten thousand — will fail to become an orderly citizen and a useful member of society, in all the relations in which he may be called to act.

There is another particular connected with the history of the subject of these sketches, which should, perhaps, be noticed just here. He joined the Church, as a seeker of religion, which, though it were no more than has been done by thousands of others, who subsequently became good and useful men, was doing that to which many, in that day, would have objected very seriously, and what many, in this day, protest against with much apparent earnestness, and sometimes venture to ridicule in no very becoming manner. A few words on this subject may not, therefore, be out of place, just here.

It was said of the blessed Savior, "This man receiveth sinners." And to whom else should sinners go? From whom, if not from Him who came to call— not the righteous, but — sinners to repentance, should the sin-stained, guilt-stricken, but sorrowing, penitent expect to receive that for which the heart pants? Is there any other Savior — any other Redeemer — any other Mediator between God and man? Is there any other name given whereby man can be saved? Surely not. But how may sinners come to Christ? First, by that Spirit which he promised, as well as by his Word, he convinces of sin and of righteousness. The sinner is warned to heed these calls and follow the teachings of this light. How? He must cease to do evil, and learn to do well. As a wicked man, he must forsake his way, and, as an unrighteous man, he must abandon his former thoughts, purposes and feelings, and *turn* unto the Lord — throw himself fully open to the teachings of his Word, and the operations of his Spirit — learn all he can as to what is his duty, as to what the Lord would have him to do, and then perform it, to the best of his ability. And now where could an awakened sinner and a sincere inquirer after truth go, with a better prospect of obtaining that for which he sought, than among the true followers of the meek and lowly Jesus? They *were* as he now is. They have experienced what he now suffers ; and, understanding his case, they are prepared to administer somewhat to his wants — at least so far as to guide his thoughts and encourage his hopes, by presenting appropriate texts of Scripture, and relating something of their own experience when they felt and struggled as he feels and struggles. If it be proper and beneficial that, under such circumstances, he should seek the sympathies, advice and counsels of Christians temporarily, why not seek them permanently? If he may go among them for a time, with prospects of benefit, why not, for the same reasons, remain among them? But he is not a Christian. True, he is not, nor does he profess to be, a Christian ; but he is deeply convinced of sin, and earnestly groaning for redemption. He desires truly and heartily to repent of his sins, and henceforth follow the commands of God, and walk in his statutes blameless. What began in him this good work? Whence these good desires, holy purposes and strong resolves against sin and towards righteousness? Came they not of God? Were they not the work of the Holy Spirit? And if God have begun in him a good work, may he not flee to the people of God, and claim all the protection and aid they can afford him, while he endeavors to become a co-worker with God, and work out his salvation with fear and trembling? It would, indeed, be hard if he were denied this privilege. If Jesus has called him — if His Spirit is working in him, and he, as best he can, is endeavoring to

heed the call and follow the teachings of that Spirit—
it were sad, indeed, if the disciples of Jesus will allow
him no place among them. No — no. The Church is
the very place to which he should go, and there, with
the sympathies, the cautions, the encouragements and
prayers of those who have trodden the same path, he
may soon find his sorrow turned into joy, and the spirit
of mourning give place to the spirit of thankful rejoicings. So it has been with thousands, and so, as
will presently be seen, it was with Samuel Patton.

But, after all, there is not, in reality, so great a difference between the views and practices of the several
evangelical Churches of the country, on this subject,
as, at first view, one might suppose. The difference
consists more in the different light in which the same
work of grace in the human heart is viewed, and the
different terms used to designate this work, than in
anything else. What some call awakenings and convictions, others call regeneration or conversion ; so
that while the individual, though in precisely the same
spiritual state, is called a seeker by some, he is regarded as regenerated by others ; and a proper understanding and due consideration of this fact would, no
doubt, contribute greatly to soften the acerbity of feeling, and quiet the controversies that sometimes arise
on this point. In conclusion, on this subject, it may
safely be affirmed, without the fear of successful con--
tradiction, that those qualifications and mental states
which, under its discipline, entitle a person to membership in the Methodist Church, would secure for
them membership in any other Christian communion
known in this country. This statement is not written

hastily, but with due deliberation, and with, also, a tolerable knowledge of the usages of all the leading sects of the land.

The feelings and course of Mr. Patton, immediately subsequent to his connection with the Methodist Church, he sometimes expressed in language substantially as follows : Speaking of having united with the Church at the time already mentioned (November, 1813), he says, "I continued seeking the Lord, as best I knew how, through the following winter — sometimes encouraged, and sometimes much depressed. In April, 1814, a quarterly meeting was held in our neighborhood. I wept much during the meeting, especially in the love-feast, on Sabbath morning, and was somewhat encouraged. After the meeting had closed, I rose on Monday morning with such a weight of discouragement and depression upon me that I knew not what to do. I had occasion to be a good deal alone that day, and revolved the subject of my having joined the Church over and over, and came to the conclusion that I could not get religion, and would leave off seeking it. I determined, however, for the sake of my character, that I would not leave the Church, but, as I had attached myself to it, I would try to live so as not to bring any reproach either upon the Church or myself. I spent the day in an uneasy and painful state of mind.

"In the twilight of the evening, I retired, according to custom, and went through the forms of private devotion. I returned about dark, and took my seat by the fire, when it seemed as though something was saying to me, 'You have not prayed; you have only pretended. This will not do. You had better go and pray again.' So strong was the impression, that I immediately arose and retired to a house which had then been recently built, and in which a quantity of seed cotton had been stowed away. There I engaged in prayer. My tenderness of heart returned, and I prayed and wept before the Lord for some time. At length I arose and took a reclining posture on the cotton, where I lay in a silent agony of meditation and prayer. While in this situation, I thought of everything I held dear on earth, and felt within my heart that I would freely give up all, and be or do anything that might be required of me, if I could only realize a sense of pardon, and feel that I had a living interest in my Savior. Just at that moment I felt a thrill of horror, as if Satan were standing before me, while my spirit seemed to fly for help to Him that is mighty to save; when a power to which I had been a stranger seized me, as in the twinkling of an eye. In the excitement of the moment, and scarcely knowing what I was saying, I distinctly remember the first words I uttered were, 'My God, come a little nigher;' and the next were, at the top of my voice, 'Glory to God and the Lamb.' I continued crying aloud and praising the Lord, until, in a few minutes, parents, brothers and sisters were with me, and I was taken into the dwelling-house, where I continued in the same exercise for some time."

Thus far Mr. Patton spoke of his conversion in some memoranda written by him, in 1853, at the suggestion and by the request of his eldest son. A brother of his, older than himself, in a letter to the present writer, gave the following account of it : " I do not recollect the precise date of his (Samuel's) conversion, but the circumstances I remember well. A little after dark, one evening, when we were all seated at the fire-side, he suddenly absented himself. We waited long for him to come in to prayers, and began to feel very uneasy, as we knew him to be in great distress ; but just as we had commenced reading the lesson, previous to prayers, we were startled by a loud shriek, issuing from a new, unfinished house, close by. In one corner of the new building, some planks had been laid across the joists of the second story, and on these planks was piled a quantity of cotton. Samuel had climbed up there to pray, and there he had been blessed. The Lord had converted his soul, and when we reached the house, as we did in a very short time, he was leaping about over the naked joists, tripping from one to another as safely as if he had been on a floor — all the while shouting and praising with a loud voice, his eyes seemingly turned upward, his arms extended above his head, and he exclaiming, ' Praise, O praise the Lord forever and ever. Come and help me to praise his holy name.' We were exceedingly alarmed, lest he should fall and be seriously hurt, as he was some distance from the ground, and a fall might have been quite a serious matter. We procured a ladder, and got him down as soon as possible, took him to the dwelling-house, and seated him on a chair. He appeared to be greatly exhausted, and soon there was something like a general calm. Again we attempted family worship. It fell to my lot to read the lesson. The chapter selected was the 19th of John. When I had read the sixth verse, closing with the words, 'Take ye him and crucify him, for I find no fault in him,' brother S. sprang to his feet and shouted, 'No, there is no fault in him ; there is no fault in him,' and added, 'Brother Edward, do you pray, and let me praise.' This course was pursued, and while we tried to pray, he shouted praise. He then exhorted, first one and then another of the family, but particularly our mother, who, at that time, was not clear as to her acceptance with God. Thus we continued in prayer, praise and exhortation, until, ere we were aware, the night was nearly spent when we retired to rest. About day-break, Samuel arose and went out for secret prayer, and awoke the rest of us as he returned to the house, shouting, as he came, ' O, father, I have found him again !' A little after breakfast time, quite a crowd of our neighbors had gathered in, and soon some were singing, some praying, and some shouting, while a few of our old friends were not a little distressed, on our account, supposing that we were deluded — half distracted — and would all go to Satan together."

Some time during the day, they all set out on a tour of visiting the neighbors, Samuel leading the way, and many following in the train. He went from house to house, exhorting the people to forsake sin and seek religion. When he would leave one house, the inmates were so affected by his conduct — to them so strange— that more or less of them would follow him to the next, and thus the number was continually increasing, so that at night, when the young missionary returned home, there accompanied him so large a crowd that the house would not contain them. The meeting that

night was one of power. Many were converted, and
a most glorious and extensive revival commenced, that
continued until hundreds were soundly converted to
God. The next day the same course was pursued, and
the same scenes enacted, and, day after day, for a week
or more, but little was done, in that neighborhood, but
to listen to the prayers and exhortations of young
Patton, or talk of the strange things that were oc-
curring. Some mocked; a few opposed; but the
greater part of all in the neighborhood were deeply
affected, as, with tears and rejoicings, they followed the
boy preacher from house to house, heard the gracious
words that fell from his lips, and witnessed the won-
drous works the Spirit of the Holy One was performing among the people.

That such proceedings were characterized by various
incidents, the reader will not be slow to believe. One
or two of these may be related. There lived in the
neighborhood a Baptist preacher, named Pegg, fa-
miliarly called "Uncle Neddy Pegg" — a man who, in
his adherence to the doctrines of unconditional election
and reprobation, was of the strictest sort — so strict
as to be a downright Antinomian in view, if not in
feeling and practice. One day, while young Patton
and his company were visiting from house to house,
they called on "Uncle Neddy." He received them
kindly, and at once a conversation on the subject of
experimental religion was commenced. Had Mr.
Patton at that time been acquainted with the leading
doctrines maintained by the different denominations,
he was in no mood to discuss them. His heart was
warm with the fresh glowings of Christian love—love

to God and all mankind — and of that he would speak,
and in that he would rejoice. His prevailing desire
was that all should enjoy what he enjoyed, and feel as
he felt. So, after a brief space, employed in this kind
of conversation, they all joined in prayer. Young
Patton led, and while he prayed the fire burned — his
heart grew warm — and his feelings found vent in loud
shouts of praise. He arose from his knees, still shouting aloud, embraced the preacher (who was a great
opposer of shouting) in his arms, and exhorted him
and all around to seek the fullness of the blessings of
the Gospel, and prove faithful until death. The old
preacher's wife, unable any longer to restrain her feelings, shouted aloud, declaring she was converted after
a new sort. These exercises continued for some time.
The old man, at a subsequent period, when relating the
affair to some of his friends, remarked, "That boy
came very near upsetting my principles, for really I
had hard work to keep from shouting, and Milley (his
wife) did shout like the mischief."

Very soon the whole neighborhood was in a blaze of
revival influence ; and so prosperous was the work,
that the little society that met at the old house in
"Horton's old field" was increased from eleven to one
hundred and forty members. Meetings were held at
their old meeting-house at least every Sabbath, and
often during the week. The society were of one heart
and of one mind, and in the enjoyment of great peace
and prosperity. But these were not allowed to remain
without the benefits of the labors of some ministers
of other denominations, who were particularly anxious
they should now be taught in the good and right

way, though, previously to this excitement, they paid
but little attention to that neighborhood, and acted as
though they thought the people were doing very well,
so long as they remained careless and indifferent, and
made no move towards the Methodists. Such preachers
may be met with in divers places. So long as a people
remain in careless indifference, so long they manifest
no special anxiety about them; but let a revival influence exhibit itself, under the ministrations of another
denomination, and, all at once, they are seized with a
wonderfully kind and tender solicitude for the welfare
of the people over whom such influence extends. So
it was in the case under notice. There were no Baptist preachers in the neighborhood alluded to, except
Uncle Neddy Pegg, and he, kind soul, was disposed to
let everybody and everything go on without interruption from him. But some of these preachers, in different sections, hearing of this work, concluded at once
it would not do to allow the people to go on thus,
without, at least, having the opportunity of connecting
themselves with the only true Church in the land; because, as no other Church happened to believe and do
just as they did, of course all others were wrong; so
they soon had appointments among them for preaching.
These appointments they attended, and at them had
much to say of the peculiarities and excellencies of
their own creed and usages, and fully as much, or
more, to say of the error and danger of other creeds
and other usages. Exclusiveness of creed and exclusiveness of feeling go together, and they reciprocally
encourage and strengthen each other. In the case alluded to, much of this feeling was exhibited. A great

outcry was made about what they called self-righteousness — being saved by works — and some other points,
which few or none believe, and the Methodists least of
all ;, and great stress was laid on the prominent dogmas
of their own sect, the most prominent of which, perhaps, is that of immersion. What success these had
in winning the people to their views, the present writer
is not prepared to say ; but the following account of
one of their meetings, given by an eye-witness, may be
repeated, especially as the subject of these sketches
took rather a prominent part : One of these preachers
had an appointment for meeting at night, at a private
house in the neighborhood. Samuel Patton, in company with four or five others, attended, though to do
so cost them a walk of six miles through snow several
inches deep. The house was crowded, and the preacher
had, as usual, much to say in opposition to Arminian-
ism, self-righteousness, and such like " filthy rags."
The people behaved well, listened attentively, but appeared not to be particularly instructed or edified.
After he had pretty much exhausted himself, as well,
perhaps, as the patience of his hearers, he sat down.
Some one in the company called on young Patton to
pray. While praying, he was blessed and revived, and
when he arose from his knees, he commenced a most
touching and impressive exhortation, and in his exhortation he preached Jesus and salvation, by faith in his
name, to all the world. Life and power were in the
word. The people were greatly moved. Some trembled, some wept, some prayed for mercy, and some rejoiced in a sense of pardoning love. The preacher
sat, looked serious, but said nothing.

The next morning, as young Patton was returning home from this meeting, in company with his brother Edward, he called by the way to see an acquaintance and old associate. Coming near the house where he lived, Samuel remarked to his brother, " I am sorry for Ned Bowers. He is frolicsome and wicked. Let us call, pray with him, and try to prevail on him to seek religion." They called, and found Mr. Bowers and his wife busily engaged at shelling corn. As they were in a hurry to get home, Samuel at once addressed his friend substantially as follows : " Mr. Bowers— Edward and myself have professed religion. We have been converted to God, justified by faith in Christ, and born anew of the Holy Spirit, and are now endeavoring to go on to sanctification. We expect to go to heaven when we die, and desire you would go with us, and have called to pray with you, that God may bless you also with the forgiveness of sins and the renewal of your heart. If you have no objections, we will pray." Mr. Bowers replied that he had none. The young men then rose, and sang that hymn of which Mr. Patton was always so fond, commencing—

" And can I yet delay
My little all to give,"

After which they kneeled to pray. Samuel prayed, and then asked his brother to follow him. While at prayer, the spirit of power came upon them, and they shouted aloud for joy in the love of God. " When we rose from our knees," says Edward, in relating the occurrence, " we found Mr. and Mrs. Bowers stretched on the floor among the shelled corn, scattering it prodigiously,

and bitterly crying aloud for mercy. Their two little
children, being terribly frightened, were crying piteously. I took them in my arms, and walked with them
to and fro, until they were pacified ; while Brother S.
continued to exhort the awakened and mourning parents. We had promised to be at home by a given
hour, and, finding our time nearly out, we were compelled to leave. We, however, propped Mrs. Bowers
in a chair, so that she could hold the youngest child in
her arms, and keep the other at her side ; then, leaving
our blessing, we departed, reached home, and went to
work."

This well meant, and no doubt well timed, effort was
not in vain. Soon after, both Mr. Bowers and his
wife professed religion, joined the Methodist Church,
and he became a very acceptable and very useful leader
of a class.

One other incident it may be well to mention in
this connection : At no great distance from the residence of Mr. Patton, there lived an uncle who, with
his wife, was a Presbyterian, but the children, of whom
there were many, were gay, worldly-minded and frolicsome. When the Pattons attached themselves to the
Methodist Church, these parents treated them very
coldly, and the children persecuted them no little ;
while they themselves, overruling their parents in the
matter, would not unfrequently have drinking and
dancing parties at the house, and seemed particularly
pleased with any opportunity that might offer to ridicule and make sport of the Methodists generally, and
of the Methodistic tendencies of the Pattons particularly. These things grieved Samuel Patton most sadly,

and, after thinking and praying over the matter for some time, he at length, on Saturday evening, proposed to his brother Edward (who seems to have been his favorite brother, and almost constantly with him) that they should go and spend the night with their uncle and cousins. He readily assented; but the father hesitated to give his consent. He rather doubted the propriety of such a course, and feared the consequences might be unpleasant. However, after giving the boys many cautions and much wholesome advice, applicable to the case, he suffered them to go. As they went, they agreed not only to conduct themselves with strictest religious propriety, but also to pray with the family, provided they could gain permission; and, knowing that they might look for a severe trial, they turned aside into a grove, and spent some time in prayer. There they solemnly covenanted with the Lord, that if he would be with them and aid them, they would strive to glorify him by their conduct and conversation, and, if they could gain permission, they would also pray with the family. With these purposes, and trusting in God for wisdom and strength, they went on. They were received with some surprise, and with what appeared to them as mock seriousness, and were treated by the younger members of the family with a sort of mock dignity that greatly dampened their feelings. However, nothing very special occurred, until some time after supper, while all were seated around the fire. The boys were asked to sing "some good song." They complied, and sang several hymns, then, in their turn, asked their cousins to sing. "O yes," said they, "we can beat that singing easily enough," and struck up, and merrily sang, a love ditty. This was worse than a bucket of cold water to the boys. They were dismayed, and just ready to give up the contest. But presently they walked out to confer together, and resolve on what was best to be done. Their purpose had been formed — their promise had been made — and they agreed they could not retreat without, at least, one more effort. So they returned to the house, and, finding that the uncle had gone up stairs to rest himself on a bed, Samuel immediately addressed his aunt, substantially as follows : "Aunt Betsey, we are trying to serve the Lord, and get to heaven. The Lord has mercifully forgiven our sins, for the sake of Christ, and we, desiring you should all go to heaven with us, have come to see you, and have promised the Lord to pray with you, if you would permit us." She, without replying to him directly, turned quickly round, and said to the family, "Some of you go up stairs and tell your father to come down to prayers." As all seemed to have been taken by surprise, no one moved to obey the order, and Samuel remarked, "I'll go, aunt — I'll go." Accordingly he went, and, as all were silent, those below distinctly heard him repeat what he had just before said to his aunt, to which the old gentleman replied, "O, oh! I'm glad you came. I'm glad you thought so much of us." Samuel took his arm, and down they came, the old man evidently in a pretty violent fit of involuntary shaking. He, however, took his seat and composed himself, while his young nephew commenced to sing the hymn —

"Plunged in a gulf of dark despair."

At first all joined, but soon a holy, melting influence

prevailed. Tears flowed freely, sighs and sobs followed, and the young Pattons were left to sing alone. Prayer followed, led by Samuel. The whole family were in tears, and, immediately after prayers, they all retired — the father, mother and eldest daughter weeping bitterly. Next morning, being the Sabbath, preparations were early made for prayers, and the young Pattons were kindly asked to lead in the family devotions, which they did, and soon after left, and, in consequence of a removal that shortly after occurred, they subsequently saw but little of these relatives ; though they afterwards treated them very differently from what they had previously done, and some of the number, not long after, professed religion, and joined the Church.

In regard to the foregoing account of Mr. Patton's conversion, and his conduct immediately subsequent to that event, it is proper, just here, to offer a few remarks, which are more especially submitted to the consideration of those who knew him in after life. They, recollecting his retiring disposition — his unaffected modesty, and simplicity of manners — will, no doubt, be surprised on reading the foregoing, and there being told how he did — especially in going from house to house, exhorting and praying with the people, and thus becoming manifestly the instrument in a most wonderful revival of the work of grace. Those who knew him well, knew that he was not of the ardent, excitable temperament of those given to conduct like this—that, though prompt in the discharge of religious duty, he was more diffident than forward ; and few men ever lived that were less likely to attempt an ostentatious display or parade. His modesty and humility were proverbial, and yet he did as stated. For the statements given, the writer has the most undeniable evidence, though, in all his intercourse with Mr. Patton, he never, to his recollection, heard him even allude to these things, and few, perhaps, except the members of his own family, knew him better, were more intimate with him, or better acquainted with his private history.

In the memoranda already referred to (see page 48), Mr. Patton makes no allusion to the occurrences immediately succeeding his conversion, other than merely to state that the next day afterwards he called to see a family to which he felt greatly attached, and merely adds, the family, including an old minister that lived with them, received him kindly. He could not have forgotten these scenes. Why, then, did he not speak of them, or at least say something more in these private memoranda, written at the urgent and oft-repeated request of an affectionate son, and of which he, doubtless, supposed no other than a private use would ever be made? There is but one reason to be assigned — that is, he instinctively abhorred and shrank from any and everything like boasting or vaingloriousness, especially in Christians, and still more especially in Christian ministers. Than this, nothing was farther from his nature, or more incongenial to his feelings. He was never accustomed to speak much of himself, and what he did was not of the self-gratulatory or self-glorious kind. One who knew him, as did the present writer, will account for the course he pursued immediately after his conversion, by the fact that his whole mind and soul were absorbed in one great leading thought — the goodness of God and the power of his grace. By a sense of these he was overwhelmed, and, losing sight of almost everything else — warmed and moved by their holy influences — he pressed forward with the same feeling that urged the Psalmist to exclaim, " Come near, all ye ends of the earth, and I will tell you what the Lord has done for my soul." The "love of Christ constrained" him — overcame his natural timidity and backwardness, and urged him forward in active efforts to spread the honors, and bring glory to His name.

These were, doubtless, the true reasons, both for the course pursued and the silence he subsequently preserved in reference to it.

CHAPTER IV.

HIS CALL TO THE MINISTRY — IS LICENSED TO PREACH,
AND ADMITTED INTO THE TRAVELING CONNECTION.

THE reader is now brought to a period in the history
of the subject of these sketches, which is at once of
the most interesting and thrilling character — the period of his call to, and entrance upon, the work of the
Christian ministry.   But who can describe the feelings,
the mental struggles, the spiritual conflicts, of a truly
converted man, who is as truly called from on high to
this holy, and yet fearfully responsible, work ?   What
language is adequate to describe the agony of his mind,
or the anguish of his heart, as, day after day, and night
after night, he struggles under a deep sense of " woe
is me, if I preach not the Gospel ?"   These conflicts,
in their full sense, and to their full extent, however,
language can no more describe than it could describe
the unutterable anguish of the blessed Savior, when,
in the Garden of Gethsemane, his sweat became, as it
were, great drops of blood falling to the ground.
They are feelings that none can know but he who ex-
periences them ; and there is nothing hazarded by the
assertion, that usually, if not universally, these conflicts, in their intensity, bear a proportion to the subsequent devotion and usefulness of him who sustains
them ; or, if the manner of expression be more accept-

able, the subsequent devotion and usefulness of the minister bear a proportion to the severity of these conflicts. The conviction is very deep, at least in the mind of the writer, that a careful and thorough examination would develop the fact that, in a great majority, if not the whole number, of cases, where ministers have been most devoted, most useful and successful in their work, they were the ones who had the hardest struggles, sustained the greatest conflicts, and overcame the greatest difficulties attendant upon the entrance to that work. He who enters and prosecutes the early periods of this work easily, is too apt, afterwards, to perform it too carelessly, and, consequently, too inefficiently ; while he who engages in it as did the subject of these sketches, will, most likely, prosecute it with a trembling sense of his responsibility, until, finally, he will —

> " His body and his charge lay down,
> And cease at once to work and live."

For this opinion there is a reason, and that reason is found deep in those principles which influence human nature, both in its regenerated and unregenerate state. To discuss those principles here, would not be altogether in place, but they are deep, abiding and operative, and will be readily suggested to the intelligent and reflective mind.

What constitutes a call to the ministry, agreeably to the views of the present writer, is stated somewhat at length in another volume, but recently given to the reading public* ; and to say that Samuel Patton was

---

* See LIFE AND TIMES OF REV. WILLIAM PATTON.

called to the ministry, would be only to utter what most of those who knew him would regard as a mere truism. He did not choose the work of the ministry merely in the light of a profession, nor yet simply because he desired to do good and be useful to his fellow-men ; much less did he regard it as a road to ease, honor or profit. He entered and continued the work from a solemn and an abiding sense of duty — duty to God, to his fellow-man, and to himself. He did it that he might "save himself and those that heard him." Of his feelings and spiritual conflicts in regard to this work, he left the following record : Referring to his conversion, he said, "I thought I would have no more trials — see no more stormy clouds, and no more feel the anguish of a desolate heart. I continued for several weeks, with but little interruption, to a triumph which I thought would be perpetual. It was not long, however, until a sudden reverse of feeling came over me. A deep depression seized upon me, and sank me almost to despair ; and yet I felt that I had an interest in Christ. This was accompanied with an overwhelming sense of the delusion and danger of sinners, and an impression that I *must* warn them to flee from the wrath to come.

"I felt that I had trusted too much in my own strength — that I had not been as humble, and realized my own helplessness and dependence, as I should have done — and yet I could not relinquish my hold on the Savior, though I felt ashamed and confounded before him. I went mourning and weeping, from place to place, and, when alone, was often praying audibly, in the field, on the road, or anywhere that I thought I would not be observed. Sometimes, when I sat under preaching, it was with great difficulty that I could refrain from rising up, and crying aloud to the people to repent of their sins.

" Many — very many — were the times that I would retire to bed, remain awake till I supposed the family were all asleep, then rise, with great caution, slip softly out of the house, and walk away to some place where I might weep and pray, and indulge in reflections on the work of the ministry, my impressions concerning it, my unfitness for it, and the abiding conviction which followed me, that I *must* preach. Sometimes I would go into the woods, lie down among the fallen leaves, and roll from side to side, in an agony of grief. My mind was weighed down ; clouds and darkness rested upon it, and yet I could not shake off the conviction that it was my solemn duty to preach. At times, after weighing the subject in my own mind, I would, with great confidence in the correctness of my judgment and decisions, determine that I ought not, and would not attempt it, and then congratulate myself on having settled a question which had troubled me so greatly. But less than one day would find me in as great an agony as ever.

" During this time, I would frequently speak in public. when called on to do so, though I stubbornly refused regular license. Nay, more ; after I had sometimes spoken to a congregation for half an hour, when there was no one else to do it, or when I was called on to lead the exercises of a meeting, I have gone from the place reproaching myself most bitterly for having spoken at all. At one time, I thought I would put the question forever at rest ; so I went into a field, kneeled down at the root of a tree, and solemnly promised the Lord I would never again atttempt to speak in public in his name.   But the agonies that followed, I will not attempt to describe.

"During the progress of these exercises, my father sold out in South Carolina, with the view of removing to the State of Alabama.   But the first year afterwards he spent in Georgia — the scene of the exercises last related.   When about leaving that State for Tennessee (whither he removed, instead of Alabama), I thought, as I was going to a strange place, where the people had no knowledge of my having attempted to speak in public, I would take that occasion to refrain altogether. But the first Sabbath after we reached the place, in Middle Tennessee, for which we had set out, I fell in with a preacher with whom I had been well acquainted, and one who knew my history.   When he had done preaching, he called on me to exhort.   I thought then it was no use for me to hide or flee, as some one would find me out everywhere I went.   Soon after I fully surrendered, and in my heart submitted, at least, to try to be a Methodist preacher."

Thus far Mr. Patton spoke of this matter in the memoranda already referred to.   But the picture falls far short of what there is good reason to believe was the reality.   His natural and cherished indisposition to talk or write of himself, connected with the fact that, in the above, he was only penning a few thoughts for the private gratification of a son, caused him to be more brief and less particular than he, perhaps, would have been, had he, at the time, supposed any

public use would have been made of what he was writing. Another account given of his mental conflicts,
while laboring under the conviction of a call to the
ministry, and previously to his engaging in that work—
an account given by the elder brother, already referred
to — is more full and explicit. It is substantially as
follows : Referring to the time, a few months subsequently to his brother's conversion, he says, " Up to
this time, Sammy had been an industrious boy, and active in the discharge of all his duties pertaining to
worldly business, but now seemed not to have the same
relish for worldly matters, nor to perform his temporal
duties with the same activity. An inward conviction
of duties more immediately connected with eternity,
and which involved the interests and destinies of the
soul, had seized upon his mind, and, the time being come
that he felt he *must* preach, quite overpowered him.
He seemed most keenly to feel the responsibilities of
the ministerial office and work ; and as he had deeply
imbibed the views then entertained by Presbyterians,
in regard to ministerial qualification, and believed no
one should, or could, preach the Gospel, unless educated somewhat after the manner in which ministers
of that Church claimed to have been trained, his sufferings were extreme. His constant plea was, 'I am
no scholar. I have no gift. The burden is too heavy ;
the task is too great.' He lost his appetite for his
daily food, slept but little, and pined away almost to a
skeleton. He would wander along the roads, in the
fields, or in the woods, as if seeking for rest, and often
desired that he might die. Sometimes he was sorely
tempted by the enemy to lay violent hands on himself,

and put an end to his existence. Then, again, he was tempted to blaspheme the holy name of God. For days he would not speak a word, unless forced by circumstances to do so ; but all the while his lips were moving. I have softly approached near him, that I might hear his whispers. They were, 'No—no ! My heart says no. It can not be. I can not do it—no, no !' and thus he would go on, for hours together. I have seen him, when trying to work in the field with the rest of us, suddenly fall on his knees, without dropping his hoe, and piteously implore his father and brothers to pray for him. It was noised abroad that he was distracted ; and his parents were greatly reproached by their relatives, for having, as was alleged, ruined him by indulging him in the Methodist delusion. O, it was a time of sorrow, indeed ! Many flocked to see him, and some tried to comfort him ; but he generally retired to himself, saying, ' God only can comfort me.' He constantly carried a Bible, either in his hand or bosom, and kept it in his bed at night."

As already stated, Mr. Patton's father and family removed from South Carolina, first to Georgia, and then to Middle Tennessee. The first removal was in the early part of 1818, and the second in the early part of 1819. During the year preceding the first removal, the family lost by death a daughter, Prudence, and a son, Thomas—both pious, and both died in the triumphs of the Christian's faith—the former in January, 1817, and the latter in the following March. A few evenings before Thomas died, he called the family around him, and, first of all, addressed his brother Samuel, and said, "Brother, I am going to die ; but, glory to God, I am going to heaven. The Lord has called you to preach the Gospel — to call sinners to repentance — and I want you to obey the call." He then exclaimed, " O, my dear brothers, I shall soon be in heaven! Thanks be to God! I thank you all for your kindness to me." Then he addressed his father and mother, and all the members of the family, one by one, and affectionately bade them farewell. But to Samuel he addressed himself a second time, exclaiming, " O, my brother, I know the Lord has called you to preach Jesus to a dying world. Fear not, nor flee. Be bold, and the Lord will be with you ; the God of Israel will stand by you." Here his strength and voice failed, and he was silent ; but one who was present says, "The room seemed filled with the glory of God." This circumstance, with the exhortation given, is said to have greatly encouraged Mr. Patton in reference to the discharge of the solemn duties he felt were imposed upon him, and, most likely, had no little to do in assisting him finally to determine his future course.

During the year the family resided in Georgia, Mr. Patton spent much of his time in solitude, as it was there that he experienced his sorest trials and most serious conflicts. The disadvantages under which he labored were many and great. The family were poor, and the mother, in consequence of mental affliction to which she was occasionally subject, was ill prepared to perform many of the duties that devolved upon her. A part of the time he worked by day, in order to procure for himself clothing, and such books as could be obtained ; while a great portion of each night was spent in reading or writing. Necessity forced him to be economical, both of time and means ; and, though he was hardly pressed for a time, the habits of economy thus formed were of incalculable service to him in all after life, and in this, perhaps, may be found, at least in part, the secret of his being able, though his annual receipts were very small, to continue in the traveling connection, and still raise and educate a family of several children. He was economical of time and money, though no man, perhaps, was ever farther removed, in his feelings and practice, from penuriousness.

During this year, also, though, as himself says, refusing to receive regular license to preach, as he was, from time to time, earnestly requested to do, he was prevailed on to travel some, in company with the Rev. William Redwine, the circuit preacher, in hopes that more frequently attending preaching, and more frequently exercising his gifts as an exhorter, would tend to open his way and relieve his mind, by leading him fully into the work to which all seemed satisfied he had been called. But still his sense of the high, holy and responsible character of the work of the ministry, and his sense of unfitness for it, overcame his convictions of duty, and he continued to hesitate. When the family removed from Georgia to Tennessee, the state of his feelings is set forth in the extract already given. During the first year spent in Tennessee, he remained mostly at his father's, alternately laboring on the farm and improving his mind by close attention to his books. Some time during this year, he was regularly licensed to preach, and, at the proper time, duly recommended to the Annual Conference, as a suitable person to be received into the traveling connection. This recommendation was presented to the Conference held at Nashville, Tennessee, commencing October 1, 1819, when he, with thirteen others, was received on trial in the Tennessee Annual Conference.

The reader will observe that Mr. P. embraced religion in the month of April, 1814. He was then in the eighteenth year of his age. He was licensed to preach some time during the year 1819, or five years after his conversion ; and, from the best information now at hand, about four of these five years were spent in that painful state of feeling, and amid those agonizing conflicts of mind, to which reference has already been made — a long time, truly, to be in such a state ; and what makes it the more remarkable is, that, in all that can now be gathered, there is no evidence, nor even an intimation, that he was, at any time during that period, backslidden in heart. Why this was not the case, can only be accounted for by the fact that he not only made every effort to retain the grace of God in the heart, but frequently exhorted, and otherwise exercised his gifts in calling sinners to repentance, and forwarding the interests of religion in the public acknowledgment of the claims of God upon him. But for this course, half reluctant, as it was, it would be difficult to understand how he could have retained faith in Christ at all. In the disobedience which he was half cherishing in regard to his call to the ministry, he certainly would have lost from the heart the life and power of godliness, but for these public ministrations ; and, even with them, what a fearful struggle did he pass through! No powers of language can express what he must have felt and suffered; and, no doubt, a recollection of these sufferings, in after life, kept him closer to the work he had undertaken, and tended to increase the ardor and diligence with which that work was performed.

Would a man possessed of feelings such as those experienced by Mr. Patton, be likely to calculate his chances for a good circuit, or the probabilities of receiving his disciplinary allowance, when entering the traveling ministry? How preposterous the thought! And if a proper sense of ministerial obligation continued to rest upon the mind, would these things ever characterize a minister? When men begin to calculate these things, and become sticklers for good appointments, as they are sometimes called — that is, appointments where there is little work, easy living and good pay — and complain when such are not given them, they have either never experienced, or have lost, the proper sense of their obligations as Christian ministers. Men truly called of God, when once given up to this work, are not apt to confer with flesh and blood, much less calculate their chances of easy work and good pay. And one important point demanding attention among preachers, is, always to cherish and keep up in their minds a deep sense of their individual responsibility as ministers of Christ; and that this may be the more easily as well as certainly done, let them sacredly cherish a constant recollection of the feelings and agonies they experienced when first they felt a solemn sense of " Woe is me if I preach not the gospel." The Church will never materially decline while the preachers are true to their work ; and they can never be true to their work unless they are true to God, and keep their own hearts with all diligence. If the love of ease, of the applause of men, or the things of the world enter into the heart, it will drive out the pure love of God, and, of course, lessen the concern for the salvation of souls ; consequently, prayers will be less ardent, and characterized by less of the agony that fills the heart that is truly imbued with the love of Christ, and a burning desire for the salvation of souls. The preaching will partake of the caste of the feelings, and be shaped so as to please men rather than God — to please men, that they may gain their applause, or win favor that may enure to their own personal benefit; and as the preachers lose their own spirituality, so will the Church likely degenerate into formality, and, becoming powerless for good, will be no blessing, if it, indeed, be not a curse to the world.

Again : while ministers retain the feelings they ought, they will never seek to bring people into the Church, or have them to profess faith in Christ, merely to build up this or that particular sect, or strengthen this or that particular Church, so much, as to honor God and save souls. The apostle rejoiced when Christ was preached, though it were done by those who thought thereby to add affliction to his bonds ; so every Christian minister rejoices in the spread of truth, in the prevalence of righteousness, and in the salvation of souls, regardless of the special instrumentalities which may be used for the accomplishment of the work. That is, he rejoices in the end, and ever prays, " Send by whom thou wilt, but save the people, O

Lord." With a ministry called of God, baptized with the Holy Ghost, and faithful to their work, the Church will ever prosper, truth and righteousness will prevail, and God's Spirit, accompanying his word in the hearts of the people, will work to the salvation of souls in every place.

In this connection it may also be remarked, that it sometimes happens that ministers, in their efforts to improve their minds, and cultivate the spirit of preaching, seem for a time to overlook the necessity of cultivating, also, the spirit of the private Christian; and yet they must attend to both, if they do all that is required of them. They have the feelings, the frailties, the imperfections, trials and difficulties common to individual Christian men, and, superadded to these, they have those of the Christian minister; and, these being by no means of the same class, the one class may be, to some extent, cultivated to the neglect of the other. The distinction between them may not be easily discovered, nor will it be, unless one mark his own feelings, and notice the operations of his mind, with great care; still the distinction exists, and he who discovers it, guards himself in this particular, and acts accordingly, will find that thereby he promotes his own spiritual welfare, and prepares himself for greater usefulness. The spiritual enjoyments and conflicts, the hopes and fears of one truly Christian heart, are substantially those of all Christian hearts, and he who administers consolation to Christian people should know experimentally what Christian people feel and suffer; hence if ministers closely study their own hearts, and keep themselves familiar with their own experience, they will thus gain at least a general knowledge of the hearts, the experience and conflicts of others. To know human nature, as it exists in one man, is to know something of it as it exists in all men ; and to know well the operations of the grace of God in one human heart, is to know something of the operations of that grace on all hearts. So while a minister labors industriously to improve his mind, store it with useful knowledge, and prepare himself to be a teacher of the intellect, he should also, by close attention to his own heart, and a frequent and careful analysis of his own feelings and motives, seek to be prepared to act as a teacher of the heart.

These remarks are made under a deep conviction that many preachers are too much accustomed to look without, rather than within — to attempt acquainting themselves with human nature, as they see it manifested in others, rather than as they may feel it in their own breasts. To read the Bible, in order to become better and still better acquainted with its doctrines and precepts, that they may be correctly taught, defended and enforced, is certainly necessary ; and it is equally necessary to the full success of the ministry that the same Bible be read with a view of applying its promises, cautions and threatenings to the minister's own heart, that it, being made to feel them in their full force, may thereby be the better able forcibly to apply them to the hearts of others. If a preacher beget, in the minds of his hearers, a reverent awe of God and things sacred, himself must feel that awe. If he inspire the desponding heart with hope, he must speak with an experimental knowledge of that hope ; and so,

likewise, of whatever else pertains to Christian experience.   When properly understood, there is a vastness
of meaning in the oft-repeated phrase, "from the heart
to the heart."

In all the particulars to which allusion is here made,
few men were ever more diligent, or exercised themselves with more cautious circumspection, than did Mr.
Patton.   All, and more than all, these excellent quali
ties, through the abounding grace of God, centered in
him.   He was familiar with his own heart, and kept it
with diligence, while he watched his life with godly
jealousy ; and hence the sweetness and submissiveness
of his spirit, the highly cultivated sensibility of his
heart, the practical power of his preaching, and the
ready ability with which he could encourage the timid,
strengthen the weak, cheer the desponding, comfort the
distressed, and caution the froward.

CHAPTER V.

HIS TRAVELS AND LABORS FROM 1819 TO 1824.

It is with the writer a matter of regret that he is no better prepared to present the subject of his sketches more fully and satisfactorily, during the five years that elapsed from the time he was received on trial in the Tennessee Conference until he took his position to live and die in the bounds of the Holston Conference. But this part of his history is now doomed, perhaps, to remain almost a blank among the records of men. The records of these years are in the hearts of a few that survive, but, for the most part, they are registered only on high. Very little is in the writer's possession that would enable him to trace the history of this good man — exhibit his joys and sorrows, his hopes and fears, his oppositions and his difficulties, his encouragements and discouragements — as he traveled circuit after circuit — attended appointment after appointment — saw prosperity here, and, with a sad heart, witnessed decline there — during these five years, which, in some respects, were the most important in his ministerial life. During this period he was — as have been many others — "troubled on every side, but not distressed ; perplexed, but not in despair ; persecuted, but not forsaken ; cast down, but not destroyed ;" because he had a treasure in an earthen vessel, that the excellency of the power might be of God. Amid the obscurity that now rests upon this part of his history, this much is well known : he received his appointments cheerfully — he went to them promptly — he labored faithfully, and with most encouraging success. His first appointment from the Conference was to the Sequatchee Circuit, lying in the beautiful and fertile valley of the Sequatchee river — a valley averaging, perhaps, five or six miles in width by fifty or sixty in length, in Eastern Tennessee, between Walden's Ridge and the Cumberland Mountain. This part of the country was then just being settled, and, of course, characterized by all those inconveniences and want of religious and other facilities usual to countries in the earlier periods of their settlement. The people, for the greater part, were poor, and, in many places, scarcely prepared to shelter the preacher, much less to afford him anything like the pecuniary support it is now common for preachers to receive ; but they could give him of their plain, homely fare, and, perhaps, help somewhat to clothe him with the products of their own wheels and looms. But he sought them — not theirs ; went to their rude cabins as they were, took the people as they were, and earnestly labored to make them as they ought to be. This is the true object of the ministry, and the true work of gospel ministers, in every time and place, and heartily did Mr. Patton address himself to the work. His success was most gratifying. Scores were soundly converted to God, and hundreds benefited for time and eternity, by his faithful labors.

Though the religious services were of necessity performed in the cabins where families resided, or in the
open air, the results proved the work to have been
none the less of God, and none the less powerful for
the reformation of society and the salvation of men.
The present writer once learned, from one who was
present at the time, that at one of Mr. Patton's extra
appointments, at a meeting held in a small house after
night, there were no less than eleven persons happily
converted to God. So elsewhere, and at other places
on the circuit, that year. A flame of revival and soul-
saving influence glowed, to the salvation of much people. His desire and design was, not to preach just so
often, or at just so many places, but to save all the
souls he could ; and with this end in view he preached,
he met the classes, he visited the families, instructed the
children, attended his regular appointments, and had
many extra ones ; by which means he extended his
work, and extended his usefulness, greatly enlarging
the boundaries of his circuit, as well as greatly increasing the number of the members in the old boundaries. He was never of that class of preachers who
seem content simply to retain what is given them, and
think they do well if a circuit do not run down on their
hands ; but, on the contrary, labored industriously to
improve "his lord's money," that it might be returned
with interest. However good and prosperous a circuit
might be, he labored to make it *more so ;* and rarely,
if ever, failed to accomplish what he undertook.

At the close of this Conference year, or in the fall
of 1820, the Tennessee Conference met at Hopkinsville, Ky., October 4th, at which he was continued on

trial, and appointed to Clinch Circuit, which was partly in upper East Tennessee, and partly in Virginia. This circuit, as to the character of the population, was much like the other, but the face of the country much more uneven, and the traveling much more difficult. The territory embraced was also much larger than in that of the preceding year; but differences like these formed no objections to a circuit, or created any impediments in his mind. It was enough for him to know that there were souls for whom Christ died — souls needing the ministrations of the word of grace; and as the constituted authorities of the Church had deemed it proper he should go there, he did so cheerfully, and labored with considerable success, though in the midst of difficulties and oppositions of no ordinary character. Some of these oppositions will be briefly noticed hereafter.

At the close of this year, the Conference met in Bedford county, Tennessee, where, after the usual examination, he was received into full connection, and, on the 11th day of November, 1821, was solemnly ordained a Deacon in the Church of God, by the venerable Bishop McKendree, and, as the Mississippi Conference had then been but recently formed, and was greatly in want of active laborers, he was transferred thither. The session of that Conference was held in December — just one month after that of the Tennessee Conference — and at its close he was appointed to the Tuscaloosa Circuit.

The reader will remember that the Mississippi Conference was formed at the General Conference of 1820, and included in its boundaries the States of Mississippi and Louisiana, and all that part of the State of Alabama south of the Tennessee River. Hence Mr. Patton, though in the Mississippi Conference, was traveling in the State of Alabama. The Alabama Conference was not organized until the General Conference of 1832.

He traveled the Tuscaloosa Circuit during two consecutive Conference years — that is, from the fall of 1821 to the fall of 1823. Each year he had charge of the circuit, and each year he had a colleague; the first of whom was the Rev. E. V. Levert, and the second the Rev. Wm. M. Curtiss. The two years preceding these he traveled alone.

Some idea may be formed of his usefulness on this circuit, from the fact that, when he was appointed there, the membership was reported to be *four hundred and seventeen* whites, and *thirty* colored; and when he closed his second year's labor, the membership was *seven hundred and nine* whites, and *two hundred and two* colored — a net increase of two hundred and ninety-two whites, and one hundred and seventy-two colored, or four hundred and sixty-four in all.

At the close of this year, the Mississippi Conference met at Natchez, on the 25th of December, and Mr. Patton, having traveled four years, was duly elected to Elder's orders, but, not being present at the Conference, he was not ordained; nor did his ordination take place until the 29th of December following, when the Conference met in Tuscaloosa, Ala. He was ordained Elder by Bishop Soule, who had been elected to the Episcopacy at the General Conference preceding, or in May, 1824. At the time of the Conference of 1823, he was on a visit to Eastern Tennessee, where, on the 27th of November of that year, he was married to Miss Nancy Morrison, of Sullivan county, with whom he had become acquainted some years previously, when he traveled on the Clinch Circuit. She survived him, and, through a course of more than thirty years of wedded life, cheerfully sustained the labors, toils and privations incident to the wife of a Methodist traveling preacher, that she might, so far as possible, aid her husband in the great work to which he had been called, and in which he was so successfully engaged.

In one of his letters to a young preacher, Dr. Adam Clarke remarked, " Marriage to you can not be an indifferent thing. It will *make* you or *mar* you. It will be a *blessing* or a *curse* to you. It will either help you to heaven, drive you to hell, or be a heart-rending cross to you while you live." This, it may confidently be affirmed, is true in reference to every preacher of the Gospel, and especially every Methodist traveling preacher. There are more of these whose work is more or less hindered — whose usefulness is more or less restricted, and whose lives are made to be a scene of anxiety and cross bearing — because of improper matrimonial connections, than there are that experience similar results from any other cause whatever ; if, indeed, it be not true that there are more injured, as to the final success of their ministry, by this than all other causes. Nor is this a mere hasty remark, but one made with due deliberation, and that, too, after many years of careful observation.

Fortunately for Mr. Patton, and for the Church for

which he labored, he chose a companion suited both to
him and the character of his work—or, in other words,
suited to him as a Methodist traveling preacher. He
chose a woman who had sense enough to know that
though she had married a preacher, she was not, therefore, necessarily the public servant of the people of
every circuit, district or station her husband might be
called to fill; and whatever claims they might or might
not have on him, those claims did not extend to her.
And she knew, also, that though the people of the
different circuits might be well pleased to see her husband as their teacher and pastor, it did not, therefore,
follow that they would be equally well pleased to see
her. She knew that though, in one sense, they were
one, in another point of view they were two. Hence
she was a keeper at home, where, by quiet industry and
frugality, she not only contributed to the comfort, and
consequently to the success, of her husband, but also
to the proper training of a large family of children.
She was content to live within her husband's means;
hence he was never embarrassed and harassed by
debts. In frugal, economical habits of life they con-
curred and co-operated, and, although they were what
many would call poor, they had food and raiment, and
therewith strove to be content; and, after all, he lived
as well, and died leaving as much behind, as many
preachers whose annual receipts from the Church were,
perhaps, twice as large as was his, and yet who located
because, as they alleged, they were not supported.
Many a man has made out worse in supporting himself
than the Church did in supporting him.

Much of Mr. Patton's success as a traveling preacher

is justly attributable to the patient industry and constant economy of his wife; and so it has been in many other cases; while, on the other hand, many a man has blighted the prospects of his usefulness, blasted the hopes of his friends and of the Church, by an unsuitable matrimonial connection. There may be, and doubtless are, cases where the wives of ministers do much good by intermingling with the people in a proper way, and with a proper spirit and motive; but there are others who do equal, if not much greater, good by industriously applying themselves at home, thereby lessening their husbands' cares, and enabling him to devote himself more exclusively and more devotedly to his legitimate work of preaching the Gospel. Such women are worthy of all praise. They do a good to the Church, and forward the interests of religion, indirectly, it may be, but none the less certainly, to an extent, perhaps, never fully understood or appreciated in this world. Such an one was the wife of Samuel Patton.

At the Conference held in Natchez, in December, 1823, Mr. Patton was appointed to the Alabama Circuit, with Rev. R. Pipkin as a colleague. On this circuit he labored with that diligence, perseverance and success that characterized him for so many years, and experienced all those trials and hardships, discouragements, privations and enjoyments incident to the life of a traveling preacher in a newly-settled country, where almost everything was yet in little else than its primitive state.

From an early period in his ministerial history, it had been a cherished object with him to become per-

manently connected with the work in that healthful and
inviting region of country afterwards embraced in the
Holston Conference ; and now it was particularly so, as
his health, not by any means very good for several years,
was obviously failing more and more.   Accordingly,
at the close of this, his fifth year in the itinerancy, he
sought a transfer to the Holston Conference, which
had been organized at the General Conference, the
preceding May, or in May, 1824.   But Bishop Roberts
was to hold the session of the Holston Conference, and
Bishop Soule that of the Mississippi ; and the former
coming on some months earlier than the latter, Bishop
Roberts felt he could not, with propriety, transfer and
give him work in that Conference, until his character
had been examined and passed by the Conference of
which he was then a member.   So, when the session of
his Conference came on, in order to accomplish what
he desired, he asked for, and received, an honorable
location, designing merely to change his Conference
relations, and place himself where he could, in his
judgment, serve the interests of the Church equally
well, and, at the same time, likely, enjoy better health.
He, therefore, remained as local from this time (December, 1824) until the next session of the Holston
Conference, which took place the following October,
at Jonesborough, Tenn., when he was regularly re-
admitted into the traveling connection, where he remained, in the same Conference, until he was called
from labor to rest.

As Mr. Patton is now introduced as a member of the
Conference in which he labored so long and so faithfully, it may be proper to give a hasty sketch of his

manner, attainments and abilities, that the reader may
be the better prepared to trace his subsequent history.

As a man, he was rather under than above the ordinary size — about five feet eight or nine inches in
height; slender, and a little inclined to stoop. Head,
small, and remarkably well shaped. Eyes, dark gray,
keen, and very deeply set. A rather square, but not
very high, forehead. Mouth and chin, round and regular. General features, well proportioned; and the
expression of countenance, intelligent, grave and impressive — particularly so when carefully examined.
In the pulpit, he usually leaned a little forward, turned
from side to side, or moved his feet, but seldom, ges-
ticulated very little, but appropriately and impressively;
had very little of what is sometimes termed mannerism,
and nothing like bombast or rant, but was always earnest and solemn. Considering that his lungs were
weak, his enunciation was sufficiently rapid, and always
distinct; so that he was easily heard in all ordinary
congregations. His preaching was both topical and
textual — mostly, perhaps, the former; but, whether
the one or the other, it was always doctrinal; and he
seemed ever to regard that excellent injunction laid
on Methodist preachers by their Discipline, to suit
their subject to their congregations. His ability, as a
doctrinal preacher, was surpassed by very few, and his
great theme was that of the atonement. On this, with
those cardinal doctrines of Christianity so intimately
connected with it, he dwelt, more or less, in almost
every sermon; and every sermon or exhortation, as
well as almost every public act of his life, plainly
said, with the Apostle, "I determined not to know

anything among you, save Jesus Christ and him cru-
cified."

As to the peculiar doctrines of the Church to which
he belonged, few understood them better, loved them
more, or were more ready to defend them to the utmost
extent of their ability; and yet he rarely, or never,
publicly attacked or opposed the doctrines of other
sects, except when forced to do so in defense of his
own. He fearlessly, but very kindly and candidly,
exhibited and defended what he regarded as truth, but
left the application of it to those who heard. With
all the power of his mind and earnestness of his soul,
he proclaimed the doctrines of original sin, atonement by Christ for the sin of the world, justification
by faith, and sanctification by the Holy Spirit; but he
did not turn aside to say that other sects believed so
and so, and were opposed to the views he expressed,
and, therefore, wrong. He seldom said anything about
them directly, and yet the hearer, feeling the force
of the truth he presented, would rarely fail to contrast
it with opposing theories or dogmas. It is not to be
understood, however, that he failed to apply the doctrines he preached, from time to time, to the hearers
present. This he always did with great pertinency
and force, and often with remarkable success. He, at
all times, preached in a manner calculated to satisfy
any intelligent, candid mind that the object was to
save sinners then and there — save them at once and
forever. In all his preaching, it is doubted if any one
ever heard a light or trifling expression fall from his
lips, or heard him say anything in a flippant manner.

He dealt with the interests of souls, and he was solemn and earnest. The love of Christ constrained him, and he was affectionate and pressing. He spoke readily and justly. His ideas and words flowed freely, but coherently. He entered at once on the explication of his subject, passed regularly and correctly on through all the parts of a regular, well-systemized discourse, applied it, and was done. It seemed, when he entered the pulpit, he well understood both what he was going to say, and how he would say it. After often hearing him at intervals, under various circumstances — before large assemblies and before small congregations — through a period of nearly thirty years, the present writer does not remember to have ever heard him make what is commonly called a failure. He never heard him when he seemed to have lost himself, and become bewildered in what he had undertaken to present. It is true, there was a difference in his sermons. Some were much more elaborate and profound than others. Some gave evidence of more thought, more research and more interest of feeling than others ; but, with all these variations, he always seemed to make out clearly what he had taken in hands, and, whether he had much or little to say — whether his sermon was long or short — one could easily perceive he never spoke at random, but had well arranged and well digested what he said.

In the pulpit or out of it — presiding in a Quarterly, or, as he sometimes was called to do, an Annual Conference — in company with one or two private friends, or in large circles — on the floor of an Annual or General Conference, or in the class-room — that which first and most deeply impressed every beholder was his meekness and unaffected humility. These shone everywhere and all the time, because they were permanent qualities of his truly converted heart, and fixed traits in his Christian character. These won for him the respect and affection of thousands, and yet this was not the purpose for which they were cherished and cultivated. He never seemed to know that he possessed them, and appeared to be always seeking the virtues which, to other eyes, shone in him most brightly.

The writer is perfectly aware he is penning lines that will be traced by hundreds who well knew the subject of them ; hence he writes the more freely. None will deny the truth of what is here written.

In all the relations of private and social life he demeaned himself with that decorum and propriety becoming the sacred office he had been called to fill. He was friendly, but never fawning ; cheerful, but not light or trifling ; serious and candid, but never sour or carping. In a word, his feelings were those of a Christian gentleman, and his conversation and conduct partook of their nature. He cherished a sacred regard for the rights and feelings of others, that prompted him ever to treat them justly and kindly; and even when compelled, by a sense of propriety or feeling of duty, to differ with his brethren, he did so with a meekness and mildness that won their hearts to him, while, perhaps, he overthrew the cherished positions or thwarted plans on which their hearts were set. As may be supposed, he had but few enemies, and these few were such, more because his position as a minister required him, from time to time, to repel attacks made upon the doc-

trines or polity of the Church of his choice, than because of anything personal to himself. As will be seen
in the course of the narrative, he was called upon to
bear the brunt of attacks, and be foremost in the defense of the Church, in two or three spirited — not to
say bitter — controversies, carried on in the country
where he labored ; and though in these he acquitted
himself in a manner satisfactory to the Church and to
his personal friends, it was far otherwise with those
who had been his opponents. Foiled in argument, and
smarting with the pain, they rather naturally, but very
unjustly, blamed and abused him. Abused him because
they were defeated — not that he had acted unfairly or
improperly, but had been the instrument through which
truth had overthrown their favorite dogmas. While
seeking to put down others, they found their darts and
bolts to recoil to their own destruction ; and there is
no uncharity in the supposition that mortified vanity
and wounded pride had something to do in the clamors
sometimes raised against him.

As Mr. Patton was well instructed in the doctrines
of the Church, so he was well informed as to her history and discipline. Immediately upon his entrance to
the Holston Conference, he was placed in charge of a
district, and for fourteen years, by reappointments, he
occupied, on different districts, the same relation. The
duties pertaining to this office he performed as faithfully and as acceptably as most men ever do. The Discipline of the Church he administered with a cautious,
firm, but exceedingly kind hand. In this respect he
scarce had an equal. No man was farther from any
disposition to cover up iniquity in the Church, or

screen wrong-doers; and yet few men were ever more patient, gentle, kind and forbearing, when dealing with offenders — none more anxious to bring back the err- ing, or ready to forgive the penitent. In all his ad- ministrative acts, he proceeded upon the principle, that the honor of the Church is best sustained, and the glory of the cross best promoted, by reclaiming the wandering, bringing the guilty to repentance, and sav- ing souls. Hence he resorted to the fearful expedient of expelling from the communion of the Church, only when the hope of reclamation had fled, or the guilty parties stubbornly and persistently refused to yield to honest efforts made to bring them to contrition and reformation. Expulsion was with him — as it should be with all — the last remedy, and never to be applied until all else had failed. It was a maxim with him that, in Christian experience, more men fall into de- spair through discouragements, than into presumption through forwardness; hence the kind, encouraging manner of all his preaching and ministrations, both in public and in private. It may have been that the peculiar cast of his own mind had something to do in fixing this conviction so deeply as it was in his mind; but, all that aside, the thought is worthy of serious ex- amination. Sin must be denounced; but the sinner must needs be encouraged to look to Christ, as a Savior from sin. Wrong is to be deprecated and op- posed; but, at the same time, the wrong-doer is to be taught to hope for a better state. Hence the more of invitation to Christ, and encouragement, given in each and every sermon, the better, because the more success- ful it will likely be.

As a private Christian, he was of the most uniform kind. As he was seen one day, so he was seen every day—uniform in his conduct and conversation, uniform in the performance of all his Christian duties, and uniform in his manifestations of Christian feelings, and his exhibitions of Christian principles. But this uniformity was not always so much in fact as in manifestation—not that he dissembled, nor that he indulged improper tempers or dispositions ; but that, whether the skies were bright or lowering — whether the soul rested in the calm sunshine of a Savior's love, or was overcast with clouds and darkness—his outward course was still the same. He was often sorely tried, sadly cast down, and in great spiritual heaviness. His conflicts were such as defied the power of language to express, and yet the world nor the Church knew nothing of them. Perhaps none, except a part of his own family and the writer of these lines, ever had anything like an adequate idea of the depth, and strength, and agonizing character of the spiritual conflicts he was sometimes called to sustain. Why these came upon him, no one could tell ; whence they came, or through what medium, no one knew. But the present writer has been again and again called to him privately, when his mind was overcast with darkest clouds, and his soul agonized almost to despair ; yet that soul would still cleave to a Savior it could not then see, and struggle still to rely on promises it could not then feel. His mind was ever of the desponding cast, rather than otherwise ; and whether these seasons of despondency and horrible gloom were partly the result of peculiarity in constitutional temperament, and partly through the power of temptation, or whether they were wholly of the latter, the reader is left to decide for himself. Of one thing, however, he may be satisfied : they were not attributable to any irregularity or impropriety of conduct or conversation. Samuel Pattou was, in the full sense of the word, a good man. And yet these seasons of sore trial and unutterable suffering came upon him ; and when in the midst of this darkness — worse, if possible, than that of death and the grave — his mental agony, and the fearful conflicts of soul, defied all the power of language to describe. The depths of his nature were stirred ; the blackness of darkness and horror seized upon him ; the fiery darts of the enemy flew so thick and fast that he and others trembled, lest he should be pierced through and through ; and yet, in that very moment, ask him if he could give up the Savior, and, with an earnestness that only a soul thus feeling could throw into words, he would instantly reply, " *Not for ten thousand worlds. No—no ; never— never !* " " The gloom is very heavy," he would say ; " the clouds are thick, and fearfully dark — the conflict is dreadful — but there must be light beyond. Jesus lives, and he will help me. He must help me, else I die. Come, Lord Jesus. Pity, help and save me out of this distress." As a man cast overboard, amid howling storms and pitchy darkness, would hold on to a rope, and struggle towards the vessel, though neither could be seen, so he would hold on to the promises of the Gospel, and struggle towards the Savior, though the latter was hid from his faith, and the former had lost, for the time, their power on his heart. All this while, he believed, intellectually, all that he ever believed, as to the reality of religion, the truth of the Scriptures, and the power of grace. The difficulty was not in the mere intellect. It perceived, apprehended and recollected as usual. It performed all its accustomed work as readily as ever, if, indeed, its operations were not more vigorous. But there was a darkness over the moral sensibilities. The soul was in gloom, and though the mind perceived truth, the heart did not feel it. Promise after promise — text after text — might be repeated, and they were all clear to the mind, but just then they did not affect the heart.

It is not sufficient that the Christian read, apprehend and understand the Word of Truth. He must also feel its power in his heart ; and how can he thus feel, unless the Spirit of the Holy One accompany that Word ? The mind may be fully satisfied of the truth of the Gospel, and satisfied, too, after the most careful and candid investigation — it may have not the shadow of a doubt as to its truth — and yet the heart may not feel — the depths of the soul may not be stirred — and, while light is in the intellect, darkness may brood over the moral sensibilities. Thus it often is with the unconverted man, and thus it sometimes is with the most faithful Christian man. Thus it is that Christians are sometimes suffered to be tried — carried thus through the flood and through the fire — though, if they still trust in Jesus as best they can, and as did Mr. Patton, the one does not entirely overflow, nor the other consume them. Of all the trials to which good men are subjected, perhaps this is one of the sorest. Outward opposition, or conflicts from without, are as nothing, compared with these inward struggles. When all is dark, how difficult to trust! When gloom and horror enshroud the soul, and the blessed promises, though clear to the mind, have, for the time, no solace for the burdened heart, what can it do? As a man in midnight darkness, standing amid horrible dangers, dares not to move, lest one step prove his utter ruin, so the soul in such a state must gather all its strength, and hold on to what little it has, waiting for heavenly light to direct its course.

It is worthy of note that, in these sore trials of faith and severe assaults of the wicked one, Mr. Patton was rarely, or never, tempted to do or say any particular thing or things. The temptation was to thoughts. Suggestions were made, as seemed to him, almost audibly, and with a quickness and force that startled him; but they all referred to his own mental operations or spiritual condition. It is almost needless to say that he came out of the scenes of trial as gold tried in the furnace — all the purer and better for the ordeal through which it had passed. And yet who, that was but limitedly acquainted with him, or that knew him only as he appeared in his every-day walk and conversation, would have ever supposed him subject to such severe spiritual conflicts? His calm exterior and uniform deportment would have offered little or no intimation of the struggles sometimes going on within. So true is it, that every heart knoweth its own bitterness.

In the private or religious circle, he would sometimes merely mention that, as other professed Christians, he had his difficulties and spiritual conflicts, but never in a complaining — much less a whining — manner or spirit. He considered it incumbent on him, as on others, to endure hardships as a good soldier of Jesus Christ, and to murmur or complain was not to endure, in the sense in which he understood that duty.

As his subsequent life was spent in the bounds of the Holston Conference, and his subsequent history will, of necessity, be in part the history of the Church in that section, it is proper now to turn aside, and briefly review the rise and progress of Methodism there, down to the period of his connection with it. Thus the reader, by having a better understanding of the nature and condition of the work he was called to perform, will be the better able, also, to understand and appreciate the man.

CHAPTER VI.

METHODISM IN THE HOLSTON COUNTRY FROM 1776 TO 1800.

It does not pertain to a work like this to trace, or attempt to trace, the civil history of any particular section of country, or point out its topographical or geographical characteristics, else it might be pleasing, and perhaps not unprofitable, to do so in reference to the country in which it is now proposed to consider the origin and progress of Methodism. But unity—an important feature in historical narrative—requires close attention to the one subject taken in hands.

At the date of the organization of the first Methodist society in America—which, though usually fixed in 1766, was doubtless, as shown by recent historical developments, a few years earlier than that—there were comparatively few families residing in all that country now embraced in the bounds of the Holston Conference. In 1754, less than a dozen families resided in the territory bounded east and south by New River and the Allegheny Mountains, and north and west by the Cumberland Mountains. From this time, however, the number was gradually and almost constantly increased by immigration from the colonies of Pennsylvania, Virginia and North Carolina, but principally from the last-named, until, some twenty years afterwards, or in 1774, there was a considerable population, made up, as may be supposed, of traders, pioneers and adventurers of almost every caste and grade. In the meantime, Methodism, from very small and inauspicious beginnings, though scarce a dozen years had passed in its American history, had widely extended itself, particularly in the South and South-west. The energy, diligence and perseverance of its preachers were equal to the emergencies upon them, and wherever men were to be preached to, there they sought to go. The difficulties of traveling, the poverty of the people, and the numberless hardships attending their work, had no terrors to them ; while, intent only on saving souls, by the spread of pure evangelical truth, they pressed on from neighborhood to neighborhood, and from colony to colony, nor thought of stopping while there were yet men, for whom Christ died, destitute of the word of life and the blessings of a Gospel ministration. Their character, their course, and their success, considered merely in the light of historical narrative, or seen only by the historian's eye, present a scene almost, if not altogether, without a parallel, and exhibit results not to be satisfactorily accounted for on any known principles of human philosophy. It was fortunate, however, for the country, at that period of its history, there were such men in it. Thousands heard the Gospel through their agency, who, but for them, would, so far as human wisdom can see, have been utterly deprived of that privilege ; and the conservative moral influence thus thrown around the scattered settlers of new countries was of incalculable advantage, not only to the immediate subjects of such influence, but to the country at large. Bad and wicked passions were thus restrained — crime was prevented — the better feelings of human nature drawn out and cultivated to an extent not only advantageous to the then existing population, but, also, to the generations that should come after them. This influence moulded society to a better and more healthy state of things than would otherwise have existed, and it is impossible now to calculate the beneficial results of labors bestowed at such a time, and under such circumstances. While a wise Providence was preparing the way for a great change in the political and civil condition and aspects of the country, the moral interests were not neglected; and that these might receive the necessary attention at the proper time, and be prepared for coming events, the Gospel of grace was sent in a way and by means such as had not been used from the days of the apostles till then. Men, suited to the age in which they lived, and to the circumstances under which they were placed, were strangely sent forth to accomplish what seemed almost impossible — to do a work involving the severest hardships and most fearful responsibilities — a work which none others, perhaps, could have done — and yet they went forth, amid all the oppositions and discouragements attending them, and labored with a success almost unprecedented in the annals of Christianity. In less than a dozen years from the date of their organization in this country, they had spread themselves, and caused their influence to be felt, from New York to the heart of the Carolinas; and in less

than twenty-five years from the first Conference of
Methodist preachers, when their number was only ten,
there was scarce an important settlement from Kenne-
bec to the Savannah, and from the Atlantic on the east
to the farthest settlements of the Western country, but
where something was known of their doctrines and
manner of life, while they then numbered their preachers by hundreds, and their membership by thousands.

It was a remarkable and, no doubt, providential feature in the early history of Methodism in this country,
that it took deep and fast hold on the minds and hearts
of the less wealthy classes of society, and those less
cumbered with wordly goods and worldly cares. These
are the classes most given to migrations from place to
place, and these are specially they who are most likely
to be first in the occupancy of new countries. Hundreds of this class pushed westwardly as fast as the
obstacles to the settlement of the country could be
overcome ; and, carrying with them the love and principles of Methodism which they had previously imbibed,
they sent back the Macedonian cry of Come over and
help us, and thus contributed very greatly towards the
spread of the doctrines and principles they loved.
This was more or less the case all the time, and helps
to account for the wonderful rapidity with which Methodism was spread in the West. No sooner was a settlement formed, if there happened to be two or three
members or friends of the Methodists in it, than a notice was sent, by the earliest opportunity, to some
preacher that they desired preaching ; and no sooner
did the preachers receive such notices than they prepared at once to go, if at all practicable. No contracts

were made — no stipulations were entered into, other than, perhaps, a promise that some of the settlers would meet the preacher at some designated point, conduct him to the settlement, and, when there, he should be welcome to such as they had. In this way, many sections were reached, and hundreds of people preached to, and brought under the wholesome restraints of the Gospel, who otherwise might have long remained in a quite different condition. Had the early conquests of Methodism in this country been confined to those in comparatively easy circumstances — the well-settled land proprietors — emigration would have been less, so far as Methodist influence was concerned, and the cause deprived of this, one of the most successful means by which its interests were spread. Herein may be seen the providence of God. A great moral work was to be accomplished in the sparsely-settled regions of the West and South-west. The foundations of society were to be laid under new circumstances, and society itself moulded anew to the circumstances attending, and the destinies that awaited it, and these the agencies, and these the means chosen for the accomplishment of that work.

It was in this way Methodism first found its way into the section of country now under notice. At an early period after its permanent organization in America, it was introduced, and made considerable progress, in the interior of North Carolina, and thence, by emigration of its members and friends, was carried to regions watered by the Holston and Watauga rivers. The settlements near the head waters of these rivers were formed principally by persons from North Caro-

lina, and a few from Eastern Virginia. Among these
early emigrants towards the West, were Methodist
members, leaders and local preachers, who, though far
removed from former associations and influences, still
retained their love for the cause they had espoused.
Hence they acted together, for their mutual edification
and benefit — had their preachings and their prayer-
meetings — solicited the attention and labors of the
traveling preachers east of the mountains, and were,
at long intervals, served by them, from time to time, as
their pressing engagements would allow.

At the Conference held in May, 1783, there was a
return made of the Holston Circuit, with sixty members; and with this year the statistical history of
Methodism in that country begins. The reader will
observe this was only seventeen years after the commonly received date of the organization of the first
Methodist society in America, and only ten years after
the first Conference, when the whole number of
preachers, as previously stated, was only ten. So it
will be seen that Methodism in the bounds of the Holston Conference dates back almost as far as in any
other portion of the country. But to the mind of the
writer, with the evidence before him, there are good
reasons to date it back earlier than this, and date its
commencement in 1776, when Drumgole, Poythress and
Tatum labored in Carolina, gathering members and
forming circuits ; or certainly in 1777, when King,
Dickens, Cole and Pride labored at the same work,
in the same regions of country. This, as the writer
believes, and not without good reason, is the date that
should be fixed for the permanent organization of Meth-

odist societies in that country, and thenceafter they were visited by traveling preachers, from time to time, as they could find opportunity, until the time when the Holston Circuit was formed and reported, as stated above. There were then (in 1783) sixty members in these bounds. Who had gathered them? Evidently the preachers who had labored there, and whose circuits lay principally in North Carolina, east of the mountains. If the reader be curious on this subject, and will take the pains to examine, he will find that, after its introduction to the Holston country, Methododism worked its way northward and eastward in Virginia, and also that the Holston work was connected with that in Carolina immediately east of the mountains, clearly indicating that from thence it found its way to that country, almost as soon as to any part of North Carolina.

At the Conference of 1783, when the Holston Circuit was formed, or, rather, reported in the Minutes, there were, in the entire connection in America, thirteen thousand seven hundred and forty members, and eighty-two preachers were this year stationed. But if the history be commenced in 1776, which the writer believes to be the proper date, there were at that time twenty-four preachers, and four thousand nine hundred and twenty-one members in the connection. So the operations of Methodist preachers, in what is now the bounds of the Holston Conference, had an early, if not a fair, start.

Jeremiah Lambert was the first appointee to the Holston Circuit, as such. The war of the Revolution being about ended, and the tide of emigration setting strongly in that direction, the number of members in the Church having increased, as well as the federal population, and this country being separated by high mountains from that on the east, it was deemed best, in laying off the work, to separate it from that with which it had previously been connected, and assign it to one man.   Mr. Lambert's circuit embraced all the settlements on the Watauga, Nollichuckie and Holston rivers, including those in what is now Green, Washington, Carter, Johnson, Sullivan and Hawkins counties, Tennessee, and Washington, Smyth, Russell, and, perhaps, Lee and Scott counties, Virginia.   This circuit he traveled during the year, but, as the country was very sparsely settled, provisions scarce, and the Indians very troublesome, his hardships must have been very great, and his sufferings severe—no accommodations, in the modern acceptation of that term, for traveling, lodging, study, or anything else—without pay, without hope of earthly reward, without earthly friends or protectors, and often without food or shelter—he made his way, as best he could, in the name, and for the sake, of Him who had said, "Lo, I am with you alway, even to the end of the world;" and at the next Conference, or in April, 1784, he returned seventy-six members, or sixteen more than he had received. This good man ended his career on earth a few years after this, and was taken to his reward on high. Henry Willis was appointed to succeed him on the circuit; but at the Conference next ensuing this, there was no return of the numbers in society, or, at least, the General Minutes of that date show none, consequently it is impossible to tell what success may, or may not, have attended Mr. Willis' labors.

At the Conference for 1785, after the organization of the Methodist Episcopal Church, and the ordination of a portion of the traveling preachers, Holston and Yadkin Circuits were connected under the charge of one Elder, and supplied as follows :

Henry Willis, Elder. Yadkin Circuit, Henry Bingham, Thomas Williamson. Holston, Richard Swift, Michael Gilbert.

This was the Conference to which Mr. Willis should have reported the members in society.

At the next Conference, or in the spring of 1786, there were two hundred and fifty members returned from the Holston Circuit—a large increase over the returns of 1784 ; but it can not now be ascertained whether this increase was mostly during the year just closed, or during the year before, nor is it at all important. This year, Salisbury was added to the Elder's charge, and the appointments stood —

Reuben Ellis, Elder. Salisbury, Thomas Williamson, Henry Bingham. Yadkin, Robert J. Miller, John Mason. Holston, Mark Whittaker, Mark More.

[1787.] This year, as the population of the country had increased, and the number of members returned was four hundred and forty-nine whites, and one colored, or nearly one hundred per cent. above the returns of the previous year, it was thought best to divide the Holston Circuit, which was accordingly done—the eastern part extending east, so as to embrace the settlements on New River. This retained the name of

Holston, though almost entirely on new territory. The western part, lying mostly in Eastern Tennessee, was called Nollichuckie.* The two made up the charge of one Elder, and the appointments were:

John Tunnell, Elder. Holston, Jeremiah Mastin, Nathaniel More. Nollichuckie, Thomas Ware, Micaijah Tracey.

During this year, the work greatly extended westwardly, as well as towards the east. Mr. Ware, in the sketches of his own life and travels, states that, in the fall of 1787, or about the middle of the Conference year, his Elder received letters from persons living low down on the Holston and French Broad rivers, informing him of their destitute condition, and imploring him to give them aid. These letters having been read at their quarterly meeting, it was, after consultation, determined that Mr. Ware should visit the people there, and attempt to form a circuit. He went in the midst of a severe winter, and, after a season of exposure, toil and suffering, such, perhaps, as few men have endured, he succeeded in forming a circuit, called French Broad. This circuit must have been principally south-west of the French Broad River, as Mr. Ware states distinctly that, before reaching the country to which he had been sent, he crossed that river. From the best evidence now in possession of the writer, the circuit embraced the settlements in what is now Cocke, perhaps part of Jefferson, Sevier, Blount and Knox counties.

The accounts Mr. Ware gives of his privations,

* For a more particular account of Holston Circuit, as thus formed, see LIFE AND TIMES OF WILLIAM PATTON.

dangers, difficulties and sufferings are most touching, and serve to show at what a sacrifice of ease and personal enjoyment, and what a cost of privation and suffering, the foundations of Methodism were laid in that country. The Indians were exceedingly troublesome, killing people, or stealing their property, in all directions ; and once or twice the preacher very narrowly escaped death at their hands. Several times he was nearly frozen to death, and at other times compelled to flee before infuriated mobs.*

[1788.] In May of this year, the Conference was held at Keywoods, in the neighborhood of King's Salt Works, Va. Bishop Asbury reached there from Burke Court House (Morganton), N. C., passing across those terrible mountains. On his way, he stopped at Cox's, one of the oldest Methodists of that country, who lived on one of the forks of the Holston River ; thence on to the neighborhood where the Conference was to meet. But, as several days would pass ere the Conference began, he turned, and visited the brethren in the vicinity of Jonesborough, Tennessee ; thence toward Kentucky, in the Powell's Valley, and then up that valley, through Lee and Scott counties, Va., to the place of holding the Conference. The session commenced on the 13th day of May, and continued three days. It was characterized by a very gracious revival of religion, of which the present writer has given an account elsewhere.†

At the Conference, the number of members returned was : Holston, three hundred and sixty whites, and

* See LIFE OF WARE, p. 132, *et seq*
† LIFE AND TIMES OF WILLIAM PATTON.

three colored. New River — or West New River, as it stands on the Minutes — three hundred and seventy-two whites, and eight colored. Total, seven hundred and thirty-two whites, and eleven colored.

It will be observed that the name of Nollichuckie Circuit disappears from the Minutes, and Holston Circuit seems to have fallen back to its original position in Tennessee, and New River Circuit embraced the territory included in Holston the previous year. There were this year three circuits in the bounds under notice, the localities of which were about as follows : The French Broad Circuit embraced the settlements already alluded to. The Holston came next on the east, and extended eastward to some distance beyond Abingdon. Then came the New River Circuit, extending to New River, or beyond, on the east and north, and north-west, so as to include the country from Giles on to Russell, and perhaps Lee counties, Va. That it included the head waters of New River, Holston and Clinch rivers, is learned from Mr. Ware's memoir, already referred to. The appointments this year were :

Edward Morris, Elder. Holston, Jeremiah Mastin, Joseph Doddridge. French Broad, Daniel Asbury. New River, Thomas Ware, Jesse Richardson.

Greenbriar was also included in the same Elder's charge, but, as the country does not lay within the limits noticed, it will not be considered.

[1789.] In the early part of this year, Bishop Asbury passed through this section of the country, on his way to the Conference in North Carolina. He preached, as occasion served, and traveled on horseback from forty to sixty miles a day; looked after the people, and attended particularly to the wants, conduct, etc., of the preachers, thus making himself what every Methodist Bishop should be—a pastor of the preachers.*

At the Conference held in April of this year, the numbers reported were : Holston, four hundred and eleven whites ; nine colored. New River, two hundred and ninety-nine whites ; six colored. Total, seven hundred and ten whites, and fifteen colored members. There was no report from French Broad Circuit, nor does the name appear on the Minutes again for some years. The probabilities are, that, as the Indian troubles were, about this time, greatly increasing, Mr. D. Asbury had failed of success, and what of the Circuit that could be retained, if any, was attached to Holston. This year the Elders in charge of two or more circuits were first called in the Minutes *Presiding Elders*—this because the number of Elders had greatly increased, and only those the more able and experienced were put in charge of two or more circuits. They were called *Presiding Elders*, to distinguish them from other traveling Elders, whose charges were confined to single circuits. At first, the practice of putting an Elder in charge of two circuits, or more, was to give the people the benefit of the ordinances of the Church, as many — indeed a great majority — of the preachers were not ordained, and many of them inexperienced. Such a course was deemed necessary, as,

* There is nothing in Bishop Asbury's journal that would clearly indicate his having passed through this country in the spring of this year ; yet Mr. Ware says expressly that the Bishop passed through his circuit, as above stated, and he (Ware) went with him to the Conference, at McKnight's Chapel, in North Carolina, and other records confirm Mr. Ware's statement.

no doubt, it was, to afford the ordinances of the Church, and a proper administration of discipline, to the people, as well as to give all possible advantages for improvement to the junior preachers. The appointments made at this Conference for the work under notice were:

John Tunnell, Presiding Elder. Holston, John Baldwin, Mark Whittaker. New River, Jeremiah Abel, Joseph Doddridge.

Greenbriar was still under the charge of the same Elder.

It should be borne in mind that there was yet no division of the work into separate Conferences, much less into Presiding Elder's districts. The work itself was spreading in every direction, and those having it in charge were guided and governed by necessities, as they arose, and seemed to look but little in advance of them, being, no doubt, fully occupied with the pressing claims of each passing day. The great question was not so much how to provide for the future, as how to meet the demands of the present.

[1790.] This year, Bishop Asbury made another visit to the Holston country, and more protracted than those previous to this. He entered the country from Burke county, North Carolina, passing the settlements on the Watauga River; thence to those on Holston, on down as far, he says, "as to the last house," intending to make his way to Kentucky. But, being much indisposed, and not meeting the expected guides, he changed his purpose, turned eastwardly, and visited the various settlements, on as far as twenty or thirty miles beyond Abingdon, Va. Here, after resting a

day or two, he set off, by the way of the Moccasin Gap,
to visit the settlements on Clinch River, and in the
Powell's Valley.   On reaching what was then called
the lower end of that valley, near the Cumberland Gap,
he met with guides and an escort, and passed across to
Kentucky, where Methodism was then taking a deep
and firm hold.   After spending some time here, he re-
passed the Wilderness, as the country between the settlements in Tennessee and Kentucky was then called,
made his way up through South-western Virginia, to
New River, and thence across to North Carolina again.
In all this route, he was visiting the different settlements, preaching, holding prayer-meetings and class-
meetings, and often stopping by the way to talk to,
and pray with, families.   In this way, he not only did
much good to the moral interests of the people, for the
time being, but opened the way for the success of
preachers whom he afterwards sent to people thus
visited.   The impression he made was favorable to the
cause he advocated, and often the preachers found a
hearty welcome for his sake.   At this very time, one
great object he had in making the tour through what
is now Russell and Lee counties, Virginia, was to see
if a circuit could not be formed there ; and that a circuit was soon formed, will presently be seen.

In the list of Conferences appointed for this year,
there was to be one in Kentucky, April 26, and one in
Holston, May 17 ; but that Bishop Asbury attended
neither at the time specified, is clear, if his journal be
taken as authority, though he met the preachers in
Conference, in both these sections, some time during
the spring or early summer of the year.

The returns of numbers show the following : Holston, four hundred and fifty whites ; fourteen colored. New River, three hundred and eight whites ; fifteen colored. Total, seven hundred and fifty-eight whites, and twenty-nine colored members — only a small increase over the preceding year. The appointments for the ensuing Conference year were —

Charles Hardy, Elder. New River, Daniel Shives. Russell, Daniel Lockett, John Pace. Holston, Julius Conner. Green, John McGee, John West.

The Bishop said, in his journal, he wished to visit Russell, to see if a circuit could not be formed there for one man ; but, as two were sent there and to Green, with only one each to New River and Holston, the probabilities are, some parts of each of these circuits were taken off, and connected with the new territory proposed to be occupied.

It will be observed, the word *Presiding*, before *Elder*, was left off, in the list of appointments, and was not restored until 1797. This, as the writer believes, was done to accommodate the feelings of some, who, though not more immediately interested than others, were, nevertheless, disposed to complain, and professedly regard this, with some other movements of the day, as evidence of a departure from the economy of Methodism. But, as there is here no attempt at a general history of the Church in that day, there need be no discussion of this point.

[1791.] The Conference for the Holston preachers met this year at McKnight's, in North Carolina. The numbers in society returned from the Holston work were : New River three hundred and twenty whites ;

sixteen colored. Russell, seventy-nine whites; five colored. Holston, one hundred and forty whites; six colored. Green, three hundred and forty whites; three colored. Total, eight hundred and seventy-nine whites, and thirty colored, or an entire membership of nine hundred and nine — an increase, in the aggregate, of one hundred and twenty-two over the previous returns. The appointments were :

Mark Whittaker, Elder. New River, Charles Hardy, John West. Russell, John Ball. Holston, J. Sewell.

Green Circuit was left off the Minutes, and in place of *four*, the work was embraced in three circuits, while Bertie, Greensville, Camden and Portsmouth Circuits, in Carolina, were added to the Elder's district. This was, however, only a temporary arrangement, made, most likely, to meet the great demand for preachers, and allow the greatest possible number of preaching-places to be supplied by the number of preachers at command. The next year, the district and circuits were arranged as during the year preceding this.

[1792.] This year, Bishop Asbury again passed through the Holston country. Entering across the mountains from North Carolina, east of New River, he passed on by way of the Salt Works, Abingdon, Hawkins' Court House (Rogersville), to the Cumberland Gap, and thence to the settlements in Kentucky. This was about the first of April. Early in May, he returned, by pretty nearly the same route, and, on the 13th of the same month, commenced the Conference, at Huffacres, in Washington county, Va., and then went on to hold another Conference of preachers in Greenbriar, a few weeks afterwards.

The reader will understand these Conferences were held once a year, to report the number of members, general state of the work, change preachers, and transact such other business as the general interests of the cause seemed to require ; and they were held without any special regard to locality or local boundaries, other than the convenience of the preachers.   The Bishop passed over all the country, exercising a general oversight of the work, and, by previous appointment, meeting the preachers in Conference at such times and places as would least interfere with their work on the several circuits.

The number of members reported this year, from the work under notice, was : New River, two hundred and seventy-eight whites ; seventeen colored. Holston, two hundred and fourteen whites ; thirteen colored. Green, two hundred and sixty-six whites ; eight colored.   Russell, one hundred and fifteen whites ; two colored.   Total, eight hundred and seventy-three whites, and forty colored — a decrease of six white members, and an increase of ten colored, or a net increase, during the year, of only four in the entire membership.

The reader, however, if he be familiar with the history of that country at this date, will recollect this was a year of great trouble, caused by the Indians. Whole settlements were broken up, much property destroyed, and many persons killed.   Considering the exceedingly unsettled and troubled state of the country, the wonder is there was not a very great decrease in the aggregate membership.   The appointments made at this Conference were :

Barnabas McHenry, Elder. Holston, Salathiel Weeks, James Ward. Green, Stephen Brooks, Wm. Burke. New River, David Haggard, Daniel Lockett. Russell, Jeremiah Norman.

It would be pleasant, did the character of this work allow it, to trace more particularly the operations of these devoted, noble-hearted men, as, amid the many difficulties that surrounded them, they prosecuted, from year to year, the high and holy work they had undertaken ; and especially to note some of the many incidents connected with them, some of which were of the most touching and thrilling character ; but it would swell this volume to too great an extent.

[1793.]   The Conference this year was held at Nelson's, not far from Jonesborough, Tenn., commencing April 3. The Bishop reached there by the route frequently traveled from Burke county, N. C., again crossing those high and rugged mountains, that no art of man has, as yet, made easy to pass. After the Conference, he went through Green county, preaching at different places through that county, and the country between that and Cumberland Gap, and passed on again to Kentucky. On his return, he passed by pretty much the same route, through Tennessee, and on by way of Abingdon, to the Valley of Virginia. The work he performed on these routes was of incalculable service to the cause in which he was engaged.

The numbers in society, as returned this year, were as follows : Green, three hundred and forty-five whites : nine colored. Holston, two hundred and seventy-one whites ; eighteen colored. Russell, one hundred and twenty-five whites ; four colored. New River, one hundred and eighty-four whites; fifteen colored. Total whites, nine hundred and twenty-five; colored, forty-six. Total membership, nine hundred and seventy-one. Increase this year, fifty-eight. The appointments were:

John Kobler, Elder. New River, Jacob Peck. Holston, John Simmons, Stith Mead. Green, Samuel Rudder, John Ray.

For some reason, Russell was left off the list of appointments this year, but returned the next. Whether, during this year, the people there were supplied by the preachers assigned to the other circuits, or some one whose name does not appear in the Minutes, is unknown to the present writer. The probabilities are, however-it was temporarily included in the work of the other circuits.

[1794.] A Conference was held this year also in the bounds under notice, but at what particular place, is now rather uncertain. It seems that Bishop Asbury did not make his annual visit to the settlements in Kentucky and Tennessee, because of indisposition.

The number of members reported were: Green, three hundred whites; seven colored. Russell, one hundred and forty-five whites; four colored. New River, two hundred and fifty-five whites; eighteen colored. Holston, two hundred and fifty-seven whites; eighteen colored. Total, nine hundred and fifty-seven whites, and forty-seven colored, or total membership, one thousand and four. Thus it will be seen that, notwithstanding all the difficulties under which they labored, and all the disadvantages attending them, they were making some progress in their work of faith and labor of love. And it should not be overlooked, that, for several years preceding this, the Indians were very troublesome — so much so, that many settlers were driven away, while many others were killed. All was commotion, and, in such a state of things, it is rather to be wondered there was any success at all. And certainly nothing but a sincere desire to save souls, induced the preachers to remain and labor there, under the circumstances that attended them, when they might easily have gone to other and more quiet places. The people of this country were collected in different settlements, about what were called stations, or block-houses, which had been erected as means of defense and protection ; and preachers passing from one settlement to another were constantly exposed to attacks from the Indians, who were skulking about to steal and to kill ; and yet not one of these preachers, it is believed, was hurt by them. The appointments this year were :

John Kobler, Elder. Holston, Francis Acuff, John Lindsey. New River, Samuel Rudder, John Ray. Russell, Jacob Peck. Green, Williams Kavanaugh, Lewis Garrett.

[1795.] This year, the Conference met at Earnest's, on Nollichuckie, on the 27th of April. Bishop Asbury says that six preachers from Kentucky met them, and they opened Conference with twenty-three preachers, fifteen of whom were members. The Bishop reached there from North Carolina, and, after the close of the Conference, went on, by the route usually traveled, to the Valley of Virginia.

Mr. Felix Earnest, at whose house most of the preachers were entertained during the Conference, was at the time, and afterward, till his death, a local preacher. Three years previous to this, he had professed religion. Wm. Burke, who was at that time one of the preachers on that circuit, relates the circumstances of the conversion as follows : Speaking of the neighborhood in which Mr. Earnest lived, he says, "It was a very wicked neighborhood. There was one, and only one, Methodist in it, and that one the wife of F. Earnest. She sometimes attended preaching in another neighborhood, some miles distant. Her husband was a very wicked man. Being one day at a distillery, and partially intoxicated, he, all at once, became deeply concerned for the welfare of his soul. The Spirit of the Lord arrested him. He immediately went home, and inquired of his wife if she knew of any Methodist meeting anywhere on that day. It happened to be the day that Mr. Brooks, one of the preachers on the circuit, preached in the adjoining neighborhood, and he immediately set off for the meeting. He arrived after the services had been commenced. He stood in the door — his shirt collar open, his face red, and tears running freely from his eyes." After preaching was over, he invited Mr. Brooks to preach in his neighborhood. An appointment was made, and, two weeks after, Mr. Burke preached in that neighborhood to a good congregation. The whole family of the Earnests, with many others, were brought into the Church, and by September there was a large society. The first preaching was in July preceding. A meeting-house was soon built, and, as already stated, the Conference met here in the spring of the year now under notice. Sessions of the Annual Conference were frequently held at the same place, from this date on to 1830, when Bishop McKendree made his last visit to that section of country.

The number of members returned this year was: New River, one hundred and ninety whites; nine colored. Holston, two hundred and sixty-nine whites; fifteen colored. Green, three hundred whites; fifteen colored. Total, eight hundred and eighty-nine whites, and forty-four colored. Total membership, nine hundred and thirty-three — a falling off from the reports of the preceding year.

In the stationing of the preachers, John Kobler remained as *Elder ;* but Bottetourt, Bedford and Sussex Circuits, in Virginia, were added to his district; while Benjamin Lakin and Nathaniel Munsey were sent to Green Circuit; Tobias Gibson and Aquilla Jones, to Holston; Lewis Garrett, to Russell, and Richard Bird, to New River.

[1796.] The Conference was held in the vicinity of Jonesborough. Bishop Asbury attended, reaching there by his old route — "up Doe and down Tow" rivers — or, in other words, crossing those huge mountains between Burke county, N. C., and Washington county, Tenn. He complained of the scarcity of preachers, and could send only one to each of the circuits in Kentucky, and only one to Green Circuit, Tenn. This is the language of his journal, though the Minutes show two preachers sent to Green. Perhaps one was sent after he made the entry in his journal.

The district was changed back to what it had been in '94. John Kobler continued *Elder*, and Green Circuit was supplied by John Page and Nathaniel Munsey; Russell, by John Dunn; Holston, by Obadiah Strange, and New River, by James Campbell.

This year, for the first time, the membership was reported by States. The aggregate number in the bounds of the work under notice was nine hundred and fifty-nine whites, and sixty-five colored, or a total of one thousand and twenty-four — an increase over the preceding year of seventy-one. During both this and the year previous, there was a considerable decrease in the numbers on New River Circuit. On this, indeed, was the principal decrease of the year before.

While in this country this year, Bishop Asbury visited the frontier settlements in the northern part of Russell county, Va., and preached to such as could be, from time to time, gathered together. He notes, while on this trip, that he had been on the waters of Nolli-chuckie, to the mouth of Clinch, all along the north, middle and south branches of the Holston, at the settlements on New River, and was now hunting up the scattered ones near the head waters of Clinch River. Indefatigable man!

[1797.] This year, the Bishop visited what he called the new territory again, intending to go to Cumberland (Middle Tennessee) and to Kentucky, but was too unwell. So, after meeting a few of the preachers in the upper part of East Tennessee, and holding the Conference, he made his way, as best he could, towards Baltimore, lamenting greatly at the prospect of his having soon to hurry from Conference to Conference, stopping only at the principal points on the way.

The number of members reported was eight hundred

and seventeen whites, and forty-five colored, or an aggregate of eight hundred and sixty-two — a considerable decrease from the year before, and the greater portion of this decrease was on the New River Circuit, which seemed to have been running down for three successive years. In 1794, it had two hundred and fifty-five white, and eighteen colored members, and now only ninety-four whites, and six colored.

The term *Presiding* Elder was this year brought again into use, and the appointments were:

Jonathan Bird, Presiding Elder. Green, John Buxton, Robert Wilkerson. Holston, William Burke, William Duzan. Russell, John Watson. New River, Joseph Dunn.

There seems to have been a gradual extension of the work this year, and a considerable increase in some of the societies, but nothing like a general revival. Mr. Burke says, in his Autobiography, that they had peace and quietness on his circuits, and that he visited and attended quarterly-meetings in the bounds of the Green and Russell — or, as he calls it, Clinch — Circuits, where things were also moving on harmoniously. Still, as will presently be seen, there was a further *decrease* in the number of members.

[1798.] In the spring of this year, the Conference met, and transacted the usual business. No reference is made to this meeting in the journal of Bishop Asbury, and, from its reading, the plain inference is, that he was not present. But yet Mr. Burke says he was. However this may have been, the usual returns were made, and the preachers re-appointed. The district remained as it had been during the previous year, and, strange to say, the Minutes report it as supplied by both Francis Poythress and Jonathan Bird, as Presiding Elders. This, however, is most likely the result of some error committed in transcribing or printing the Minutes. The writer of this recollects to have once heard Mr. Bird say that, some time during the year, he was sent to supply this district, because Mr. Poythress had either failed in health, or been removed to some other field of labor, but does not now recollect which. The impression is, that Mr. Bird was traveling with Bishop Asbury when Mr. Poythress' health failed, and he was sent to take his place on the district. As to the circuits, they were supplied by Thomas Allen, on New River; Obadiah Strange, on Russell; Thomas Wilkerson, on Holston, and Henry Smith, on Green. As to extension, these circuits, from the first, embraced the principal settlements in the section of country already described, and the only extension they could have was by increase of appointments, as new settlements were formed, and the federal population increased.

The number of members reported was eight hundred and three whites, and fifty-one colored. Total, eight hundred and fifty-four — a still farther decrease. One cause for this might, no doubt, be found in the fact that, as the Indian troubles were now less, and much being said of the excellency and fertility of the country in Kentucky and Middle Tennessee, there was a considerable emigration from this to those sections, which emigration included, no doubt, many Methodists. Then, again, as new settlements were rapidly forming on the other side of the mountains, both west and north-west, and there was an increasing demand, in that direction, for additional preachers, there were not left in the Holston country enough to supply the work, even as well as it had previously been supplied. But there were other reasons for the decrease, some of which will, perhaps, come under notice hereafter.

[1799.] There was no Conference held this year in the Holston country; nor does it appear the Bishop passed through that section. He had now been twenty-eight years in America, performing labors and enduring hardships and privations, such as few men would, or could, have done. He was becoming very feeble, often traveling and preaching in great pain of body, as well as depression of mind. Hence it is not at all surprising he did not pass through all parts of the now widely extended work.

The district was changed, so as to embrace all the Holston country, all of Middle Tennessee, all of Kentucky, and a part of Ohio. The valleys of the Cumberland, of the Tennessee, of the New River, and of the Miami rivers, were all in the same Presiding Elder's district. Francis Poythress was the Elder. Bishop Asbury was sometimes wont to remark, in reference to his hard rides, "Kill man, kill horse — kill horse first;" but in the case of poor Poythress, there seemed a good prospect of killing both. This was the district to which, when, a year or two later, Mr. (afterwards Bishop) McKendree was appointed, he quietly remarked, if Mr. Asbury could furnish him an immortal horse, he, perhaps, could then travel it.

The circuits in Holston remained as before, only that Holston and Russell were united under one

preacher — John Sale.   New River was supplied by
Lewis Hunt, and Green by William Lambeth.   The
people were moving off to Cumberland, to Kentucky,
or the North-western Territory, and the preachers
were sent after them.

The numbers returned were eight hundred and forty-
six whites, and sixty-four colored.   Total, nine hundred
and ten — a slight increase over the returns of the
year before.

As these hasty, but, as it is believed, correct, sketches
have now been brought down to the commencement of
the present century, and as some important changes
were soon after made in the character of the work, it
will be proper to defer further notices for another
chapter.   Were the design to give anything like a full
history of Methodism in that country during the period
passed over, chapters and volumes would be required
for what is merely glanced at in a few pages.   In no
part of the whole continent, perhaps, unless it were
Kentucky, was Methodism introduced, planted and
sustained amid more serious difficulties, or more formidable oppositions, than in the particular section to
which reference is now made.   The early preachers
there suffered and endured, labored and toiled, far beyond that of which the masses of their successors of
the present have any adequate idea; nor can such idea
be formed without a general and correct knowledge of
the circumstances which attended both them and the
people whom they served.

CHAPTER VII.

METHODISM IN THE HOLSTON COUNTRY FROM 1800 TO 1816.

THE Conference for 1800 was appointed to be held at Dunworth's, on Holston, commencing the first Friday in April. Bishop Asbury did not attend it. At that time, he was in the South, in bad health, slowly making his way on towards Baltimore, where the General Conference was to meet on the first of May. The Conference was, however, held, and the usual business transacted. The numbers in society were reported as one thousand and fifty-five white, and eighty-six colored members. Total, one thousand one hundred and forty-one. In the stationing of the preachers, the district was left to be supplied, and, as it embraced all of South-western Virginia, all of East Tennessee, all of Kentucky, and all the settled parts of Ohio, or the North-western Territory, as it was then called, the probabilities are, there was no particular anxiety on the part of any one man to supply it, provided he had to be that supply.

The settlements in Kentucky were rapidly enlarging and being filled up, and all the Western preachers who could be spared were taken for that work; so that only three were left for all the Holston country. New River, Holston and Russell Circuits were united under the care of John Watson and John Page, while James Hunter was sent to Green. One preacher only (William Lambeth) was all that could be, or that was, afforded to the Cumberland, or West Tennessee, country, while there were seven in Kentucky. Regarding the facts connected with the early history of the Church in these different sections, and seeing the manifest advantages given to the Kentucky settlements, the reader would naturally expect to find Methodism there greatly in advance of what it was in the other sections. And this was the case for many years; but the precedence thus gained was not well sustained, and, in process of time, the others not only overtook, but, in many important respects, outstripped, their early favored sister. A close inquiry into the reason of this, prosecuted with a cool, philosophic pen, would reveal facts, and the operation of principles, important to Methodists everywhere, and through all time. But such an inquiry pertains to the general historiographer of the Church.

Very soon after the close of the General Conference of this year, Bishops Asbury and Whatcoat (the latter of whom had been elected and ordained at that Conference) made a tour to the West. Passing through the Valley of Virginia, and on by way of Wythe Court House and Abingdon, they entered East Tennessee, and passed on to near the mouth of Nollichuckie. Thence they turned northward, and, by way of Bean's Station and the Cumberland Gap, entered

Kentucky. After spending some time in the various settlements there, they set off for Mero District, or the Cumberland country, by way of the "barrens," in the south-western part of Kentucky. This was Bishop Asbury's first visit to this region. He preached at Nashville, and various other points in Middle Tennessee, and then, passing across the Cumberland Mountains by the old route — Spencer's Hill and the Crab Orchard—he returned to East Tennessee, and preached at various points, from South-west Point (Kingston), to the mouth of Nollichuckie, where he had left his carriage, when going out. From this last-named place, he went south, by way of the Warm Springs and Buncombe Court House, in North Carolina. As these journeys were made by stages of from twenty to forty miles a day, and often by zig-zag routes, opportunity was given to see and preach to many people, as well as attend the Conferences, and superintend the general interests of the work.

[1801.] After spending some time in the Carolinas, the Bishop took a jaunt eastward, through Virginia, then on to Maryland, Pennsylvania and Delaware, then back, through Maryland and the Valley of Virginia, to the Holston country. After crossing New River, at Pepper's Ferry, he passed through parts of Wythe, Tazewell, Washington, Russell and Scott counties, Va., and to Ebenezer Meeting-House, in Green county, Tenn., to hold the Conference. This was in October of that year (1801). A Conference had been appointed, and was most likely held, in May preceding this; and a little explanation may be necessary, just here, in order to prevent mistakes. In the General Minutes for 1801, it is stated that no reports of numbers had been received from Tennessee or Kentucky. Now the annual round of Conferences for that year commenced with the South Carolina, January 1st, and ended with the New England Conference, which began, according to appointment, July 17, 1801; so that the Annual Minutes were, most likely, published some time between the last of July and the first of October, of this year; and when the publishers say that there were no returns, they must have had reference to the Conference held in May; and the preachers then appointed to the several circuits, traveled them from May until October, only. Then, when Bishop Asbury came on, and held the Conference at Ebenezer, in October, 1801, he reappointed the preachers who remained on the appointments then given, until the Conference held in the Cumberland country, in October, 1802; and the returns made at the Ebenezer Conference, in 1801, appear in the General Minutes of 1802. The Bishop did not attend the Conference in May, and his annual round for 1802 commenced at Ebenezer, in October, 1801, and ended with the New England Conference, held in the Province of Maine, July 1st, 1802.

The appointments made for the Holston work, at the Conference in May, were: For Green Circuit, Samuel Douthet, Ezekiel Burdine. Holston and Russell, James Hunter. New River, John Watson. The district remained as before, embracing all the Western country, almost, and Wm. McKendree was Presiding Elder.

At the Conference in October, of the same year, the

Holston country was separated, and formed into a district, and the appointments were as follows :

HOLSTON DISTRICT — *John Watson*, P. E.   Green Circuit, Moses Floyd, John A. Grenade.   Holston, Samuel Douthet.   Russell, James Hunter, six months, and then L. Blackman.   New River, Ezekiel Burdine, Louther Taylor.

The numbers in society, as reported to this Conference, and published in the General Minutes of 1802, were only three or four more than had been reported eighteen months before.

In the fall of 1802, Bishop Asbury twice passed through the Holston work, preaching at various places, and otherwise attending to the interests of the Church. His annual round of Conferences commenced in Tennessee, in October, 1802, and closed with the New York Conference, July, 1803.

The Conference year from October, 1801, to October, 1802, was one of great prosperity. The total membership, in the country under notice, in 1801, was 1,057 whites, and 86 colored, or 1,143 in all ; and at the succeeding Conference — the one held in Cumberland, in October, 1802—the numbers were 2,811 whites, and 170 colored. Total, 2,981 ; while the number of circuits was increased by the addition of two. This was about the beginning of that extensive revival which swept so extensively over that whole country, and which, for a year or two previously, had been prevailing in Kentucky. The appointments made at the Conference of 1802 were :

HOLSTON DISTRICT — *John Watson*, P. E.   Holston, Thomas Milligan, John A. Grenade.   Nollichuckie,

Henry Smith. French Broad, Louther Taylor. Powell's Valley, Benjamin Young. Clinch, Moses Black. New River, L. Blackman.

In 1801, names indicative of locality were prefixed to Presiding Elders' districts, and, the next year, the same was done in regard to Conferences; and the district of country which, in 1801, was embraced in the *Kentucky District*, with nine circuits, and W. McKendree for Elder, was, in 1803, or two years later, the Western Conference, with four Presiding Elders' districts, and twenty-six circuits — so rapid and so great was the extension of the work.

[1803.] This Western Conference met for this year at Mount Gerrizim, Ky., on the 2d of October, when the numbers in society, reported from the Holston District, were 2,933 whites, and 205 colored, or a total of 3,138, or an increase of 157 over the reports of the preceding year. The stations of the preachers for the ensuing year were:

HOLSTON DISTRICT — *John Watson*, *P. E.* Holston, Thomas Milligan. Last year his station had been changed to Clinch. Nollichuckie, Samuel Douthet. French Broad, John Johnson. New River, Elisha W. Bowman. Clinch, Joab Watson. Powell's Valley, Moses Black. Wilderness, Jacob Young.

It may be satisfactory to the reader, briefly to refer to the geographical position of these several circuits, as now arranged. New River Circuit included the country lying west of that river, from the Carolina line, on north and north-west, through Tazewell and Giles counties, in Virginia. Holston Circuit came in next, on the west, and embraced the country on both sides of the main traveling route, from somewhere west of Wythe Court House, to considerably west of Abingdon. Clinch included Russell, Scott and part of Lee counties, Va., and a part of Tennessee lying north of the Holston River. Powell's Valley embraced all the settled country lying between Clinch River and the Cumberland Mountains, from about Lee Court House, in Virginia, on as far west as the settlements extended. Nollichuckie included the upper part of East Tennessee, down as low as about the western line of Green county. French Broad came in immediately west, and occupied country on both sides of the French Broad and Holston Rivers. The Wilderness, to which Jacob Young was sent, lay in the mountainous country lying north and west of the Valley of East Tennessee.

This year, as on the three preceding, Bishop Asbury visited a large portion of all the prominent settlements in this country, contributing what he could to the advancement of the work, and the prosperity of the cause of God. No work possible to be done was too arduous for him to undertake; and much of that zeal and aggressive, as well as persevering, spirit, characterizing the Methodist preachers of that day, was, doubtless, owing to the example they ever had before them, in the course pursued by their Bishop.

[1804.] The Conference met again at Mount Gerrizim, in Kentucky. Bishop Asbury attempted to reach the place, but, after traveling several hundred miles, was taken with a severe illness, when within a few days' ride of the seat of the Conference, and compelled to relinquish his purpose, and return eastwardly. Several preachers were this year received on trial in the traveling connection, some of whom labored long and faithfully, doing much good for the Church and the general interests of Christianity.

The numbers in society, reported from the Holston District, were 3,122 whites ; 182 colored. Total, 3,304, or 166 more than the year before. There had been remarkable prosperity attending the Church, in the bounds of the Western Conference generally ; but it had been more marked and extended in Kentucky and Middle Tennessee than in the Holston region. There were no important changes made, either in the district or circuits, other than their gradual enlargement, so as to meet the increasing wants of a country still being settled up ; and in this respect the course and conduct of the preachers was worthy of all commendation, as also of constant imitation. The promptness with which they visited new settlements, and sought to carry the truths of the Gospel to every part of the country, and, if possible, to save all the people — in every place — proved them to have felt the importance of the work they had undertaken, and to have been alive to the worth of souls, and the value of the truth they preached. Facts and incidents connected with the history of the men and the times, now in possession of the writer, present them in a light very different from that in which they have too often been viewed.

The appointments made at the Conference referred to, and which stood from October, 1804, to October, 1805, were :

HOLSTON DISTRICT — *Jonathan Jackson, P. E.* Holston Circuit, Joab Watson, William Houston. Nollichuckie, William Ellington, Thomas Lasley. French Broad, Elisha W. Bowman, Joshua Oglesby. New River, Anthony Houston. Clinch, Moses Black, Obed Noland. Powell's Valley, Thomas Milligan.

These labored on their several circuits, as best they could, under the circumstances attending them, until the Conference for 1805.

[1805.] The Conference met in Scott county, Ky., and there they reported a membership of whites, 2,773 ; colored, 171. Total, 2,944, or 360 less, in the aggregate, than at the preceding Conference, though a new circuit — Carter's Valley — had been formed, and was returned as having forty members.

It were useless to stop here, and inquire into the probable causes of this decrease in the number of members, though satisfactory reasons might be assigned, did it comport with the character of this work. Several similar cases will yet pass under notice ; and if the writer stop to account for one, he must, also, for the others, which would require more space than can be allowed to these notices.

There was no change in the district or circuits, other than the addition of the circuit just alluded to. Thomas Wilkerson was appointed Presiding Elder. Anthony Houston and William Vermillion were sent to Holston Circuit; Moses Black, to Nollichuckie ; Ralph Lotspeich, to French Broad ; Joseph Williams, to New River ; John McClure and George C. Light, to Clinch ; William Hitt, to Powell's Valley, and Thomas Milligan, to Carter's Valley. Some of these were most excellent men and faithful laborers.

[1806.] The next session of the Western Confer-

ence was held at Ebenezer Meeting-House, Green
county, Tennessee, commencing September 15, 1806.
Bishop Asbury attended, and notes that the preachers
were in want, and could not help themselves; so he
parted with "his watch, his coat and his shirt," to relieve them, as far as possible. Last year, the Bishop
merely passed through the Holston country, on his
way from Kentucky to the Carolinas. This year, he
entered the country from the Valley of Virginia, and
spent some time visiting and preaching at different
points, from New River to the place of holding the
Conference. After the close of the Conference session,
he went south, by his old route, as far as to Buncombe
Court House; but from there, instead of passing out
by the head of French Broad, as usual, he turned eastward, and crossed the mountains at Mill's Gap. He
preached at several places in North Carolina, west of
the mountains, and, among others, on Turkey Creek,
at what he called "a sort of camp-meeting," where four
or five hundred persons were present.

. The return of members this year was 3,023 whites,
and 182 colored. Total, 3,205 — 261 more than the
year before, but still not equal to the number returned
two years previously. No change in the district, except a circuit, called West Point, was formed, and left
to be supplied. This embraced the country about, and
west of, Kingston, which, at the next Conference, was
returned with the name of Cumberland, and as having
forty-five members; but no separate appointment was
made there the next year, or for several years; and
when, finally, an appointment was made, it was to a
circuit called Tennessee Valley. Until then, these

forty-five members, with others, were included in a circuit previously formed. Thomas Wilkerson was continued as Presiding Elder, and the circuits were supplied as follows:

Holston, Ralph Lotspeich, J. Crane. Nollichuckie, William Houston. French Broad, James Axley. New River, Thomas Milligan. Clinch, Richard Browning, George C. Light. Powell's Valley, John McClure. Carter's Valley, Joshua Oglesby. West Point, to be supplied.

[1807.] The Conference this year met at Chillicothe, Ohio, commencing September 14th. During the Conference year now closing, there had been some prosperity in the Holston work, and a net increase in the number of members of 101 ; the returns showing a membership of 3,108 whites, and 198 colored. Total, 3,306. The preachers, for the greater part, had labored faithfully, extended the area of their work considerably, and witnessed a good degree of prosperity. No change was made in the district, other than already noticed in the case of West Point, except, for some reason, now unknown, New River was left off in the list of appointments. The probability is, that, in the scarcity of preachers, supplies could not well be commanded, and, by slight alterations, that territory was embraced in the Holston Circuit, and, to do this, the changes may have affected two or three circuits.

Thomas Wilkerson located this year, and Learner Blackman was appointed to succeed him on the Holston District; and the circuits were supplied by Caleb W. Cloud, and Hezekiah Shaw, to Holston ; Nathan Barnes and Obadiah Edge, to Nollichuckie ; Benjamin

Edge, to French Broad ; Miles Harper and Thomas Trower, to Clinch ; Abbott Goddard, to Powell's Valley, and John Henniger, to Carter's Valley.

It would be exceedingly pleasant to trace the personal history of these men, and note some of the incidents therewith connected. It might serve a valuable purpose, but, if done, it must be at another time.

[1808.] The Conference for this year was held at Liberty Hill, in Tennessee, commencing October 1st. Bishop Asbury attended, passing through Kentucky to reach there, and then, after Conference, visiting East Tennessee, and preaching at divers places. As this Conference was much nearer to them than that of the previous year, the attendance of Holston preachers was larger than at the preceding session ; but they wore the marks of hardships and toil. One who was present once stated to the writer, that the appearance of the whole Western Conference, as a body, was strongly indicative of hard labor, privation and suffering. Their clothes were of the plainest homespun ; their shoes (for boots they had none) were of strong, coarse, home-tanned leather, and there was not what could have been regarded as a decent overcoat among them. As to pecuniary compensation, they received almost none at all.

The total number of members returned this year, from the Holston District, was 3,199, or 107 less than the number returned at the preceding Conference. Two new circuits were formed, but mostly of territory which had been previously occupied, to a greater or less extent, by those traveling the circuits already existing. These new circuits were Watauga, lying partly in the upper or eastern part of East Tennessee, and partly in South-western Virginia, and, perhaps, occupying a part of Ashe county, in North Carolina. The other was called Tennessee Valley Circuit, and the name will clearly indicate the locality, to those acquainted with the country.

Learner Blackman was continued on the district, and the circuits were supplied as follows:

Holston, Wm. Pattison, Moses Ashworth. Watauga, T. Milligan. Nollichuckie, Thomas Trower, Horatio Barnes. French Broad, Nathan Barnes, Isaac Lindsey. Clinch, Isaac Quinn, Lewis Anderson. Powell's Valley, James Axley. Carter's Valley, Moses Black. Tennessee Valley, Milton Ladd.

This seems to have been a good supply. Several of these were men of no mean ability, and characterized by a spirit of devotion to the Church, and great earnestness in their efforts to promote her interests; and yet, during the year following the Conference just alluded to, there was a decrease, in the aggregate membership on the district, of *one hundred and nineteen*—a decrease even greater than during the Conference year just closed.

It would not be fair to attribute this decrease in numbers, and apparent want of success, to any lack of efficiency, industry or diligence on the part of the preachers, as that would be contrary to the facts in the case; nor would it be proper to look for the cause in the emigration of the people, though this had been the case in other years. The country was now filling up, as indicated by the formation of the two circuits alluded to; and although there were many removals from, there were many immigrants to, that section of country.

The true cause for this decrease in the number of members, for two years in succession, lay back of all these things, and was to be found in an honest mistake on the part of the preachers, together with outward opposition, which will come under notice in another chapter. Much well-meant, honest ministerial labor was lost, because misdirected.

[1809.] The Conference for 1809 was held at Cincinnati, Ohio. The territory of the Western Conference, at that time, embraced almost the entire Valley of the Mississippi ; and preachers who one year traveled in East Tennessee, or South-western Virginia, might the next year travel in Ohio, Indiana, Illinois, Missouri, or Louisiana, and still be in the same Conference. A case occurred at the Conference under notice. Isaac Lindsey, who, at the Conference of 1808, was appointed to the French Broad Circuit, in Holston District, was, at the next Conference, sent to Cold Water Circuit, in Indiana District. French Broad Circuit lay in East Tennessee, and mostly south-east of Knoxville, while Cold Water Circuit—his next appointment—lay west of the Mississippi River, and north of the city of St. Louis ; yet Lindsey traveled both.

Not many of the Holston preachers attended the Cincinnati Conference. The distance was great, and they were ill able to incur the expense of the travel ; and had it not been that they traveled on horseback, riding their own horses, and were but seldom charged for their lodging at night, still fewer, if, indeed, any of them, could have attended. Bishop Asbury was present at the Conference, and, after its adjournment, passed through the Holston country, to South Carolina. As already stated, the returns show a further falling off in the membership, the total number this year being only 3,080, of whom 2,887 were whites, and 193 were colored. The stations of the preachers on the Holston District were :

Frederick Stier, P. E. Holston, James Axley, John Brown. Saltville, James King. Nollichuckie, William Pattison. French Broad, Thomas Trower. Clinch, William B. Elgin. Powell's Valley, Lewis Anderson. Carter's Valley, John Bowman. Tennessee Valley, William Young.

[1810.] On the first of November, the Western Conference commenced its session for this year at "the New Chapel, Shelby county, Kentucky." Bishops Asbury and McKendree were both in attendance, and the former spoke of it as a very pleasant and profitable session. Twenty-six preachers were admitted on trial, and ninety-five were stationed. In the membership of the Church, there had been, during the Conference year now ending, an increase of four thousand in the bounds of the Western Conference ; and the net increase in the whole Church, during that year, was *ten thousand and seven.*

After the close of the session, the Bishops passed hurriedly through a portion of Middle and Eastern Tennessee, and on to the South. They preached at but few places on the route, but prayed in every house they visited, except, says Bishop Asbury, *in one case.* Where this was, he does not inform us ; nor have we now any means of knowing *why* there was any exception. The probabilities, however, are, that, in their journeyings, the good Bishops chanced upon a family where they were utterly forbidden to hold prayers, though such families were very difficult to find, in all the Western country, during the early periods of its history. They may have been careless and prayerless themselves — and many were so — but there was a respect for things sacred, that forbid their denying to others the privilege of doing what themselves neglected.

There seems to have been but little change throughout the Holston country, except a gradual going forward in the various departments of the work. There was, during the year, a net increase in the membership of .625 ; the total being 3,705, of whom 230 were colored. The district still contained eight circuits, to which the appointments this year were :

Holston, Thomas Trower. Saltville, Josiah Crawford. Nollichuckie, Samuel H. Thompson. French Broad, William Pattison. Clinch, Samuel Hellums. Powell's Valley, John Brown. Tennessee Valley, Thomas Hellums. Carter's Valley, Richard Richards.

[1811.] The session of the Western Conference this year was held at Cincinnati, Ohio, commencing October 1st. A few of the Holston preachers attended.

The year now closing had been marked by signal displays of Divine power in different parts of the Holston District. At a camp-meeting in Blount county, there was a most extraordinary season of revival influence, and scores were gathered into the fold of Christ. In Lee, Tazewell and Washington counties, Virginia, and in Green, Washington, Hawkins, Knox, and other counties of Tennessee, the work was power-

ful, and the ingathering great ; so that, notwithstand·
ing the feeble supply that had been made to the dis·
trict, there was a net increase of members of 654 ; the
whole number, as returned at this session, being 4,359,
of whom 291 were colored.

This year, also, a number of half-breed Cherokee
Indians were converted and received into the Church—
perhaps the first instance of the kind that had ever oc·
curred in the South-west.

The name of Saltville Circuit was left off the list,
and the societies there attached to other circuits.
Frederick Steir was continued on the district, as on the
year previous, and the appointments for the circuits
were :

Holston, Lewis Anderson, Jesse Cunnyngham. Nol·
lichuckie, Samuel Sellers.   French Broad, George
Ekin, Josiah Crawford. Clinch, Samuel H. Thompson,
Richard P. Conn. Powell's Valley, Thomas A. King.
Carter's Valley, John Henniger. Tennessee Valley,
Wm. B. Elgin.

At this date, the whole Western Conference, which
embraced, as already noticed, almost the entire Valley
of the Mississippi, and had its preachers operating in
almost every settlement, contained only *thirty thousand
six hundred and forty-five* Church members — less than
are now in the bounds of the Holston Conference,
which then composed only one Presiding Elder's dis·
trict.   In the territory of the old Western Conference,
and that opened out west and south-west of it, there
are now nearly twenty Annual Conferences, with half
a million of Church members ; and yet men who la-

bored in the Western Conference, ere its division, still live to behold and wonder at the works God hath wrought.

[1812.] At the General Conference which met in May, of this year, the Western Conference was divided, and the territory previously embraced in it was, by the division, embraced in the Ohio and Tennessee Conferences, formed this year. The following boundaries were agreed upon as the limits of those two new Conferences, to wit :

"The Ohio Conference shall include Ohio, Muskingum, Miami, Kentucky and Salt River Districts."

These districts, be it remembered, embraced a part of North-western Virginia, a part of Pennsylvania, all of Ohio, nearly all of Kentucky, and a good part of Indiana. But, large as was the territory of this, it was much less than that allotted to the Tennessee Conference. The boundaries of this, as defined in the Discipline of that date, were given thus :

"The Tennessee Conference shall include Holston, Nashville, Cumberland, Wabash, Illinois and Mississippi Districts."

Consequently, South-western Virginia, all of Tennessee, and all the settled portions of Illinois, Missouri, Arkansas, Mississippi and Louisiana, with a part of Alabama, were embraced.

The first session of the Tennessee Conference was appointed to be held at Fountain Head, Tenn., commencing November 1, 1812 ; but, from some cause or other, it did not commence until the 9th of the same month. Bishops Asbury and McKendree were both present, and the former spoke of it as a profitable ses-

sion, and also spoke of the great need of more preachers for the Mississippi country. After the close of the
session, the Bishops again passed through the Holston
country, by pretty much the same route as on their last
visit, previous to this, and, on their way, preached at
several points, baptized much people, and rejoiced
greatly in the great prosperity of the work throughout
the bounds of the new Conference. The numbers in
society, as returned from Holston District, were:
whites, 5,794; colored, 541. Total, 6,335, or an increase over the previous year of 1,976 members.

There was still but one district in the country under
notice, though another circuit or two was added, and
the names of some others changed. The appointments
were:

HOLSTON DISTRICT — *James Axley, P. E.* Abingdon,
Baker Wrather. Nollichuckie, L. Anderson. French
Broad, George Ekin. Tennessee Valley, Thomas A.
King. Clinch, John Henniger, W. Douthet. Carter's
Valley, William King. Powell's Valley, Mumford
Harris. Knoxville, Samuel H. Thompson. Holston,
Sela Paine.

[1813.] The Conference for 1813 was appointed to
be held at " Rees' Chapel, to commence on the 1st of
October." Bishop Asbury was present, though in
great feebleness. He spoke of it as a pleasant and
profitable session ; and, after its close, he made his
way hastily, through East Tennessee and Western
North Carolina, to the South.

The numbers in society, from the Holston District,
were: 5,549 whites, and 577 colored. Total, 6,126 —
a considerable falling off from the reports of the

previous year. But it should be remembered, this was in the heat of the war with England, when hundreds of Church members, in common with others were pressed into the service of their country, many of them to find gory beds of death, and many others to experience what is worse than that — a backsliding from God in heart and in life. When communities are excited, as this country then was, it tries the Church, and often separates "the precious from the vile."

At this time, there was a larger membership in the Holston than in any other district in the Conference, the entire membership of which was *nineteen thousand seven hundred and seventy-six whites*, and *nineteen hundred and thirty-nine colored*, distributed through six Presiding Elders' districts, Holston having as above stated.

There was an additional circuit formed. this year, and the appointments were :

James Axley, P. E. Abingdon, George Ekin. Nollichuckie, Sela Paine, Nicholas Norwood. French Broad, John Hartin. Tennessee Valley, Jesse Cunnyngham. Clinch, Benjamin Malone, Wm. Stribling. Carter's Valley, Thomas A. King. Powell's Valley, William King, John Manifee. Knoxville, Richard Richards. Holston, John Travis, William Douthet. Cumberland, John Bowman.

From this list, it will be seen that John Bowman, of whom a more particular account has been given in the LIFE AND TIMES OF REV. WILLIAM PATTON, was sent to Cumberland — not the Cumberland so well known, and of which so much was said and written, in periods of Methodist history somewhat earlier than this, but a district of country, exceedingly mountainous and rugged, which divides East Tennessee from Kentucky, settled by a people as primitive in their manners as could likely be found anywhere in the United States. Mr. Bowman seems not to have accomplished much among them, as we hear no more of Cumberland Circuit for some time afterwards.

In the list of appointments there is another name that will call up reminiscences of a character very different from those associated with the name of Bowman. It is that of Richard Richards—a man of strong mind, well cultivated, and once of great popularity and usefulness. But alas! that bane of human society — strong drink — was his ruin. For many years he was out of the ministry and out of the Church. The present writer was his pastor during the closing months and scenes of his life. He had returned to the Church, with a wrecked fortune, a ruined reputation, and himself but the mere wreck of a man, and, amid the bitterest tears of repentance and keenest pangs of remorse, spent the last periods of life, and at last died, casting himself on the mercy of Him who died to save sinners.

[1814.]   The next year, Conference was held at " the New Chapel, Logan county, Ky., commencing Sept. 29." Bishop Asbury was present, and recorded of the session, that it was one of great peace and harmony. The people were very kind, though they were much crowded. " We sit," says he, " six hours a day in Conference. Poor Bishops — sick, lame, and in poverty!" Both the Bishops were in attendance—both in very feeble health. Bishop Asbury was suffering under the weight of age and many infirmities, and Bishop McKendree had re. received an injury some time previously, under which he was suffering greatly. Their condition prevented them from going to Mississippi, as they had contemplated ; so, after the close of the session, which was on the 6th of October, they passed on, through Middle, and part of East, Tennessee, to the South, to attend the South Carolina Conference.

At this same session, where the Bishop says they sat six hours a day in Conference, they also spent two hours a day in the chapel, arranging the appointments, *etc.*, and four hours more at the preaching-stand. Well might he exclaim, " Poor Bishops !"

Although there was but little increase in the traveling ministry this year, it was quite otherwise among the local preachers. Their numbers had greatly increased. Many had moved into the bounds of the Conference from other sections, and many others had been licensed, and set apart for that work. The aggregate membership returned this year, from the Holston District, was 5,513, or over six hundred less than at the previous session. The war with England still raged, distracted the country, and tried the Church most sadly. One new circuit was formed in the district, and the appointments for the year were :

HOLSTON DISTRICT — *James Axley*, P. E. Abingdon, Sela Paine. Nollichuckie, Benjamin Malone. French Broad, John Henniger. Tennessee Valley, J. Manifee. Clinch, Wm. Hart. Carter's Valley, Jesse Cunnyngham. Powell's Valley, James Porter. Knoxville, James Dixon. Holston, G. Ekin. Lee, Thos. Nixon.

James Dixon, this year appointed to Knoxville, was, in many respects, a remarkable man, and one who, subsequently to this, was the subject of a most remarkable

providence.   He was an Irishman by birth, finely educated and highly gifted.   At this time, he was in the
prime and vigor of manhood — an able preacher, and
an able exponent and defender of the doctrines and
polity of the Church to which he belonged.   He was
once led into a protracted controversy, which was carried on through the public prints, with the celebrated
Dr. I. Anderson, of the Presbyterian Church — one of
the ablest ministers that Church ever had in Tennessee, and one who, no doubt, felt it to be his duty to
oppose, with all his ability, the doctrines and polity of
the Methodist Church ; and, in justice to his memory,
as well as to the truth of history, it must be said, if
such were his duty, he was faithful in the discharge of
it.   A portion of the published matter in the controversy alluded to is in the possession of the present
writer, and, whatever Dr. Anderson and his friends
may have thought of the result, Mr. Dixon and his
friends had no cause to regret the controversy had
been thrust upon them, or to feel ashamed of the manner in which he had conducted it, or of the results which
followed.   This year he acted his part well.   The next
year after this, he was sent to Natchez, where his
health failed, and for two or three years he was on
the list of superannuated preachers.   In the fall of
1819, having been partially restored to health, he was
again sent to Knoxville, and, at the Conference for
1820, he was appointed to Knoxville and Greenville ;
but, during the year, he was suddenly stricken down
with apoplexy, or epilepsy, and, for a remarkably long
period, remained helpless, and almost entirely uncon-
scious.   After some weeks, during which he was, with

great difficulty, kept alive, he was restored to consciousness, but not to a recognition of anybody or anything around him. He had forgotten his own name — forgotten the names and faces of his most intimate friends — forgotten how to read — forgotten, even, the letters of the language — forgotten everything. Nor did he. ever recover, to any considerable extent, what he had then lost. He learned his letters, learned again to read, and slowly recovered a part—but only a small part—of what he had been, by disease, bereft. Some eight or ten years after his first attack, he had so far recovered as occasionally to give a short exhortation at religious meetings, and, a few times, attempted to preach. Later in life, he became worse, his affliction exhibiting much more of mental derangement, sometimes going off into frenzy, then into dementation. At last, his friends were under the painful necessity of sending him to an asylum, where his sufferings were, a few years ago, ended by death.

[1815.] The next year, the Conference was held "at Bethlehem Meeting-House, in Wilson county, Tennessee, commencing October 20th." Bishops Asbury and McKendree were both present, the former for the last time. This was the fifty-fifth year of his ministry, and the *forty-fifth* of his labors in America, during which he was constantly traveling and preaching. Did ever mortal man labor as he did? But he was now nearly done. Soon after this, he went to his reward on high.

The Conference was eight days and a half in session, and did a great deal of business. Fourteen preachers were admitted on trial, and a like number were received into full connection. The reports of the progress of the work, in some parts of the Conference, were of a gratifying and encouraging character, but not so from the Holston District. There was a still further decrease in the number of members, though not so great as during the year before.

It will be recollected that, early in this year, peace had been proclaimed between the United States and England ; and, soon after, large tracts of country were opened, in the West and South-west, for occupancy ; and to these hundreds of persons emigrated, from the bounds of the Holston District, among whom were many Methodists, which may, at least in part, account for the decrease in membership, notwithstanding some extensive revivals were experienced. And then there was a peculiarity in the mannerism of some of the preachers who had labored there, that manifestly militated against the success of the Church. This may come up for notice in another place. The appointments were :

HOLSTON DISTRICT — *James Axley*, *P. E.* Abingdon, James Porter. Nollichuckie, John S. Ford. French Broad, John Bowman. Tennessee Valley, Wm. Hart. Clinch, Ivy Walke. Carter's Valley, Nathan Barnes. Powell's Valley, John Seaton. Knoxville, John Henniger. Holston, John Hutchison. Lee, Josiah B. Daughtry. Tazewell, G. Ekin.

At the session of the Conference under notice, delegates were chosen to the General Conference, which was to meet in May, 1816 ; and P. Cartwright, Samuel Sellers, James Axley, Jesse Walker, T. L. Douglass and James Smith were chosen, all of whom were present at the opening of the session, and subsequently bore their part in the doings of that body.

The work was extending in every direction — being pushed forward, as far as practicable, into every neighborhood ; so that all — of every class and of every grade — might be blessed with the privilege of hearing the Gospel, and enjoying the benefits of the institutions of the Church, in all their purity, simplicity and power.

The whole number of traveling preachers in the connection, at this time, was *seven hundred and sixteen*— a small number, compared with the present, when there are more than six thousand, yet a large number, when it is recollected that, forty-three years before, the whole number was only *ten*. The entire membership of the Church was *two hundred and twenty-four thousand eight hundred and fifty-three*. The net increase this year was over ten thousand.

There is that in the spirit, progress and success of Methodism, the philosophy of this world can never explain. The excellency of its power " is not of men, but of God ;" and, while its ministers are true to it, to themselves and to God, the world can not stand before it. It must, and will, succeed and triumph.

CHAPTER VIII.

METHODISM IN THE HOLSTON COUNTRY FROM 1816 TO 1824.

THE General Conference of 1816 was, in many respects, one of great interest and importance to the whole Church, and particularly so to the Church in the South and West. Some of the measures then adopted worked to the great advantage and success of the Church in the West, while some others were rather detrimental than otherwise to her rapid progress. A particular examination of these points would not, however, come properly in place here, hence it is waived.

The organization of the Missouri and Mississippi Conferences, which was effected at this time, took from the Tennessee Conference the greater portion of her territory, but left her with a large majority of the membership of the Church, as well as of the preachers.

[1816.] The session of the Annual Conference this year was held at Franklin, Tenn., commencing October 20th. Under the new arrangement of boundary lines, there were over fifty preachers remaining in this, while scarce more than thirty were set off to the Missouri and Mississippi Conferences.

The work in the Holston country was divided into

two Presiding Elders' districts, and one or two more
circuits were organized. Eleven preachers were received on trial at this session, two of whom spent many
years in the Holston country. Of them, one — Rev.
T. Stringfield — a great and good man, has just passed
away.* The other — W. S. Manson — perhaps, still
lives, but lives as a monument of human frailty, and an
example of the necessity of daily watching unto prayer,
lest, after a man preach the Gospel unto others, himself
become a castaway.

Notwithstanding favorable reports, as to the general
state of religion, and the peace and prosperity of the
Church throughout the bounds of the Conference, there
was a still farther decrease of the aggregate of members in the circuits of the Holston District. The whole
number, as reported this year, was 5,378, against 5,397,
reported the year before. The appointments were :

HOLSTON DISTRICT — *Jesse Cunnyngham, P. E.* Ab-
ingdon, John Bowman, Wm. Ashley. Clinch, G. Ekin.
Carter's Valley, W. S. Manson. Holston, Nathan
Barnes, John Dew. Lee, Benjamin Edge. Tazewell,
Isaac Quinn.

FRENCH BROAD DISTRICT — *John Henniger, P. E.*
Nollichuckie, J. B. Daughtry. Little River, Wm.
Hart, Benj. Peeples. Knoxville, Nicholas Norwood.
Powell's Valley, John Hutchinson. Tennessee Valley,
Hugh McPhail, John Seaton.

These, for the most part, were men good and true,
who labored faithfully, and whose labors were blessed
of the Lord, to the salvation of much people.

This and a few succeeding years were characterized

* Mr. Stringfield died in peace, June 12th, 1858.

by a great scarcity of money, and consequent depression, or total stagnation, of business in the various departments of trade and commerce, which, though it affected very little any enterprise of a secular character the Church then had — for it scarce had any — it, nevertheless, affected greatly the comfort of the preachers.   They were generally without money, and very frequently almost without clothes, and were constantly subjected to a great many serious inconveniences, and to numberless discouragements.   However, they bore it, somehow or other, and pressed forward in the work they had undertaken, and God crowned their efforts with most gratifying success.

[1817.] The next session of the Conference was, according to the Minutes, appointed to be held at the same place as the last — Franklin, Williamson county, Tenn. — to commence on the 30th of October. The returns made at this time do not show as great an aggregate prosperity as during some previous years; yet there was a most blessed revival influence abroad in parts of the Conference, and a considerable ingathering of members.   In the Holston country, the decrease still went on, and this year the reports show a less membership, by about twenty, than the year previous; being, in the aggregate, 5,357, against 5,378, the year before.   Emigration was, at this time, going on, from that country, very rapidly; and the removed members, though lost to that particular section, were not lost to the Church; and while their removal diminished the aggregate number of members there, it swelled the numbers elsewhere, so that, in the general aggregate, the Church steadily and rapidly increased.

The two districts remained this year pretty much as they had been the year previously. One new circuit was formed, and the appointments were :

HOLSTON DISTRICT — *Jesse Cunnyngham, P. E.* Abingdon, George Ekin. Clinch, Edward Ashley. Carter's Valley, Wm. S. Manson, Holston, Thomas D. Porter. Lee, James Witten. Tazewell, James Porter. Ashe, Jesse Green.

FRENCH BROAD DISTRICT— *John Henniger, P. E.* Nollichuckie, Nathan Barnes. Little River, Nicholas Norwood. Knoxville, Josiah B. Daughtry. Powell's Valley, B. Edge. Tennessee Valley, T. Stringfield.

[1818.] The next session of the Conference was held at Nashville, Tenn., commencing October 1st. A large class, mostly of young and promising men, were admitted on trial, some few of whom, to the present, remain faithful in their Master's work, but most of them have gone to their final reward. There were several, also, who, this year, located. A gratifying success had attended the labors of the preachers, in various parts of the Conference, and great numbers had been added to the Church. The increase in some parts of the Conference was very considerable ; but in the Holston country it was small, though enough to show that the tide was turning. The aggregate membership in the two districts, as reported at this session, was 5,399, of whom 461 were colored. There was little or no change of importance in the districts or the number of the circuits, with the exception of Sequatchee, which was formed this year ; and their boundaries, so far as is now known, remained much as they had been for some time previous. The appointments were :

HOLSTON DISTRICT — *Jesse Cunnyngham, P. E.* Abingdon, to be supplied. Clinch, Jesse Green. Carter's Valley, Obadiah Freeman. Holston, G. Ekin. Lee, John Dever. Tazewell, D. Adams. Ashe, Clinton Tucker.

FRENCH BROAD DISTRICT — *James Axley, P. E.* Nollichuckie, William S. Manson. Little River, George Locke. Knoxville, George Atkin. Powell's Valley, Nicholas Norwood. Sequatchee, James Porter. Tennessee Valley, James Witten.

As already remarked, the whole territory was pretty much occupied, and had been, for many years previously to this ; and the chance for the increase of circuits depended almost solely on the increase of population ; and, as this was slow, the progress of the work — geographically, at least — was correspondingly slow. This must be regarded as the true and only reason why circuits were not more rapidly increased, and not because of any want of zeal, energy or efficiency, on the part of the people. But if the work seemed to progress slowly, it progressed certainly ; and the different theological controversies which characterized that section of country, and which will hereafter be noticed, led the people to hear, read, think and learn, until they became quite familiar with the distinctive doctrines of the different sects engaged in these controversies, and well indoctrinated in the peculiar tenets of the Church to which they belonged.

[1819.] The next session of the Conference was

appointed to be held at Nashville, where the last meeting had been, the session to commence on the first of October.

Quite a number of preachers were received on trial, and among the rest was the subject of these sketches, as already noticed. The year was one of great prosperity throughout the connection, and in few, if any, places was that prosperity greater than in the bounds of the Tennessee Conference. The net increase of members, in the entire Church, was nearly *sixteen thousand*, and in the Tennessee Conference it was little less than *two thousand five hundred*, though the two districts in the Holston country did not share so extensively in the revival influence that was abroad, as did other parts of the Conference. The net increase in these districts was only fifty members, the whole number being 5,449, of whom 454 were colored. There was but little change in the districts or circuits, and the appointments were :

HOLSTON DISTRICT—*Jesse Cunnyngham*, P. E. Lee, John Kesterson. Clinch, David Adams. Tazewell, Abraham Still. Abingdon, James Porter. Ashe, Obadiah Freeman. Holston, John Bowman, Josiah Browder. Carter's Valley, George Ekin.

FRENCH BROAD DISTRICT—*James Axley*, P. E. Nollichuckie, Wm. S. Manson. Powell's Valley, George Locke. Tennessee Valley, Benjamin Edge, Elisha Simmons. Sequatchee Valley, Samuel Patton. Little River, John Bradfield. Knox, Robert Hooper. Knoxville, James Dixon.

Nicholas Norwood was left without an appointment, by the order of the Conference, in consequence of some difficulties which involved his moral character, and, the next year, was expelled from the Church.

[1820.] At the next session of the Conference, which was held at Hopkinsville, Ky., commencing on the 4th of October, the statistical reports exhibited a most gratifying state of prosperity. The net increase in the membership, in the bounds of the Conference, was no less than *eleven thousand three hundred and ninety-five !* which was more than half of the net increase in the bounds of the whole Church. The net increase in the two districts more immediately under notice was *eleven hundred and sixty-seven* ; the total membership being 6,616, against 5,449, reported the previous year.

Rarely, if ever, was there a more deep, widely-spread and genuine revival of religion than that which, this year, swept over the State of Tennessee. Many interesting accounts of it have been published, again and again, and need not to be repeated here. It was a most extraordinary season.

The General Conference, which met in Baltimore, in May, 1820, changed the boundaries of the Tennessee Conference, and, by the organization of the Kentucky Conference, took a large portion of the territory, and fully half of the membership. The Conference had consisted of seven Presiding Elder's districts ; but, by this new arrangement, three were taken off, and formed the principal part of the Kentucky Conference, leaving the Tennessee Conference with four — two in the Holston country, and the other two principally in Middle Tennessee. The appointments made at this session, for the Holston work, were :

FRENCH BROAD DISTRICT — *James Axley, P. E.* Nol-

lichuckie, James Cumming. Powell's Valley, Jesse
Green. Tennessee Valley, Obadiah Freeman, Robert
Hooper. Sequatchee Valley, John Kesterson, John
Paulsell. · Little River, Abraham Still, Wiley B. Peck.
Knox, D. Adams, Jesse Cunnyngham, sup. Knoxville
and Greenville, J. Dixon. Hiwassee, Thos. Payne.

HOLSTON DISTRICT — *John Tevis, P. E.* Lee, James
Witten. Clinch, Samuel Patton. Tazewell, John
Bradfield. New River, ———. Ashe, John Bowman.
Abingdon, Ancil Richardson. Holston, William S.
Manson, Wm. P. Kendrick. Carter's Valley, George
Ekin.

It will be seen from the above, that one or two additional circuits had been formed; and New River
Circuit, which, for some time previous to this, had been
in the bounds of the Baltimore Conference, was turned
over to this, in accordance with the arrangements made
at the General Conference preceding this session.

In every part of the Conference, the country was
being more and more thickly settled; and, as the population increased, societies were multiplied, and all the
operations of the Church pushed forward to meet the
increasing demands, and, as will presently be seen, the
efforts of the faithful ministers were crowned with
much success.

[1821.] The next session of the Conference was
held in Bedford county, Tenn., commencing on the 7th
of November. Twenty-six preachers were received on
trial in the traveling connection, a few of whom yet
remain in the work, while a majority have gone to
their final reward, and the remainder long since located.

The work had advanced rapidly in the Holston

country, the net increase of members in the two districts being 1,587, and the whole number, 8,203, of whom 777 were colored. Perhaps no part of the Conference shared so largely, during the year just closed, in the reviving influences of truth and grace, or enjoyed so large a proportionate increase. In the stations of the preachers, there was one appointment less this year than the year previous, the towns of Knoxville and Greenville being thrown into the circuits; but there were more preachers sent into these bounds than ever before. This year, there were twenty-nine, and the year before, there were twenty-two, which had been thought a large number for that "hill country." But now Methodism began to assume a position never before occupied, and though the Church was, from this time forward, during several years, severely and sorely tried, as will be noticed hereafter, she maintained her stand, and continued to press forward her work. The appointments for the districts and stations were:

FRENCH BROAD DISTRICT—*John Dever, P. E.* Nollichuckie, G. Ekin, Abraham Harris, and James Axley, sup. Powell's Valley, Richard W. Morris. Tennessee Valley, Lewis S. Marshal, John Rice. Sequatchee Valley, John Craig, John Bradfield. Little River, David Adams, James Cumming. Knox, Samuel Harwell, John Kelley; J. Cunnyngham, sup. Hiwassee, James Witten.

HOLSTON DISTRICT—*John Tevis, P. E.* Lee, John Paulsell, David B. Cumming. Clinch, Abraham Still. Tazewell, Ancil Richardson. As he, John Kesterson. New River, Jesse Green, William P. Kendrick, Wm. Patton. Abingdon, George W. Morris. Holston,

Wm. S. Manson, George Horne. Carter's Valley, John Bowman, Thomas J. Brown.

From the position assigned him, it may be learned that the strong-nerved, strong-minded and faithful Axley was now failing. Such, indeed, was the fact. Hard labor and great exposure, in the new settlements of the North, West and South, together with those to which all traveling preachers of his day were subjected, even in the older settlements of the West, were fast wearing him down. The next year, he located; and, though he lived until 1838, he never after resumed the traveling ministry. But John Dever, who this year succeeded him on the district, was a man among men; but his valuable services were soon lost to the Church. A year or two after this, he located, and shortly after his location, he was called by death to his final reward. There were several others appointed to the Holston country this year, of whom mention might be made, did the present limits allow.

[1822.] At the next session of the Conference, which was held at Ebenezer Meeting-House, Green county, Tenn., no less than thirty-nine preachers were received on trial, which, considering the size of the Conference, must be regarded as a very unusual and extraordinary number. But a genuine revival influence had been abroad, and such seasons rarely or never fail to supply the Church with an increased number of ministers. There were still but two districts in the Holston country, and the same number of circuits this year as during the last; but the number of preachers traveling was increased from twenty-nine to thirty-one, and the number of members, from 8,203 to 10,590, or a net

increase of 2,387. Of the whole number of members,
1,078 were colored, being an increase, among them, of
310. And just here let it be recorded, as a fact which
came under the writer's own observation, that violent
outcry from the pulpit against slavery, which had characterized many of the preachers of that day, for some
years previous to this, and which has been alluded to
already, was now giving place to a more calm and
prudent course of procedure, and, as a consequence,
there was reported a large increase in the number of
colored members. Less noise was made by the preachers about the social condition of the colored people,
and more attention was given to the interests of their
souls ; and like causes will produce like results everywhere and all the time.

This session of the Conference was remarkable, not
only for the number of preachers received on trial, but
for the number of people who attended the public
preaching, the number of local preachers who were
present, either for ordination or as visitors, and for
the impression for good that was left on the minds of
hundreds and thousands of people who attended during
the session. They collected there from great distances
in every direction, saw the preachers, heard many of
them preach, and went away with impressions, as to the
character of the Church and ability of its ministers,
greatly differing from those they had previously entertained. It is true, the Conference — or rather a Conference — had been held there before, several times ;
but it was when the country was more thinly settled —
when Methodism was but little known, and the meeting
of a few preachers in Conference attracted but little

attention. This was regarded and long talked of, among the people, as *the* Conference. The appointments for the country under notice were:

FRENCH BROAD DISTRICT—*John Dever, P. E.* Tennessee Valley, Samuel Harwell, Josiah B. Smith. Sequatchee Valley, Thomas J. Brown, William Cumming. Hiwassee, J. B. Wynn, J. Y. Crawford, T. Smith. Little River, James Cumming, Barton Brown; J. Cunnyngham, sup. Powell's Valley, George Horne, Wm. Johnson. Nollichuckie, G. Ekin, J. Rice, D. B. Cumming.

HOLSTON DISTRICT—*John Tevis, P. E.* Lee, G. W. Morris, Josiah Rhoten. Clinch, John Paulsell. Tazewell, Wm. Patton. New River, Jesse Green, John Bowman, A. McClure. Ashe, John Bradfield. Abingdon, Wm. P. Kendrick. Holston, Abraham Still, D. Adams. Carter Valley, Wm. S. Manson, Isaac Lewis.

[1823.] The next Conference was held at Huntsville, Ala., commencing November 26th; and, as the General Conference was to be held in May following, it devolved on the preachers, at this session, to elect their delegates, which they did, by the choice of the following persons: Hartwell H. Brown, Thomas Stringfield, Wm. McMahon, Robt. Paine, G. Ekin, J. W. Kilpatrick, J. Tevis, T. L. Douglas and Thomas Madden, who were present in Baltimore at the opening of the General Conference, and bore their part in the business that was transacted. But as the doings of that Conference do not come properly under review in this place, no further reference need be made thereto.

The Conference year now closing had been one of considerable prosperity, and a net increase in the membership of 4,343 was reported. Of this increase, 481 were among the colored members. The aggregate membership in the Conference was *twenty-five thousand five hundred and nine*, of whom 2,982 were colored.

In the Holston country, the progress of the work had been very gratifying. The number of members increased from 10,590 to 13,669 — an increase of 3,079 — a large majority of all the increase of the entire Conference.

Several new circuits were also formed, and a new impulse given to the work, so that it was extending rapidly, and, as it took a wider range—embraced more and more persons in its influence — it was bringing thousands to a " knowledge of the truth, as it is in Christ Jesus." The appointments made at this Conference, for the Holston work, were as follows :

KNOXVILLE DISTRICT — *Thomas Stringfield, P. E.* Tennessee Valley, Jacob Hearn, Isaac Easterly. Sequatchee Valley, Abraham Overall, Robert Kirkpatrick. Hiwassee, James Cumming, Felix Parker. Tellico, David B. Cumming, James D. Harris. Little River, G. Ekin, James G. H. Speer. Knox, Thomas Madden, F. A. Owen. Powell's Valley, John Bowman, Thomas J. Brown. Newport, J. B. Daughtry, J. Cunnyngham. Green, Wm. S. Manson, J. Y. Crawford.

HOLSTON DISTRICT — *John Tevis, P. E.* Lee, John Bradfield, Wm. C. Cumming. Clinch, Wm. Patton. Tazewell, Abraham Still. New River, Lewis S. Marshall, Isaac Lewis, Josiah R. Smith. Ashe, John Craig. Abingdon, William P. Kendrick, Elbert F. Sevier. Holston, D. Adams, J. Rhoten. Carter's Valley, J. Kelly, C. Fulton. Hawkins, Edward T. Peery.

Through a much more extended space than was at
first designed to be thus occupied, the reader's attention has been called away from the immediate subject
of these sketches, to contemplate the field and previous state of the work in which he was subsequently to
be engaged, and with which he was so closely identified during the greater portion of his ministerial life.
A perusal of the foregoing pages will prepare the
reader more fully to understand, and more properly to
appreciate, the circumstances under which his labors
were performed. Hasty and imperfect as is the view
taken of the history of Methodism in that country, the
facts and dates are, nevertheless, believed to be correctly given, and will be of some interest to many
readers. The main difficulties, however, which lay in
the way of the more rapid success of the Church, are
yet to be noticed. These consisted in the violent opposition raised and kept up by some ministers and
members of other denominations. Every inch gained
in that country by Methodism — especially in the
earlier periods of its history, was gained on the field
of theological controversy ; and, as already intimated,
few people, in any country, were ever better informed,
as to the leading tenets held by the different sects who
preached among them. These tenets were themes of
discussion, in public and private, to an extent almost
without a parallel in the history of the Church, in all
this country. Scarcely a sermon was preached, or a
public exhortation delivered, in which there was not
more or less bearing on the points at issue, and, as
may reasonably be supposed, the people caught the
spirit, and private discussions were much more frequent

and animated than those carried on in public. That this could all be justified, is not asserted, nor is it maintained that it led to no harm, or did no injury. The contrary is believed to have been the fact in the case ; yet the good preponderated, and the people were better informed, by these means, than they would have been, but for their use.   Controversies, though often — if not, indeed, generally — carried on with too much warmth — not to say bitterness — are, in many cases, of great importance to the cause of truth.   By these means, errors have been detected, exposed and exploded ; while truth has shone the more brightly for the ordeal through which it had been caused to pass. But, as the reader has now been brought down to the period of the organization of the Holston Conference, and near the time of Mr. Patton's permanent connec·tion with it, both these events, together with something of the future history of both, will be considered in subsequent chapters.

CHAPTER IX.

ORGANIZATION OF THE HOLSTON CONFERENCE — BOUND-
ARIES — NUMBER OF MEMBERS — CONDITION OF THE
COUNTRY, AND PROSPECTS OF THE CHURCH.

AT the General Conference of 1824, provisions were
made for the organization of the Holston Conference,
within the following limits : to include " all that part
of the State of Tennessee lying east of the Cumberland
Mountains, and that part of Virginia and North Carolina embraced in the Holston District ; and also the
Black Mountain and French Broad Circuits, formerly
belonging to the South Carolina Conference ;" which
organization was effected at Knoxville, in October, of
that year — Bishop Roberts presiding, and most of the
preachers attending.   The whole number of traveling
preachers belonging to the Conference, at its organization, was *forty-two*, nine of whom were this year received on trial.   One was superannuated, and the
number stationed was forty-one.   The membership in
the bounds of the Conference consisted of *thirteen thousand four hundred and forty-three white, and one thousand
four hundred and ninety-one colored persons.*   Thus it
will be noticed that, when the Tennessee Conference
was thus divided, largely over one-half of the entire

membership of the Church fell into the new Conference ; but while only forty-two preachers were assigned
to them, *sixty-three* were left to supply the work in the
Tennessee Conference, whose membership was not so
large, by more than two thousand. And in this estimate, no account is taken of the numbers who were
transferred to the Holston, from the South Carolina
Conference, along with the Black Mountain and French
Broad Circuits. Only those are estimated who belonged to the two districts previously connected with
the Tennessee Conference. Including those who had
previously been included in other Conferences, the entire membership of the Holston Conference, as now
organized, was largely over fifteen thousand, to supply
whom there were, as just stated, but forty-one effective
preachers, or a ratio of one preacher to a fraction
over three hundred and sixty-five members. This, in
later days, would be regarded as a meager supply, and
so, indeed, it would have been, even then, but for the
presence and hearty co-operation of a large number of
local preachers, who did faithful and effective work in
extending, building up and sustaining the Church.
Few sections of the country were ever better supplied
with this useful class of men, and few men of this class
ever labored more zealously, indefatigably or successfully. The Great Head of the Church performs his
work in his own way, and works by whom he will ;
but, viewing these things in the light of history, it is
difficult even to conjecture how the Church there could
have enjoyed the prosperity, and gained the influence,
she did, but for the important part borne by the local
preachers. Many of the members of the Conference

were young, and consequently inexperienced, and, taken as a whole, the traveling preachers of the Conference, at the time of its organization, were not equal in numbers, by more than one-half, nor superior in any respect, to the local preachers scattered throughout its territory.   These formed a sort of standing army, to man the forts, and protect and defend the various posts, established for the well-being of the Church, while the itinerants were engaged in pushing forward the war, and making new conquests.   And right manfully did they acquit themselves in this work.   As many of them were not only sound, but profound, theologians, able debatants, and zealous for God and his cause, the opponents of truth had good reason to dread a collision with them, and, as far as practicable, to keep out of their way.   Such men as Mitchel, Yost, King, White, Garrett, and scores of others that might be named, could do service in a good cause, that would not be despised.   Methodism owes much to their memory.   They expounded the doctrines, enforced the precepts, maintained the discipline, and defended the usages, of the Church with a zeal, an energy and an ability beyond that which could have been done by a majority of their traveling brethren.   And yet how harmoniously did they all labor together in the same field, and for the accomplishment of the same ends — the up-building of the Church, and the salvation of souls!   They mutually protected each other's rights, respected each other's feelings, were not jealous of each other's talents, position, popularity or success. Their harmony of feeling led to concert of action, and concert of action gave them that success for which the

Conference has been so justly distinguished. This union of feeling and of effort was most fortunate for the cause they advocated. Had it been otherwise — had there been dissensions and discords among them — a failure to accomplish the work they had undertaken would have been inevitable. The opposition they were called to encounter was formidable, and of a very firm, decided character; while their means of contending against it were, in the eyes of the world, "weak and contemptible." There was not, at that time, in all the bounds of the Conference, a single school, of high grade, under their control, or over which they could exercise any important influence; and, though the religion of the country was decidedly Protestant, there was by no means a unanimity among the sects. The Presbyterians — and it is recorded of them without the most remote design to censure — had obtained the control of every important educational institution in the territory embraced in the Conference. There were the Washington and Greenville Colleges, both founded in 1794; the East Tennessee College, afterwards the East Tennessee University, founded in 1807 — all of which, together with the South-western Theological Seminary, at Maryville, Tennessee, were under their influence, and had been manned by such men as the Doaks, Carricks, Coffins, and Andersons — men of decided ability, of very respectable attainments, and of high moral worth, who were as thoroughly anti-Methodistic, and as decidedly Presbyterian, in their opinions, feelings and manner, as it is usual to find men anywhere. Besides, nearly every Presbyterian minister, in all the country, had a

school, in connection with his ministerial and pastoral
work, by which he was enabled not only to secure a
better support for himself and family than his Church
was, perhaps, able to give, but also to do something as
a teacher, in the way of gaining influence as a minister.
These, all deeply imbued with the peculiar tenets of
the Church to which they belonged, felt it incumbent
on them to do all in their power to counteract the tendency, and curtail the influence, of Methodism. They
were sincere, earnest, and, no doubt, conscientious, in
this opposition. Honestly believing, as they did, that
Methodism was erroneous, they opposed it from a
sense of duty ; and, although they may have carried
this opposition to an unjustifiable extent, they were
not to be blamed for a rigid adherence to what they
believed to be true, and an honest antagonism to its
opposites. On no point did they insist with greater
earnestness, than on the necessity for a classically
educated ministry ; and, however much may be said in
support of that view, there can be but little doubt
but that, in this case, it was pressed too far, and
did an injury. In the first place, by this means, an
undue prejudice was excited against well-informed,
pious, talented and useful men, simply because they
were supposed to have a very imperfect knowledge, or
no knowledge at all, of the dead languages ; and, in
the second place, it tended, in the end, to lessen the
influence of the very class of men who were so earnest
in its advocacy. They talked and wrote so much on
the subject, that expectations were raised in the public mind, which they could not meet ; and, upon a well-
known principle of human nature, by just so far as they

failed to meet the expectations themselves had raised, by just so far they failed to get full credit for what they really deserved. The undue prominence given to this one single point, and its constant reiteration before the public, caused the people to look for, and, perhaps, tacitly demand of them, more than they could possibly give ; hence, in influence and success, they fell below what they otherwise might have experienced. And further : It soon occurred to the public mind, that learning consists in the acquisition of ideas, and that some knowledge might be acquired of the so-called dead languages, while the same man might, to a very great extent, be destitute of a store of those practical and useful ideas necessary to the various avocations of life, and particularly to the successful discharge of the duties of a minister. At the same time, there were men all around, who did not claim to be "versed in classic lore," yet possessed minds well stored with a large fund of useful knowledge, which they could easily bring to bear upon the every-day occurrences, and for the every-day purposes, of life, and thereby gain great success as ministers. Men will judge of the importance and value of learning, as they judge of other things, by its practical results ; and, estimating by this standard, they, perhaps, in the instance referred to, were led, in the end, to place a lower estimate on classical learning than that to which it is really entitled. Hence, regarding these things in the calm, clear light which the history of the past, in connection with more recent experience and observation, affords, it must be admitted, that on this, as well as other topics discussed at that day, the parties ran to opposite extremes — the

one placing too high, and the other too low, an estimate on this particular means of human culture — one
giving it an undue importance, to the neglect of other
things of equal value, and the other, in some cases, ignoring it altogether.

In the influence the Presbyterians had over the
literary institutions of the country, and the active part
they took in the education of the youthful mind, they
possessed a very great advantage over the Methodists.
They had here a lever of wonderful power, and, at
first view, it is rather remarkable it was not used with
greater efficacy and success.

The educational institutions are the controlling
power in any and every country. As are the schools,
so is the country ; and as are the teachers, so are the
schools. A denomination controlling the schools
ought largely to control the country. Why, then,
was it not so in the case under notice ? They once had
the control of the schools, as stated ; and though, as a
denomination, they have sustained themselves, and,
doubtless, done much good, the Methodists have greatly
outstripped them in numbers, at least equaled them in
influence, and now have a much more controlling influence in the educational operations of the country.
There is no reason to suppose they were unfaithful to
their trusts, as educators, or that their interest and
zeal for the success of Christianity, as developed
through their ecclesiastical organization, had at all
abated. But there was a counter influence found in the
economy of Methodism, which, when carefully considered, at once reveals the reason for this change. It was
their system of itinerancy. Men may be educated out

of schools, as well as in schools ; and, while Presbyterians were lawfully and laudably educating hundreds in schools, the Methodists were educating thousands out of schools, and these thousands were scattered throughout the entire country, and included persons of all ages, ranks and conditions. The system of itinerating carried the preachers along the highways and along the byways — among men in easy circumstances, and among the poor and obscure. They had access to all, and upon the minds of all left the impress of their doctrines. Silently, but certainly, these influences worked out their own legitimate results, and the change alluded to was effected. Had the Presbyterians, in connection with the advantages possessed by their influence in the institutions of learning, adopted some system by which their ministry could have reached the great masses of the people, in all parts of the country — stirred the public mind to its depths, in every department of society — their influence would have been almost resistless. But this was not done, nor even attempted, until the field had, for the greater part, been pre-occupied. Some few years subsequent to the date now referred to, some attempts of this kind were made, through the agency of the Home Missionary Society, but without those results that, in all probability, would have followed like efforts made at an earlier date.

The system of itinerating, as practised by the Methodists, not only gave to them important advantages over their brethren of other denominations, but it was also the means of carrying the Word of Life to thousands and tens of thousands who, but for this system, might have long remained destitute of it. Whole dis-

tricts of country, in the bounds of that and other Conferences, might be pointed out, where no other than a
Methodist preacher was seen or heard, for years
together; and, but for the attention of these preachers,
the thousands who inhabited these districts might have
remained destitute of the means of grace for an indefinite period of time — destitute, perhaps, until the
present hour. The system was carried on with severe
toil, much sacrifice, and under great privations; but it
brought its reward. It laid wide and deep the foundations of Methodism, in almost every neighborhood,
and gathered men by thousands into the fold of Christ.
Never, perhaps, since the days of the Apostles, has
there been adopted more efficient means of filling the
mission of the Christian ministry, especially in reference to preaching the gospel to the poor, and calling
all to repentance, than by *going*, so far as possible, into
all the world. It has accomplished much, but its mission is far from being ended. There is still for it an
open road and a great demand; and, whatever may be
said in favor of independent Churches, and a settled
ministry, there are thousands upon thousands of per-
ishing souls who are not at all likely ever to be reached,
except by the joint efforts of federated Churches, and
an itinerating ministry.

Another advantage the Methodists possessed over
other denominations, in the country under notice, was
found in the doctrines they preached. Without any
design or desire to institute a comparison between
these doctrines and those inculcated by Calvinistic
teachers, it may be proper to remark, that those of the
Methodists were peculiarly adapted to the whole

people — of all classes and conditions, and in every place. Regarding all men as sustaining naturally the same relation, both to the moral government of God and the atonement of Christ — believing the Savior died for all, and that all might be saved — they went forth and preached to all — offered life and salvation 'to all, upon the same terms—"repentance towards God, and faith in the Lord Jesus Christ"—offered a sufficient and a present Savior, to be received by faith alone. Hence the doctrines of original sin, of justification by faith in Christ, of regeneration and sanctification by the Holy Spirit, were themes of constant and earnest discussion before the people. These were days of doctrinal preaching. The leading points of difference between the Calvinistic and Arminian theories were kept before the public ear and eye, and the advocates of each maintained their views with all the zeal and ability they could command. There was then no temporizing. The doctrines of predestinarianism, in all their peculiar shades and bearings, were boldly avowed and ably discussed by the ministers of the Calvinistic denominations, and as boldly opposed by those of the opposite faith. The struggle was earnest and long continued, both parties claiming victory at the last, though it is undeniable that thirty years have witnessed a great change in the manner of presenting the leading doctrines of predestination before the public, where these things occurred. The views held and taught by the Methodists impressed the public mind as being most consonant with the character and moral government of God, most favorable to the idea of a great brotherhood among men, and most in accordance

with the scriptural teachings, as to justice and righteousness, goodness, mercy and love.

These things are given as a matter of history, without any direct reference to the merits of the doctrines
referred to. In subsequent chapters the reader will
find a more particular account of the controversies
which were carried on in the country under notice, as
also of the points discussed, together with the persons
engaged in the discussion. The present design is to
present, as accurately as may be, the religious condition
of the country, and the influences against which Methodism had to contend, as well as the advantages and
disadvantages attending its operations.

Next to the Presbyterians, the Baptists were the
most formidable opponents of Methodism, and these
operated among a class of the community to which the
others had gained but little access. The former were
mostly in the villages and populous neighborhoods,
while the latter had extended their labors and influence to the remoter sections; and justice to them
demands it be said that they did much for the religious interests of the poorer and more obscure classes
of the people. Next to the Methodist itinerants, they
were most assiduous in preaching the Gospel to the
poor. But their views of Methodism, as a system,
were no more favorable than those entertained by
Presbyterians. Both were then rigidly Calvinistic in
theory, and while the one met the approaches of Methodist doctrines at the towns, villages and populous
neighborhoods, the other, with less ability, perhaps,
but no less zeal and earnestness, did the same in the
less prominent and more remote sections; so that one

thing is clear : If Methodism be a system of error, or if it be in any way detrimental to the public weal, or has entailed evil upon the people of the country under notice, the Calvinistic ministers of that day were not chargeable with its introduction and subsequent propagation. It was no fault of theirs. It was not through apathy, inattention or indifference on their part these things were done. They opposed them with whatever zeal, industry and ability they could command.

It is not, however, to be understood that they made no distinction between what they regarded as the errors of a system, and the people holding and teaching those supposed errors. This was not the case ; and, however strong and uncompromising was their opposition to Methodism, they, as a general thing, cherished and manifested a becoming respect for the feelings, rights and privileges of Methodists, as a people ; and to the honor of both parties be it written, this was duly reciprocated, and the instances of departure from a course alike honorable to both were comparatively few. It was not with each other, but with each other's doctrines, that the controversy existed and was carried on. Each believed the other to be wrong in theory, and the theories were respectively opposed and combated, with but occasional allusion to each other's feelings and practices. Each regarded the other as believing and teaching much sound and wholesome truth, but mixed with a good deal of error, and as readily acknowledged the one as they opposed the other ; hence they often met on a common ground, preached, prayed, praised and rejoiced together, and demonstrated a truth, of which the public should never lose sight, that truly Christian people, while they, perhaps, necessarily differ in their views on some points of Christian doctrine, are, nevertheless, one in Christian feeling, being baptized with the Spirit. The religion of the Bible consists in supreme love to God and universal love to man ; and that this may exist, in its saving efficacy, amidst a great diversity of opinions on minor points of doctrine, there can be no reasonable doubt. That it did exist, to a greater or less extent, among the different parties, at the time alluded to, there can be no question. There were thousands who, though strong religious partisans, were moved, in all the friendly offices and charitable deeds of life, as readily towards one of a different as towards one of the same religious persuasion. They felt the softening, refining influence of grace, acknowledged, in a Bible sense, the brotherhood of man, and were ready, as far as in them lay, to do good to all men. In all the pro-tracted and earnest controversies which characterized that country, it was only once or twice, and then for comparatively short periods, that the social relations of life were disturbed, and this because the intemper-ate zeal of a very few mistaken or bad men led them to leave the field of fair and honorable disputation, and make unjustifiable and inexcusable attacks upon the personal character and reputation of their oppo-nents. This course once commenced, those concerned were, properly enough, perhaps, under the then existing circumstances, met on the field of their own choosing, and made keenly to feel the error they had committed, by a violent and destructive reaction against them-selves. But these were exceptions, which, fortunately, were few in number, and of short continuance. They disturbed rather the surface than the depths of religious feeling pervading the community. The effects soon passed away, and the holding of religious meetings, preaching, praying, singing, praising, and, except the Baptists, communing together at the Lord's table, by the ministers and members of the different denominations, exhibited the pleasing fact, that they acknowledged a common Savior — a common Christianity — had imbibed the same spirit from on high, and were seeking the same rest in a brighter and better world.

There was one thing more that greatly tended to extend and build up Methodism in that country, and should be specially noticed. It was the extensive circulation of denominational books. These were engines of moral and theological power, that had tremendous force in moulding the public mind, and directing popular opinion. From the first, the Methodists have regarded the Press as a powerful agent for the accomplishment of good in the world, and no people have used it more diligently or more successfully than they. Their books and periodicals have gone co-extensively with their itinerants, and acted as silent, but efficient, monitors, when the preachers themselves were elsewhere. What has been accomplished by these means, the light of eternity only can fully reveal. The country immediately under notice was, until very recently, cut off from the hurry and bustle of the commercial world. The avenues of trade were few, and the inducements to engage in speculations, by no means great. The people were almost wholly engaged in agricultural pursuits, and consequently could command much time for reading, the improvement of the mind, and the cultivation of the social feelings. Where goods had to be brought by wagons over a rough, hilly country, on uneven roads, for a distance of from three to five hundred miles, at a cost, for freight, of from five to ten dollars per hundred pounds, merchants were not likely to buy many books. The cost of transportation was too great, and the profits on sales too small, to induce them to go beyond a few of the commonest kind, and they were kept merely for the accommodation of customers who purchased largely of other things. These circumstances all combined to make this an inviting field for the sale of the publications of the Church, and well did the preachers improve the opportunity. To scatter these books was both their duty and their interest—their duty, because it was part and parcel of their work, as Methodist preachers, "to see that each society was duly supplied with books;" and their interest, in that, by the arrangements then existing at the Publishing House, at New York, they could realize a small profit on the sales made, and thus add to their scanty receipts from the Church. During that period in the history of the Holston Conference which properly comes under notice in this work, the amount of Methodist books sold and scattered among the people was astonishing. Though the territory was small, compared with that embraced in some other Conferences, the people generally poor, and the difficulty of procuring the books considerable, yet, from 1824 to 1854, there were sold, estimating at catalogue prices, not less, it is believed, than one hundred and fifty thousand dollars' worth, or an average of five thousand dollars' worth a year. For nearly twenty of the thirty years alluded to, the writer of this was either a committee or one of the committee to settle, annually, the accounts of the preachers for books purchased of the Book Concern, and he knows well it was no uncommon thing, with several of the preachers, to pay from three to five hundred dollars each for books bought and sold by them during the year preceding the Conference session at which the settlement was made. From 1834 or '5 to 1844 were the years during which most was done in this way. Subsequently to the last-named date, much less was done than previously, owing to the increased difficulties of procuring books, and the temporary derangement of affairs, growing out of the division of the Church.

This amount of books, of the character they were, scattered over the country, could not fail to exert a happy influence in behalf of the Church. Besides their general theological character, they set forth, explained and defended the distinctive theology of the Church, together with its government, history and usages. They were teaching constantly, and, by finding their way, as they did, to the cottages of the poor, as well as the dwellings of those in easier circumstances, they impressed all classes. The preacher might not be able to defend the doctrines, or discipline, or usages of the Church with the ability the emergency demanded; but he could, and did, circulate books that did the work effectually. As a consequence of this course, there is not, perhaps, to be found, on the continent, an equal number of Methodists who, as Methodists, are more intelligent, or better indoctrinated in all the dis-

tinctive peculiarities of the Church, than those in the
bounds of this Conference. And what is true of them.
in this respect, is true, also, of the aggregate of the
members of other denominations in the same country.
The controversies carried on from the pulpit and
press — the full, free and able discussions of the points
of difference in the creeds of the sects, respectively —
were such that the public mind became well informed
in regard to them, and, as there was little or no theo-
retical infidelity in the country, a very large majority
of the whole people were classed as adhering to one
or the other of the religious sects.

Besides the denominations already referred to, there
were some others of the Protestant faith, though less
numerous and influential than these; while. until
within a few years past, a Romanist — and more
especially a Romanist priest — was scarce known or
heard of in all that country.

The settled and homogeneous character of the people
was another circumstance favorable to their religious
culture. They, or their immediate ancestors, had lived
near to each other, in the same neighborhoods. from
the earliest settlements of the country, where children
of different families had grown up, side by side, and
common interests, under common dangers and privations, had led to the formation of friendships, which
lasted through successive generations. The various
political and social changes of the country affected all
alike. The difficulties, dangers and privations incident to the settlement of a new country, infested by
savages, were alike shared by all, and many bonds of
a strong character combined to unite and hold the

people together. There was a strong feeling of dependence, one upon another, and a ready willingness to acknowledge, at least in theory, the dependence of all upon the constant watch care and never-ceasing supervision of an All-wise Providence.

There was also a strict and systematic recognition and observance of the claims of family religion. God was acknowledged in the family. Prayers were held in the family, even by some who were not regarded as members of the Church ; and to partake of the regular meals without first asking a blessing — or, in the parlance of the day, saying grace — was regarded as next to brutish. Children were taught and indoctrinated, as to the claims, requirements and duties of religion, by the parents themselves, which was done by religious parents, from generation to generation. The truths of the Bible were taught *as the parents understood* these truths ; consequently, the children of Methodists or Presbyterians were trained in the faith of their parents ; and, though this may have made them sectarians, it did not make them bigots. If their religious information were less general than that possessed by children of later days, it was more positive and practical. They may not have learned as much of the Bible, as to its history and chronology, but they learned more as to its moral precepts and its leading doctrines. And then they were taught that the parents were their natural and proper educators, to whom they should look for instruction, as well as support and maintenance, and to whom reverence, honor and obedience were ever due. With these influences around them, it was common for the children of several generations to remain under the care of the Church to which their parents had belonged.

As the Methodists visited and formed Churches in the country under notice, at the earlier periods of its settlement, they not only had a fair start, but, in many places, the pre-occupancy; so, at the period of the organization of the Holston Conference, their prospects were as good — perhaps better than — those of any other denomination. They certainly had a very firm hold upon the masses of the people. But, in one thing, human wisdom would pronounce they greatly erred. They had neglected to make special or earnest efforts to impress their doctrines upon, and cause their influence to be felt by, that class of society whose position gave them great influence, for the time being. In this they differed from their Presbyterian brethren. These commenced at once with the very class to which reference is made; hence the position they soon gained, in regard to the literary institutions, as already noticed. The Methodists commenced among the common people; and, though they were heard gladly, and did good, the fruits of which, in some respects, were immediately seen, it was not until they had improved the common people, and indirectly elevated them to place and power, that they attracted the notice, and gained the influence, that gave them a place in the literary halls of the country, and caused their name to be honorably mentioned in the various circles of educated, as well as uneducated, men. They worked themselves up, by working up society, which, after all, is the better way to secure the most desirable, because the most enduring, influence.

CHAPTER X.

MR. PATTON IN THE HOLSTON CONFERENCE — HIS FIRST
CONTROVERSY AND LABORS — FROM 1825 TO 1830.

THE time and manner of Mr. Patton's connection
with the Holston Conference have already been given;
but it will be remembered that, from January, 1825, to
October of the same year, he was not regularly connected with any Annual Conference, but had located,
in order to effect the desired transfer from one Conference to another, for reasons heretofore assigned. If
any suppose, however, that, during the period in which
he was, in form, though not in fact, a local preacher,
he was idle, as to the duties and work of a minister,
they greatly mistake the character of the man. He
was not a man to be idle anywhere, at any time, or
in any relation to the Church. He spent this time in
diligent and active labors. And it so happened that
just then there was a special demand, in the section
of country in which he resided, for just such labor as
he was competent to perform. But, in order to a full
understanding of the circumstances under which he,
in common with others of his ministerial brethren, was
placed, it is necessary to introduce a historical sketch
of the sect, or rather the *no* sect, of people with whom
he came in collision.

In the early part of the present century, there arose, rather simultaneously, in various parts of the United States, but principally in New England, Ohio and Kentucky, a party who assumed to themselves the appellative of " Christians," boasting that they had no creed, confession of faith, or anything of the kind, and took the Bible only as their rule of faith and practice. They were loud in their denunciations of what they were pleased to call "the bondage of creeds," and still more so with reference to that bondage of discipline that prevailed, as they alleged, in all other Churches. The fact that many of the active promoters of the new *no-sect* party had been expelled from the communion of orthodox Churches, for the denial of some important point of doctrine, or refusal to submit to wholesome discipline and government, may somewhat assist in accounting for their strong opposition to the " bondage of creeds and discipline."

This sect or party, or whatever else it may be termed, claimed, according to some of their best authorities, a threefold origin. The first members of their sect in New England were originally members of the regular Baptist connection. Those in the West were from the Presbyterians, and in the South from the Methodists.[*] These authorities also maintained that the Churches were constituted on the following principles : "The Scriptures are taken to be the only rule of faith and practice, each individual being at liberty to determine for himself, in relation to these matters, what they en-

---

[*] See an account of the Christian connection, or Christ-ians, as given by the Rev. J. V. Himes, in the ENCYCLOPÆDIA OF RELIGIOUS KNOWLEDGE.

join. No member is subject to a loss of Church fellowship on account of his sincere and conscientious belief, so long as he manifestly lives a pious and devout life. No member is subject to discipline and Church censure, but for disorderly and immoral conduct. The name 'Christian' to be adopted, to the exclusion of all sectarian names, as the most appropriate designation of the body and its members. The only condition or test of admission, as a member of a Church, is a personal profession of the Christian religion, accompanied with satisfactory evidence of sincerity and piety, and a determination to live according to the divine rule, or the Gospel of Christ. Each body is considered as an independent body, possessing exclusive authority to regulate and govern its own affairs."

This is according to the Rev. Mr. Himes, just referred to, who was an influential minister among them. He also gave the following, as a synopsis of their doctrinal views :

" That there is one living and true God, the Father, Almighty, who is unoriginated, independent, and eternal, the Creator and Supporter of all worlds ; and that this God is one spiritual intelligence, one infinite mind, ever the same, never varying ; that this God is the moral Governor of the world, the absolute source of all the blessings of nature, providence, and grace, in whose infinite wisdom, goodness, mercy, benevolence and love have originated all his moral dispensations to man : That all men sin, and come short of the glory of God, consequently fall under the curse of the law : That Christ is the Son of God, the promised

Messiah and Savior of the world, the Mediator between God and man, by whom God has revealed his
will to mankind; by whose sufferings death and resurrection, a way has been provided by which sinners
may obtain salvation, may lay hold on eternal life;
that he is appointed of God to raise the dead, and
judge the world at the last day: That the Holy
Spirit is the power and energy of God, that holy influence of God by whose agency, in the use of means,
the wicked are regenerated, converted and recovered
to a virtuous and holy life, sanctified and made meet
for the inheritance of the saints in light; and that, by
the same Spirit, the saints, in the use of means, are
comforted, strengthened, and led in the path of duty:
The free forgiveness of sins, flowing from the rich
mercy of God, through the labors, sufferings and
blood of our Lord Jesus Christ: The necessity of repentance toward God, and faith toward our Lord
Jesus Christ: The absolute necessity of holiness of
heart and rectitude of life to enjoy the favor and ap-
probation of God: The doctrine of a future state of
immortality: The doctrine of a righteous retribution,
in which God will render to every man according to
the deeds done in the body: The baptism of believers
by immersion; and the open communion, at the Lord's
table, of Christians of every denomination, having a
good standing in their respective Churches."*

These views may have been, and doubtless were, entertained by him who penned them, and may, also,
have been entertained by many of his co-laborers,

* See ENCYCLOPÆDIA OF RELIGIOUS KNOWLEDGE, vol. 1, p. 363.

though they certainly were not believed, or not understood, by the preachers of this party who first found
their way into the bounds of the Holston Conference,
and commenced their operations, not far from the time
of Mr. Patton's return to that country, in 1825. They
were then called by various names, as "New Lights,"
"Schismatics," "Arians," etc. ; and, as to doctrines,
they were Arians, in the fullest sense of the term,
going to an extent of error greatly beyond that which
characterized the celebrated founder of that sect. In
preaching they were loud and vehement, and, in their
meetings, frequently gave way to excesses of feeling
that led to scenes of great disorder and confusion.
Almost their sole, and certainly their main, efforts
seemed to be to pull down other sects, and build their
own upon the ruins. Proselytism, as though they had
taken it for a watchword, was exhibited in all their
sayings and doings ; and, whether in private families
or public congregations, it was foremost in all their
proceedings. To unsettle the minds of the members of
different Churches, and alienate their feelings from associations previously formed, was a part and parcel of
their constant work. Being men of one idea, it absorbed their minds, employed their thoughts, formed
the theme of their public and private ministrations,
engaged their conversation, and employed their time ;
and, by the operation of a well-known principle in
the laws governing the human mind, the more, and the
more intently, they looked at, examined and revolved
this idea, the more it was magnified in the mind's eye,
until, at last, they could scarce see or think of anything
else. Hence, while denouncing bigotry, they them-

selves were the greatest and most intolerant of bigots.
While violently opposing all sects, they became among
the most exclusive of sectarians, and, in some instances,
went so far in their opposition to the "bondage of
creeds" as to run into the wildest latitudinarianism;
while their opposition to the Trinitarian doctrine led
them to downright deism, the more objectionable because it claimed to find authority in the sacred records.   As might have been expected, they succeeded
much better in pulling down than in building up, and,
after comparatively a few years, they either passed
away entirely, or became identified with the followers
of Mr. Alexander Campbell, to whom, in theory and
practice, they were so nearly allied.   Considering the
great similarity — indeed the almost perfect identity —
both of the doctrines and manners of these people
with those of the followers of Mr. Campbell, it is difficult to suppose they had not a common origin; and,
in the waning of the first party, this gentleman, by
greater talents, greater boldness, or by the two combined, formed a sort of nucleus, around which the
fragments were gathered for the formation of a new
one, combining, essentially, the same elements.

Many, indeed most, of these preachers were men of
much plausibleness before the masses of the people;
and the boldness — not to say effrontery — with which
they promulged their peculiar notions, and attacked
and denounced others, drew the attention of the mul-
titudes, and led hundreds astray from the paths of
sober truth and sound doctrines.   Many Baptist
Churches that had existed for years, peaceably and
prosperously, were entirely broken up, and many others

were much divided, greatly to the detriment of their peace and prosperity. It was among these the agitators first began their work of distraction and division, and, flushed with every new success, they became more and more bold, pushing forward their work under a full conviction, as they assured the people, that, in a short time, they would pervade the entire country, having overcome and demolished all opposition. Their bold, confident manner, though it offended the more intelligent and refined, gained them influence among the illiterate, and, for a time, they not only excited much attention among the masses of the people, but threatened, also, to make sad havoc in several Churches.

It was not to be expected that regular ministers of evangelical Churches, however much they might be in favor of peace and quietness, would tamely stand by and witness desolations among their people, without an effort to counteract the influences by which such desolations were to be brought about. They might contemn the infatuation that was spreading abroad, and pity the subjects of it, but the evil was there, doing its legitimate work. The authors of it were active and zealous, and neglect to notice them publicly made them the more arrogant. They construed, or affected to construe, the silence of prominent ministers of the orthodox Churches into a tacit acknowledgment of the weakness of their cause, and out of this sought to make capital for themselves. Following other ministers from place to place, making appointments as near theirs as practicable, to controvert their doctrines, and frequently, with great flourish of style, challenging them to public debates on the points at issue, at length

aroused them to engage in what the others had professedly sought — an earnest controversy — which soon
checked the progress of, and finally completely overthrew, the *no-sect* party.

It so happened that, in the section of country where
Mr. Patton was, at this time, residing, and for a considerable distance on every side, there were but few
Baptist, and only one or two Presbyterian, preachers;
so that on the Methodists principally devolved the
duty of meeting and contending with the *no sect* agitators, and they put forward Mr. Patton for that especial
work.   It was a work foreign to his inclinations and
tastes, and one in which he never could have engaged,
but at the imperative call of duty.   No man loved the
peace of Zion more than he, and none were ever more
ready to exert themselves, in any and every way consistent with duty, to promote and perpetuate that
peace ; but from what he believed to be the line of
his duty, no earthly power could cause him to swerve.
His brethren believed it to be his duty to engage in
the controversy now referred to, and, in deference to
their opinions, he yielded to their urgent and oft-repeated requests, overcame his natural disinclination to
such work, and went forward to meet the opponents
on the ground of their own choosing.   His plan, at
the first, was to explain and defend, as best he could,
the leading doctrines which had been so much opposed — particularly the dogma asserting the supreme
divinity of the Savior, and the personality and divinity
of the Holy Spirit, without saying much directly referring to those from whom the opposition came.   But
this did not satisfy the over-confident agitators.   They

must needs have a more direct reference to their positions and arguments, and at once sought this, by various
methods. Mr. Patton, with other Methodist preachers,
was discussing the commonly received views on these
solemn and important truths, through several counties
in Upper East Tennessee and South-western Virginia ;
and had the *no-sect* party been content with a like pre-
sentation and discussion of the views they entertained,
the people, after hearing both sides, might have been
left to judge, and choose between them. But, by pressing the matter more and more closely, and urging,
with great vehemence, that their arguments be answered, if it could be done, and if it could not, that
their opponents should acknowledge their force and
truth, they drove Mr. Patton and those engaged with
him into a particular notice of their positions and arguments, as well as of themselves and their doings
generally.

In one of these special notices, made in a sermon
delivered by Mr. Patton, in Scott county, Virginia, on
the 25th of September, 1825, his exposé of the errors
of Arianism was so strong and conclusive, in the estimation of those who heard it, that a large number
present, including ministers and members, and among
them several of the most prominent men in all that
country, solicited a copy for publication. The request
was granted, and, as the opposite party had industriously circulated copies of an address on the " Unity
of God and the Sonship of Jesus Christ," originally
written by the Rev. Thomas Smith, of Kentucky, and
republished by some of the " Elders in the Christian
Church," Mr. Patton took occasion, in connection with

this sermon, to publish some strictures upon the views there set forth. Both the sermon and the strictures were well received by the public, and, as they were of a character that would have done credit to an older and more experienced writer, they were, of course, very satisfactory to his friends and the friends of the cause they advocated.

Although this year witnessed the beginning of this controversy, so far as he was concerned, it was by no means closed with the year. As already stated, at the session of the Conference for 1825, he was re-admitted into the traveling connection, and appointed in charge of the Abingdon District, which embraced the sections of country where the controversy was raging; and in this country he remained, either in charge of the district or the church in the town of Abingdon, until the Conference of 1829, or four full Conference years— three on the district and one in the town; consequently the same people were to be addressed, and the same influences to be met, to a greater or less extent, during the whole of this period. But this was not all. There was another controversy going on at the same time, that agitated the country much more than this; and, though Mr. Patton was in no proper sense a leader in any other than the one already noticed, he necessarily, from the position in which he was placed, had much to do with the other. He could not shun it, any more than he could have shunned the first. It met him at every point, and demanded attention from every quarter.

Of the three Presiding Elder's districts then in the Conference, he had charge of one, and the late Thomas

Stringfield of another; and these two districts embraced the greater part of the country agitated by
these controversies — one with the Arians, as just
noticed, and the other with the Hopkinsians; and it
must be kept in mind, that a large majority of all the
Presbyterian ministers in that country were at that
time regarded as having embraced the peculiar views
set forth by Dr. Hopkins. These subsequently, for the
greater part, were identified with the New School
party, and included some of their ablest men. Some
allusion has already been made to a controversy carried
on, in the papers of Knoxville, Tenn., between parties
who were understood at the time, and afterwards acknowledged, to be the Rev. Dr. Anderson, of Maryville,
on the one part, and the Rev. James Dixon, then in
charge of the Methodist Church at Knoxville, on the
other. This grew up from some views the former had
published, which were regarded by the latter as looking, indirectly at least, towards a union of Church and
State. Whether Mr. Dixon were right or wrong in
the view he took of Dr. Anderson's doctrines, is not a
subject of inquiry at the present, the matter being alluded to only in historic narrative. The year before
this, or in 1819, the Presbyterians had presented a pe-
tition to the Legislature of Tennessee, praying for an
act incorporating the Theological Seminary at Maryville, and, with that, asking also for the incorporation
of the Synod of Tennessee, which prayer was not
granted. This produced some feeling, and they ap-
pealed to the public, through various channels, for
support in behalf of the Theological School, thus indirectly ignored by the Legislature. It is, however,

proper to add, that the probabilities in favor of secur-
ing an act of incorporation for the seminary would
have been much greater, had not the petitioners included in their prayer the request for the incorporation
of the Synod, also.

As a general thing, the Methodists gave little or no
aid towards building up the seminary, while many of
them opposed the measure altogether.   For this or
some other reason, sundry severe, and some very objectionable, publications were made in the public
prints, in regard to their doctrines, government, polity,
and supposed general designs.   This was done at
various periods, from 1819 to 1823.   An unusually
large number of sermons, tracts and pamphlets were
printed, and industriously circulated through the
country — all of them controverting some feature in
the doctrines or discipline of the Methodist Church.
There was also put into vigorous action, about this
time, a system of home missionary operations, through
that country, which, though well meant, no doubt, and
calculated to do good, had they been properly carried
on, were so managed as to give no little offense to
ministers and members of other denominations, and
impress them with the idea that there was an unwar-
rantable sectarian exclusiveness in the whole matter.
The managers and employees of the society fell into
the error of ignoring, in their reports, the services,
and even the very existence, of any ministers of religion, except those of their own denomination — an
error that was, in the end, fatal to their full success,
and somewhat detrimental to their good name.   For
instance, in a publication of theirs, made through the

Western Monitor, published at Knoxville, Tenn., June 11, 1819, they reported the States of Indiana, Mississippi and Louisiana, with the Territories of Alabama, Illinois, Michigan and Missouri, to contain a population of 350,000, with nearly the same number of square miles as the whole of Europe, excepting the Russian Empire; "yet, in this vast region," say the authors of the report, "we can not ascertain, after much inquiry, that there are more than seventeen competent and stated preachers of the Gospel." In another publication, made near the same time, Georgia was reported to have had "not more than ten qualified ministers," and Virginia was declared to be " totally destitute of the means of grace, or in the hands of illiterate men."* Similar reports were made of various sections of the country embraced in the Holston Conference. The ignoring of all ministers, save those of their own denomination, can not be justified, nor their manner of reporting excused altogether; yet it is due that they should be regarded as referring to ministers of their own denomination only, when they wrote as they did of the destitution of particular places. True, this ought to have been expressed, and they should also have been more guarded in the use of the phrase, "competent or enlightened ministers." This distinction was regarded as invidious, and called out many severe strictures from the pens of others, and especially from the Methodists, who seemed by no means to relish the idea of having sections of country which they had pioneered, and where they had gathered numerous large and

* See "Address of the Charitable Society for the Education of Indigent Young Men for the Ministry," pp. 8, 9.

prosperous Churches, reported as moral wastes, in utter destitution.

In the mean time, a monthly periodical, called the "Calvinistic Magazine," was started at Rogersville, Tenn., under the editorial management of some four of the ablest Presbyterian ministers in all that country, and, during its continuance, it served as the main channel through which they carried on their part of the written controversy. This publication, though conducted with considerable ability, was marked by extreme violence in its opposition to the Methodist doctrines and discipline, and distinguished for the severity, both of sentiment and style, with which its pages were filled. It was alleged, and not without good reason, that many false charges were made, both in reference to the doctrines and polity of Methodism, that were, or ought to have been, known as false by those who made them.

While these things were going on among the Presbyterians, the Methodists were far from being idle. In addition to their preaching and disseminating the general publications of the Church, they were circulating books and tracts specially suited to the necessities then existing, and everywhere, by all means in their power, inculcating their own doctrines, and vigorously combating their opposites, as well as seeking to give due attention to the existing state of things around them.

In the fall of 1823, Rev. Thomas Stringfield, a man of vigorous mind, well stored with that kind of knowledge that prepared him for the occasion, was placed in charge of the Knoxville District, and thus thrown in the midst of this controversy, at the very time when the presence of such a man seemed much needed. He was then in the prime of life, of great mental and physical activity, indomitable energy, untiring perseverance, and by nature endowed with great powers of endurance. For several years previous to this, his studies had been specially directed to the peculiarities of Hopkinsian and Calvinistic doctrines, and, perhaps, few men in the Methodist Church in all the West, or elsewhere, were more familiar with these doctrines, or better understood how to oppose them. He was at that time, and had been for some time before, publishing a periodical, at Huntsville, Ala., called " *The Western Armenian and Christian Instructor*," which publication was continued for some years after he went to the Holston country; and finally both the place of publication and the name were changed, without any change in the main design, and the "*Holston Messenger*," issued by him monthly, at Knoxville, Tenn., became his chief organ through which to carry on the controversy.

It was frequently alleged that, previously to the coming of Mr. Stringfield, the Churches were at peace, but the facts are as just stated. The controversy had commenced in 1819. Mr. Stringfield went to the Knoxville District late in 1823, and, previous to this date, the Hopkinsians had published and circulated numbers of sermons, conversations, expositions, letters and pamphlets, of different titles, principally in opposition to Methodist doctrines and discipline ; and, though he entered into the controversy fully, and carried it on spiritedly, he seldom or never raised a new point for discussion, or departed from the paths his opponents themselves had marked out. His topics were those which the other party, in opposing Methodism, had previously presented, either from the pulpit or from the press, and, by the manner of presenting them, had opened the way for, and indirectly invited, discussion. He was in this controversy what Mr. Patton was in the controversy with the Arians — the leader — with this difference, however: this was more violent, of longer continuance, and the opponents much more learned, intelligent and formidable.

As these things were carried on, from first to last, for nearly ten years, the reader will not be slow to admit that the discussion was not only extensive as to the points embraced, but extensive, also, as to the numbers engaged. Nearly every preacher, and almost every member, of both the Churches, had, at some time or other, more or less to say on the subject; while the points of difference, and the arguments by which they were maintained and opposed, were more or less familiar to all. Ere it finally closed, it took a still wider range, and became identified with the somewhat celebrated "Central Virginia controversy," in which Mr. Stringfield was led to take a very prominent and efficient part; but, as that does not properly come under notice in this work, a particular account of it will not be expected.

Considering the spirited manner, and the plain dealing, on the part of the speakers and writers concerned, it is somewhat remarkable these things disturbed the personal relations and social intercourse of the people no more than they did. With very slight exceptions, these remained in a pleasant condition, and the members of the different denominations continued occasionally, as opportunity served, to worship and commune together, as before, which is to be accounted for on the grounds that they, though entertaining different views on some important points of doctrine, still regarded each other as true Christian men. The few cases where the debatants so far forgot what was due to themselves, as professed Christian ministers, and what was also due to honorable antagonists, as to descend to personalities, found little favor in the public generally, and, in the end, such persons were by far the greatest sufferers.

Of the effects of these controversies, so far as they concerned the Methodist Church, some idea may be formed from the fact that, during their continuance, the membership in the bounds of that small Conference was steadily increased, in the aggregate, by something over two thousand a year. What the increase was, during the same period, in the Presbyterian Church, the present writer has not the means of ascertaining. Doctrinal preaching, or a free and full discussion, *pro and con.*, of theological dogmas, if carried on with the right spirit, and in the right way, never tends to the hindrance of the work of grace in the human heart. On the contrary, it promotes, and is sometimes necessary to it. They who would address themselves only to man's sensitive nature, greatly mistake the true principles of success. Ordinarily, the heart feels, and the conduct is influenced, only as the mind perceives. Truth must be presented to the intellect, and, as it perceives, apprehends and understands, the sensibilities will feel, and the conduct be influenced. Practical sermons, as they are usually called, to be effective, must be based on doctrinal teachings. If duties are to be taught and performed, those duties grow out of obligations, and those obligations spring from relations, and these relations involve the whole range of Scriptural theology. If this or that be urged as a duty, it devolves on those urging it to show *why* it is a duty, and this leads him back, step by step, to fundamental doctrinal principles. It is vain to hope for good success in practical preaching, unless it be founded in, and ever intimately connected with, Scriptural doctrines, which must first be promulged, explained, and, in some good degree, understood ; hence the more preaching of sound doctrines (using the word in its proper acceptation), the better for all concerned. What is usually passed off for practical preaching, requires but little study, and less research, and, however well it may suit the convenience, and accommodate the habits, of idle ministers, is not likely greatly to promote the growth of intelligent piety in the Church.

During the period of Mr. Patton's history now referred to, he attended to his work with that punctuality, and performed it with that fidelity, which characterized him through all his ministerial career. The district embraced a large extent of territory, much of which was exceedingly mountainous and rugged. His quarterly-meetings were often great distances from each other, but, almost without a single exception, were promptly attended, and his work faithfully performed. The prosperity of the Church was most gratifying, many of his quarterly and camp-meetings being marked by extraordinary displays of Divine power, in the awakening, conviction and conversion of souls. Hundreds were added to the Church, and thousands more, who previously had stood aloof, were brought, directly or indirectly, under its influences.

At the session of the Conference in the fall of 1827, after he had served two years in charge of the Abingdon District, he was appointed to the charge of the Church in the town of Abingdon, being the second Methodist preacher that had, up to that time, been stationed in that place — the talented and lamented George Atkin being the first. He had labored and died there the year before. Here Mr. Patton acquitted himself with great usefulness, commanding, almost universally, the confidence and respect of the people generally, and more than ever endearing himself to the members of the Church. He was, at the same session of the Conference, elected one of the delegates to the General Conference that was to be held at Pittsburgh, the following May. This he attended, in common with the other delegates, and bore his part in the transaction of the business that came before the body. At this General Conference, final action was taken in regard to those radical movements which, for eight or ten years previously, had so agitated the Church, and of which the present writer has given a full account elsewhere.* Mr. Patton was found on this, as he was on every other subject pertaining to the interests of the Church, sound, conservative, and on the side of genuine Methodism, in respect to its polity, as well as its doctrines. The interest he felt in all the proceedings was manifested by his making extended notes in refer-

* See LIFE AND TIMES OF REV. WILLIAM PATTON.

ence to what was done, from day to day, and the written reflections he made thereon. These exhibit not only attention and interest at the time, but also a clear, sound judgment on the important questions before that body. His notes in reference to the charges, specifications and pleadings, in several important appeal cases that came before the Conference, were full, and of special interest — particularly so in those cases, from the Baltimore Conference. which grew out of the radical controversy. He was also particular in his notes on the debate in regard to the setting off of the Canada Conference.

After his return from Pittsburgh, he devoted himself to the work of his charge, and prosecuted it with diligence and fidelity, until the session of the Conference, when he was returned to the charge of the Abingdon District, and his place in the station supplied by another.

The history of his immmediate successor in the Abingdon Station affords another melancholy proof of the evils often resulting from a neglect to pay due attention to the apostolic injunction, " Lay hands suddenly on no man." A man of fine appearance, graceful manners, winning address, and great sprightliness, suddenly appeared in that part of Virginia. Whence he came, no one seemed to know. His antecedents were entirely unknown to the people there, and seldom referred to by himself. But, as he had evidently been well educated, and, to all human appearance familiar with refined society, and was, withal, believed to possess a good degree of skill in his profession, being, or professing to be, a regularly trained physician, he found it easy to gain access to, and influence among, the people of all classes. Soon he was attending the Methodist meetings, conducting himself with strictest decorum and propriety, and professing deep interest in religious matters generally. Ere long, he made a profession of religion, and was received into the Church. Thus far, all seemed right and proper. But he had been in the Church but a short time, until he must preach. His love and zeal for the cause of God were so ardent, *he must preach*. Well, he was allowed to try—to make the experiment. He did so, and Dr. Chalmers himself would not have astonished or delighted the people more. They were enthusiastic in their admiration of his wonderful powers of eloquence. Although some experienced and grave old men shook their heads in doubt, it did no good. The people were delighted — enraptured — and clamorous for him to be regularly licensed to preach. He was licensed, recommended to the Annual Conference, received on trial in the traveling connection, and appointed to travel on the Abingdon Circuit; but the Bishop was careful enough to place another man in charge, and make him the assistant. During the year, he sustained himself so well, and became so popular, that, the ensuing year, the people of the town of Abingdon must needs have him as their stationed preacher. He was appointed there, but soon failed in almost every sense in which a preacher ought not to fail, and, for several years afterwards, the name of Albion C. Taylor was a byword and a reproach upon the whole Methodist community.

Mr. Patton's third year on that district was spent

pretty much as had been his first and second, with this difference, perhaps, that, in the Arian controversy, the Methodists had conquered a peace, and that with the Hopkinsians was declining, or rather, as already intimated, had been transferred mainly to Central Virginia ; so that, in the bounds of the district, there was more quietness, with, perhaps, increased religious prosperity. There were many gracious visitations of Divine power, during the camp-meeting season especially ; and a considerable increase of members, with a general advancement in all the interests of the Church, characterized the labors of the year.

The respect he had for the rights, and his tender regard for the feelings, of the preachers who labored with him on the several districts of which he had charge, not only made Mr. Patton an agreeable companion and a popular Presiding Elder, but so united the preachers, and enlisted them in a common cause, as to secure a hearty co-operation in all proper measures for carrying on the work, and, with this co-operation, there was always more or less success in building up and establishing the Church. Few men were ever more tender of the feelings of others than he, and yet none, perhaps, were ever farther removed from the spirit of fawning and flattery. He dealt plainly, but in greatest kindness, and with utmost tenderness ; and if, under his instruction, and with the example his upright walk and exemplary life afforded him, a young preacher did not improve, there was but little hope he would ever do so under the instructions or examples of another.

CHAPTER XI.

LABORS FROM 1830 TO 1840.

THERE is, perhaps, no class or profession of men whose lives and labors are characterized by so many or so varied incidents as those of Methodist traveling preachers. It is their lot to go into every part of the country, among almost all classes of people, and they are compelled to witness the variety of changes which occur in society, from its gayest to its gravest forms. One day they are amid the festivities and joyousness of hymeneal scenes, where all are cheerful and gay, and the very next, perhaps, they stand by the cold remains of some departed one, whose grief-stricken and heart-broken friends mourn, as though they never would or could be comforted. Now they enjoy the sweet influences of Christian and social communion, with friends who know and love them, and whom they, in return, love most fervently ; and, a few hours afterwards, they are in the midst of railers and scoffers, by whom their company is desired least of all others, and by whom they are not always treated even with cold civility. After days of hard labor and severe toil, they often find themselves at the house of a friend who is such indeed — whose eye and voice, and hand and heart, all bid them welcome ; and the succeeding evening, after a day of equally hard labor, they are at the house of one whose every look and every tone tells them they are *permitted* to be there, though, in reality, not desired; and this, too, when they feel their motive is pure, their object commendable, and their work the work of the Lord Most High. Often do they, or rather did they, in times past, meet receptions like this, when scores, and sometimes hundreds, of miles from home and friends, and, perhaps, not one dollar in their purses. Sometimes they were comfortably lodged, in houses kept by those who had just pretensions to cleanliness and decency, and at other times it would have been a privilege highly prized to have exchanged the lodgings they had for a mow of hay, a rick of straw, or a pen of clean shucks. In one part of their circuits they met with men and women of intelligence and refinement, whose society it was a privilege and an advantage to enjoy; and in other parts they were, day after day, thrown with those whose ignorance and viciousness were of the most pitiable character — persons who verily believed the sun, moon and stars passed round the earth, and only a few miles distant from it, and scoffed and ridiculed the idea of the earth's spheroidal form, or of its annual and diurnal revolutions, though they firmly believed in witches, wizards, ghosts and hobgoblins.

The reader need not be startled when told, as he now is, that there were not a few such as these in the bounds of the district Mr. Patton traveled from the fall of 1829 to the close of the Conference year for 1833, or during four full Conference years. It was so, and the present writer is witness to the fact. In the bounds of that same district, he came very near to losing his influence for good, in one whole society, because, at the request of an old gentleman—the most prominent and influential in the society—he undertook to show the reason of the difference between solar and sidereal time. It was in private conversation, at the good brother's own house, but the moment reference was made to the revolution of the earth, he cried out, " What! you don't think the earth moves, do you?" " Certainly," was the reply. " Well," said he, " I don't, and, if I did believe that, I'd never have a Bible in my house again. You don't believe the Bible, if you believe that." He was assured the Bible was believed heartily, but it would not do. The mischief had been done, very innocently, it is true, but done, and, for the remainder of the year, the circuit preacher was looked on suspiciously by the people of that neighborhood, because it was understood he believed " the world turned over." And yet these were well-meaning people. Their greatest fault, perhaps, was that they were ignorant and bigoted, and *would* not learn.

At the session of the Conference held at Abingdon, Va., in December, 1829, Mr. Patton was appointed to the charge of the Greenville District, which, at that time, embraced a considerable extent of territory, partly in Virginia, and partly in Tennessee. As already intimated, he continued to travel this district, by successive appointments, made annually, for four years. His family were located in the bounds thereof, at the only place they ever regarded as home ; and what time, though it was very little, he was not engaged in attending his appointments, and performing his regular work on the district, he occupied in active

and diligent labor on his little farm, in order to be the
better able to supply the temporal wants of those de-
pendent upon him. To this course he was compelled
by the very limited and meager support — if support
it can be called — afforded him by the people of the
district. A careful examination of the records as to
the finances of the Conference in those days, reveals
the fact that he much oftener received under than over
two hundred dollars a year from the Church, for the
services he rendered, and some years his receipts
scarce reached to half that sum. In most parts of the
district, the people were comparatively poor, and,
whatever else they may have had, they had but little
money. They were far removed from markets, and,
by their geographical position, cut off from commercial
marts and thoroughfares, and, to get money, they must
needs raise stock, and drive it some two or three hundred miles southward, or, at those seasons when the
rivers were swollen, freight their produce, in flat-bot-
tomed boats, down the rivers, to a distance of from
one to two thousand miles, by the course of the rivers,
or, lastly, to haul, in wagons, their flour, bacon or
iron a distance of some hundreds of miles. It may be
readily supposed that money procured in this way was
pretty highly prized, and the lovers thereof would be
somewhat careful the preachers were not spoiled by
their liberal benefactions. There was in the country
a good degree of energy, industry and enterprise, else
the people had scarcely lived at all, and it may be
seriously questioned whether the people of any other
part of the whole country ever did better for themselves, when all the disadvantages that attended them

are fully considered. Besides this, the people, it must be confessed, had been badly trained in regard to their duty in such matters.

In the earlier periods of the history of the Church's operations in that country, it was not uncommon for the preachers, in the exuberance of their zeal, to notify the people in every place, that they sought not theirs, but them, and to more than intimate their disapprobation of the idea of a hired salaried ministry, or " preaching for money." This was a great mistake, as well as a great imprudence. The people caught the idea readily, found it very agreeable to their notions of things, and entertained and cherished it most fondly — so much so, that, in after days, the mere mention of the propriety or necessity of contributing something to aid the preacher in the support of himself or family, was enough to cool the ardor of the most glowing zeal of many. True, this was not the case with all. There were those who took a more enlarged, liberal and common-sense view of the subject, and, to some extent, acted accordingly; but, with the great masses, there was a most lamentable lack in regard to this important duty. As time rolled on, and the people became better informed, there was a corresponding improvement in their conduct; but never, during the lifetime of the subject of these sketches, was there done what ought and might have been. It is but just to the people to add, that in many cases where the preachers had families who were removed from circuit to circuit, these families were usually supplied with the necessaries of life by the united contributions of the people, made in the articles of corn, flour, pork, beef, or whatever else they had to give, and the preacher's family needed ; so that the preachers themselves had less need for money than would otherwise have been the case. This, however, as is believed, did not apply to Mr. Patton. It was known he had a little home of his own, and a little farm which yielded him something. How much it yielded, the great majority of the people on the district had never learned, nor had they inquired. The simple fact that he had such a home was made, by many, a sort of pretext for the neglect of their duty, or, what is equivalent, made an excuse for their withholding those contributions they, perhaps, would otherwise have made ; and, from some cause or other, he rarely, if ever, presented or urged his pecuniary claims, as many others were accustomed to do.

During the years of his labors on that district, a steady progress marked the various departments of Church interests. The pure doctrines of the Bible were faithfully preached, and, under the preaching, the people became more and more enlightened, and more and more confirmed in those doctrines ; while the influence thereof became more and more widely diffused, and more and more of the people were brought into connection with the Church, and made partakers of its benefits. On the subject of religion, it is with communities as with individuals : They continually progress or recede — are continually growing wiser and better, or losing what they may have previously gained, and gradually returning to their first estate ; and to keep either going forward, requires continual effort. Such is man's relation to his fellow-man, and

such their mutual dependencies and influences, that each
must work for the other, as well as for himself; and
each can best promote his own interest by laboring at
the same time to promote the interest of his fellows.
Men are not usually, if ever, saved or lost alone.
They carry others with them, whichever way they go;
and, as communities are but the aggregation of a number of individuals, as go these individuals severally, so
go the communities. A proper and progressive state
of religious feeling in any community is kept up by
the proper efforts made by the individuals of that
community; and these individuals find it indispens-
able, in order to the end proposed, that they be constantly watchful, prayerful and vigilant, in all that
pertains to Christian duty, and especially that they
stir themselves and each other up to still greater
fidelity. So whole communities of Christians must be
constantly reminded of duty, constantly urged to its
performance, and exhorted to diligence, patience and
fidelity. A preacher never leaves his work as he finds
it. He never leaves any people exactly as he found
them. He draws them nearer to, or drives them
farther from, the Fountain of all truth and the Source
of all happiness. He always gains or loses; and, notwithstanding the downward tendency of human nature,
and the many surrounding influences calculated to increase that tendency, he who labors properly in the
cause of right, never labors in vain. He improves
himself, and he improves others. Faithful ministers,
therefore, in the performance of their proper duties,
never fail to do good. In the nature of things, it can
not be otherwise; and he who does no good, may

be sure it is owing either to the fact he is not laboring in the cause of right, or he is not laboring in the right way. So Mr. Patton, and those associated with him during the period referred to, did good — perhaps not all they might have done, but they did great good. The Church was built up, her borders were enlarged, her membership increased, and her influence greatly extended. Scores and hundreds passed away from earth, to find their home in a brighter and better world ; and scores and hundreds of others were awakened, converted, and brought to occupy their places, and fill up the ranks in the armies of Israel below. .

In some of these years, the camp-meeting seasons were times of rejoicing, indeed. Thousands of people were collected, and efforts, corresponding to the importance of the occasion, were made to expound and enforce the doctrines of the Bible, warn sinners to flee the wrath to come, and exhort them to believe on Jesus Christ, as a present and all-sufficient Savior. And rarely did these efforts fail of producing immediate results. The influence and example of Mr. Patton as Presiding Elder, at a camp-meeting, were of the most salutary kind. He seemed fully to realize the importance of the occasion, and keenly to feel the responsibility that rested upon him. He knew well these might be made the occasions of great good to a community, and they might also be so perverted and abused as to become the occasions of much harm. Hence the deep interest he manifested, and the watchful care he exercised at such times, was worthy of all commendation. He has been known to remain upon his knees, in the preacher's tent, during the whole time

of a brother's sermon, earnestly imploring the aid of
the Holy Spirit to be granted to the preacher and to
the people, that the Word might be delivered aright,
and then made the power of God unto the salvation
of souls. He carefully guarded, so far as he could,
against everything like disorder and confusion in his
congregations, believing that all things there, as well
as elsewhere, should be conducted " decently and in
order ;" and, satisfied it was easier to prevent than to
cure evils of this kind, he watched the small beginnings — the under-current of feeling — the outbursts
of which might have led to disorder. His plan was
to work as much as possible in private, by calm and
respectful appeals to men, made privately, and never
giving publicity to bad conduct at meetings, unless it
became really necessary. In this way, he won over to
the side of order and propriety many who might otherwise have been disorderly, and produced a great deal
of annoyance to those really desirous of worshiping
God. To enlist the ringleaders of mischief and
rowdyism in the cause of good order at camp-meeting,
was almost sure to result favorably. Flattered by
private appeals made to their sense of honor and
propriety, and proud to have it thought that their influence was considerable, they often engaged most
readily to see that good order prevailed on an encamp-
ment, during the continuance of a meeting ; and valuable auxiliaries they often proved themselves to be.
The ill-disposed, having thus lost their leaders, were
less inclined to be troublesome, and, withal, had some
good reason to fear these self-same leaders, then, for
the time being, pledged to the other side, might

soundly flog them, if they ventured far beyond the rules of propriety. Such instances did sometimes occur.

Mr. Patton was a close student, and read men, as well as books, was well acquainted with human nature, and, in all proper ways, addressed himself to it, that he might the more easily, as well as the more effectually, accomplish his mission. He closely studied the various characters with whom he was brought in contact, and most generally succeeded in carrying forward the interests committed to his care, without giving cause of offense. His reproofs given in public were very few, and then always mild — so much so, that none would scarce fail to perceive that the necessity for them gave him deep pain. Few men ever succeeded better in managing large assemblies, or exercised a better judgment in arranging the order of exercises, and selecting ministers, from time to time, to fill the pulpit. The quiet manner in which his work was done, and his unaffected kindness to all, scarce ever failed to command the respect, and win the confidence, of those around him.

At the close of his second year's labors on this district, the session of the Conference was held at Athens, Tenn., by the venerable Bishop Hedding, and Mr. Patton, together with T. K. Catlett, J. Henniger, J. Bowman, T. Stringfield, James Cumming, W. G. Brownlow and G. Ekin, was elected a delegate to the session of the General Conference, to be held at Philadelphia, the following May; although, in view of the state of his health, he asked, before the election came on, that his brethren would excuse him, and prepare

their ballots with reference to others. Several bal-
lotings were had, ere the delegation was chosen, and,
at the urgent request of divers members of the Conference, publicly and privately made, he withdrew his
request, and allowed himself to be voted for, when he
was at once elected, by a majority amounting almost
to unanimity. He attended the General Conference
and took his part in the proceedings, and performed
his work with that promptness, fidelity and modesty
that ever characterized him.

It was at this General Conference that a resolution
was introduced, by two delegates from the Holston
Conference, instructing a committee, which had just
been appointed to consider what changes, if any, were
necessary to be made in the section of the Discipline
referring to slavery, to inquire, also, and report as to
the true meaning of the rule which forbids the " buying
and selling of men, women and children, with an intention to enslave them." The resolution was debated
during a good part of one day, resumed the next day,
and finally, on motion of Dr. W. Fisk, who himself
argued that the rule referred only to the African
slave trade, was indefinitely postponed, much to the
disappointment and chagrin of the original mover
who was a strong, not to say violent, anti-slavery
man — a thorough emancipationist — and had hoped,
no doubt, by this means, to gain the sanction of the
General Conference to the views he entertained.
Men sometimes look so long and so intently on a
cherished thought, that it is not only magnified in
their estimation, but, in proportion as it is magnified,
other things, and especially its opposites, dwindle into

comparative insignificance. Thus it most likely was
with the good man—for a good man he certainly was—
to whom reference is now made. He had taken a
one-sided and too partial a view of the question of
slavery; and, though he did not go so far as many
have since gone, he went far enough to bias his judgment, and often to give utterance to sentiments by
which he was placed in no enviable attitude before his
Conference, the Church and the world; and, if they
have been preserved, whoever has the private papers
of the late Rev. John Bowman, may find among them
the record of his disappointment and mortification at
the failure of the resolution above referred to, in the
General Conference of 1832. He may also find some
strong animadversions on the spirit which, he thought,
the Conference indicated by the vote it gave, and still
stronger ones on the speeches made on that subject, by
some of the most prominent members of that body.

After his return from the General Conference, Mr.
Patton addressed himself to his work, with his accustomed earnestness, and prosecuted it with his usual
zeal, industry and energy, although the state of his
health, which, for some time, had been precarious, was
evidently getting worse and worse. The demands for
his services were numerous and urgent. His brethren
in the ministry were loth to entertain the idea of his
retiring from the regular and active work in which he
was engaged, and which he performed so much to the
satisfaction, and so greatly to the benefit, of the
Church; and he himself shrank from the idea of being,
as he sometimes expressed it, laid away, like a piece
of cracked china; so he went as long as he could go,

and perhaps went often when, in the end, it might have been better, both for himself and the Church, had he remained quiet, and sought that rest and recuperation he so greatly needed. But he persisted in going forward, and doing what he could — often attending his appointments for quarterly or camp-meetings, when in weakness and affliction so great that it was difficult for him to reach the place, and, when there, impossible to do more than take a sort of general oversight, and counsel his brethren what to do and how to proceed.

At length, in the fall of 1833, or near the close of his fourth year of labor on that district, it became obvious to all that his field of labor must be greatly lessened, and his burdens lightened, or he must desist entirely from efforts to do the work of a traveling preacher. The former was agreed upon, and, at the Conference held for that year, he was assigned to the towns of Kingsport and Jonesborough, though not less than twenty-five miles apart, with rivers, creeks, hills and very bad roads between. At each place there was a Church and a respectable society. He was expected to preach on Sabbaths only, and alternately at each place, besides keeping a general oversight of the Churches, and contributing whatever he might be able towards their general welfare and prosperity. This, in more recent times, would be considered work enough for a man whose health was sound and vigorous, and so, perhaps, it might be, but it was less, by two-thirds or three-fourths, than he had been accustomed to perform. Here he remained during two successive Conference years, or until the fall of

1835, when, greatly to the gratification of his friends, it was found his health had been partially restored, and he reported himself desirous of being considered as efficient, and as able and willing to work as in former days. He had taken good care of the Churches at Kingsport and Jonesborough. They had enjoyed a good degree of prosperity, and made considerable advancement in the knowledge and love of the truth.

At the Conference for 1835, he was, for the third time, elected to represent his brethren in General Conference. The delegation from the Holston Conference consisted of S. Patton, W. Patton, T. K. Catlett, and D. Fleming. They were all present at the opening of the Conference, in Cincinnati, May 2, 1836, and all bore their full part in the work there performed. At this Conference, as in 1828, Mr. Patton made copious notes of the proceedings, from day to day, interspersed with remarks and reflections, which proved him to have been a judicious, as well as an attentive, observer, and also exhibited, on his part, great familiarity with, and great love for, the doctrines, discipline, usages and interests of the Church. Here, again, there was manifested by a member of the General Conference — a delegate from the New England States — a tendency towards Abolitionism, more direct, and palpable than that shown and voted down in the Conference of 1832 — voted down by every member of the Conference, except the mover, whose vote, when given, "solitary and alone," on the opposite side, caused some one facetiously to cry out, "Athanasius contra mundum." At Cincinnati, the member from New England ventured to deliver a public lecture on the subject, which fact, coming to the knowledge of the Conference, resolutions, strongly condemning both the principle and the practice, were introduced and passed, with only a very few dissenting votes.* These were days previous to the departure of the great body of Methodists, in the Northern States, from the old landmarks of Methodism,. and the true Scriptural grounds on which such questions rest.

At the session of the Holston Conference for 1835, Mr. Patton was appointed to take charge of the Abingdon District, which he did, and performed the duties pertaining to the charge as he had long been accustomed to perform similar duties elsewhere. It is almost needless to say he was acceptable and useful. But, ere the year had closed, it was found he and his friends had calculated upon more strength than he, in reality, possessed; and, although more vigorous than he was three years previous to that time, it was evident he was again declining; so, at the next session of the Conference, his field of labor was changed from the Abingdon to the Greenville District, where his rides would be shortened, and the vigor of his labors somewhat abated. Here he was heartily welcomed by his old and well-tried friends, whose good opinion and Christian confidence he had so long enjoyed, and for whose interests he had labored so long and so faithfully. Had the body been as strong and vigorous as the mind, he could, and would, have performed there, during the year, much more work than he did. But it was not so. The spirit was willing — the heart was

* See Journals of the General Conference, vol. 2, p. 447.

in the work, the soul was alive to God and his cause; the longer it tried the service of God, the more delighted was it with that service; the more deeply and frequently it drank of the fountain of Divine love, the greater was its anxiety for all others to enjoy like privileges and blessings — but "the flesh was weak." The sword was too keen for the scabbard, and was about to cut its way out. There was a rich jewel in a frail casket, that daily gave increasing evidence of early dissolving, and permitting the treasure it bore to return to its rightful owner.

This and the succeeding year were years of great pecuniary embarrassment throughout all that region of country, as, indeed, in almost all parts of the United States; and it fell out badly for many of the traveling preachers, whose means of support were thereby greatly curtailed. It is notorious that a large portion of the people in every place, in times of pecuniary embarrassment, first lop off the contributions they may have been accustomed to make to objects of benevolence, and stint themselves in regard to the demands of their mental and moral natures, long before they determine to deny themselves the usual gratification of the senses. Many men have found themselves so hardly pressed by the stringency of the times, as to be unable, as they supposed, to aid any of the great benevolent enterprises of their day, and unable to afford more than one-half or one-third the amount usually contributed for the support of their ministers; and, all the while, their manner of living, and their various self-indulgences, were the same as before—not curtailed in the least. Unconsciously to themselves, perhaps, their selfishness thus operates, and thus manifests itself. They think they are right, and are sincere in their belief, but forget that a man may as sincerely believe a glaring falsehood as a sober, wholesome truth ; his sincerity or insincerity affecting in no way whatever the nature or character of the thing believed. This selfishness in human nature, to which the teachings of the Bible and the spirit of Christianity are always opposed, is, after all, one of the most serious and formidable drawbacks to the progress of right principles with which men are called to contend. It is so insidious — can so easily and readily hide itself amid specious pretexts — that it is often exceedingly difficult to recognize it; and yet, wherever it exists, its legitimate work is sure to be done. Very often, with great plausibility, it denies even-handed justice to others, while, at a greater expense, it seeks its own sensual gratification. It can readily see why the hardness of the times should curtail the amounts usually set apart to works of benevolence, but can not see why the same cause should at all lessen annual expenditures for the personal enjoyment, whatever it may be, of fine dress or luxurious living. It is sad to contemplate the havoc this principle sometimes makes among the beautiful things in the Church of God, and sad to witness how keenly ministers of the Gospel are made to feel the effects of its workings. Of course, Mr. Patton and those connected with him were made to feel the effects of " the hard times," by the lessening of the aggregate of their receipts from the Church, which, though at no time equal to the wants of themselves and families, were now even less than before.

If any be curious in reference to these so-called
hard times, and will examine carefully the history of
the past, they may ascertain that such times have
visited this country since 1817, at intervals of from
seven to ten years; and, in almost every instance, they
have been succeeded by extraordinary revivals of
religion, as if a merciful Providence thus checked the
career of worldly prosperity, that the people might
pause, and think of the source whence their help came;
and all experience confirms the fact that, when men
who live in a country enlightened by the Gospel can
be brought to think seriously of their dependence
upon, and obligations to, the Giver of all good, there
is then comparatively but little difficulty in successfully persuading them to seek, through the merits and
mediation of Christ, the favor of Him on whom they
thus depend.   Many men continue in moral estrange-
ment from God, more for want of due and proper re-
flection and consideration than from the active operations of willful and obstinate perversity.   It is not
that they positively hate righteousness, truth, justice
and mercy, considered as abstract qualities — on the
contrary, they love them — but it is that they do not
bring the claims of these to bear directly on themselves, carefully scrutinize the motives and feelings
that impel them, or properly consider their responsibilities and obligations to God, in connection with the
consequences that must inevitably result from the
course they now pursue.

At the close of the Conference year for 1837, it was
found that Mr. Patton's health had been much farther
impaired during the year, and it was necessary again

to make some change in the character of his work. Accordingly he was appointed Agent for Holston College — an institution of learning, under the fostering care of the Conference, which, for a number of years previous to this, had been in operation, at New Market, Tennessee.

The nature of Mr. Patton's affliction, at this time, was of a character that tended more to operate against his preaching than to prevent his transacting ordinary business, or performing such duties as pertained to a college agency. The condition of the institution for the benefit of which he labored from the fall of 1837 to the fall of 1839, or two years, was such as to require the services of some man of standing and influence, and the Conference, at that time, had no one who, it was believed, could meet the emergency so well as he. Of the history of that college, much has been given elsewhere,* and need not to be now repeated. Mr. Patton addressed himself to the work assigned him — though, upon careful examination, he found things in a worse state than had been anticipated — and prosecuted it with a degree of success at least equal to that experienced by any who had preceded him. By patient perseverance and hard labor, he succeeded in relieving the institution, to a great extent, from the heavy and embarrassing debts that hung over it, and did much, also, to establish it on a more firm basis, though all his efforts, as well as those put forth by others, failed to give perpetuity to the college. It gradually declined, until finally abandoned by the

* See LIFE AND TIMES OF REV. WILLIAM PATTON.

Conference, after years of toil and large sums of money had been expended. It was not, however, without its use to the Church and the community generally. It was compelled to contend, from the first, with influences and prejudices adverse to its true interests and final success; and, although those influences prevailed, it was not until many — very many — excellent men had received there a training, both of mind and heart, that enabled them, in after days, to accomplish much good to others; and the failure of this enterprise seemed but to arouse, in the minds of the Methodist people, a determination to carry out their ulterior objects, in regard to their educational interests, in other ways, and at other places; so that this had not entirely failed, ere two or three other larger and better institutions were in active and successful operation in different parts of the Conference.

The interest Mr. Patton felt on the subject of general education, was manifested by what he did for the cause — not merely in regard to the college just referred to, but by what he said in his sermons, and public and private lectures — by what he wrote. by the pains he took to have his own children well educated, and by what he gave of his own time and means to assist in the founding and sustaining of good schools. Through all periods of his ministry — in whatever relation he sustained to the Conference and Church — he was careful to preach expressly on the subject of education, and the right training of children; and, during the two years he acted as College Agent, while traveling extensively over the territory embraced in the Conference, he had fine opportunities to arouse the public mind on this important subject, and assist in guiding it to profitable results when so aroused. These opportunities he embraced, and used with good effect. He was never what some have called a one-idea man, or a man to choose particular subjects or favorite themes, until they became hobbies, to be ridden, not only to their own death, but also to the disgust of those who, even on the first, second or third hearing, might have been much pleased ; but he was a man that tried to do well whatever he under-took to do at all, and always labored to perform his work so as to accomplish the greatest good to the greatest number.

His manner of transacting temporal business, or managing the finances of the Church that, from time to time, were committed to his care, was correct, faith-ful and prompt, consequently entirely satisfactory to those concerned. In truth, he never parted from his religion, but let it govern him at all times, in all places, under all circumstances, and in whatever duty he was called to perform ; and this, after all, was the secret of his success.

CHAPTER XII.

LABORS FROM 1840 TO 1846.

AT the session of the Conference for 1839, Mr. Patton was again appointed to the charge of the Abingdon District, although his health had by no means been fully restored. No Bishop attended that session. Rev. T. K. Catlett was chosen to preside, and he, in connection with the other Presiding Elders, found great difficulty in providing for the several districts, unless Mr. Patton would consent to take charge of one, which, at the earnest solicitations of his brethren, he did. On this district he remained, by successive annual appointments, during four Conference years, or from the fall of 1839 to the fall of 1843. At this latter period, he was removed to the charge of the Rogersville District, where he remained one year ; was then sent once more to Abingdon Station, where he labored during the following year, or until the fall of 1845, when he was assigned to Knoxville Station, of which he had charge until the close of the Conference year for 1846.

Having thus briefly stated where he was during the periods alluded to in this chapter, it will be proper, in the next place, to give some notice of what he did.

At the session of the Annual Conference for 1839,

in connection with E. F. Sevier and T. K. Catlett, he was elected a delegate to the General Conference of 1840, and, with his characteristic promptitude, was present at the opening of that Conference, in Baltimore, May 1st, and, throughout the session, bore his part in the labors performed.

At this General Conference, much was done affecting the interests of the Church generally; and on the particular subject which, four years later, led to a division of the Church, the doctrines promulged at this Conference were sound and conservative. The subject was brought up at different times, and in different ways, but always with the same results, so far as it concerned the majority of the Conference. In the letter to the British Conference, and also in the report on the somewhat famous Westmoreland case, the position which a Church should occupy, agreeably to the teachings of the sacred Scriptures, was clearly set forth and ably maintained. Both before and after the division of the Church, Mr. Patton was a strictly conservative man, on that and all other subjects affecting the welfare of Zion.

Returning from the General Conference, he devoted himself to the work assigned him, and prosecuted it with the earnestness and fidelity which had so long marked his course, as a minister of the New Testament, but not without difficulties attending him at almost every step. The old controversy with the Presbyterians was being revived, in the bounds of his district, and the severe and repeated attacks made on some of the doctrines and general polity of the Methodist Church, in set sermons, delivered by able and influential Presbyterian ministers, within these bounds, necessarily called his attention in that direction, and demanded a more direct and explicit exhibition and defense of these, on the part of himself and those associated with him. At the same time, the "Radical Controversy" was revived in parts of the same territory, and, superadded to these, he was much persecuted and greatly harassed by a number of persons who professed themselves injured by the course he felt called upon, as an officer of the Church, to pursue,.in regard to some difficulties between influential brethren, and which grew mainly—if not entirely—out of partisan politics. It may well be supposed that, when all these things came at the same time, besides the pressing engagements of his regular work on the district, his head, and heart and hands were well filled. How he passed through these, will be learned, to some extent, as the history progresses.

As the controversy with the Presbyterians was more fully developed subsequently to the period embraced in this chapter, and will claim due attention at the proper time, there is no necessity for anticipating that time, and noticing it here; but with the "Radical Controversy" it was otherwise. This had its beginning and its ending, so far as Mr. Patton was engaged in it, during the period now under notice.

In 1831, when a few members in the town of Abingdon, Va., seceded from the M. E. Church, and subsequently connected themselves with the Methodist Protestant Church, then but lately organized, the affair produced some excitement at the time, but, after a few months, all was again comparatively calm, and so re-

mained, with but little interruption, for several years.
For some reason or other, not clearly apparent, even
at the time, several of the more prominent members,
and one or two of the ministers, of the Protestant
Methodist Church, seemed to possess less kindness
of feeling towards Mr. Patton than towards the ministers of the M. E. Church, generally. Whether it was
that his talents and influence were regarded as more
formidable than those of others, or whether they
really believed him to be more opposed to their movements than were his brethren, is difficult to determine,
though it is quite clear he was more frequently alluded
to, and oftener censured, by them than were others.
They seemed to attach a greater importance to what
he said or did; and things which passed unnoticed
when said or done by others, were regarded as of a
very grave and serious character when said or done
by him. He was well known to be exceedingly cautious as to what he said of others, and much guarded
in his expressions as to the principles and practices of
those known to differ with him; and there were many
preachers in that region of country as thoroughly
episcopal in their views and preferences, as to Church
government, as he was, and much more free in the expression of these preferences, yet, of all, he was
singled out by Protestant Methodists as their opponent
and enemy — not that he had said more or done more,
but there may have been a private conviction in their
minds, that no one, in all that country, was likely to
exercise a greater influence by what they might say,
or whose opinions would likely have greater weight.
So it was; he was pretty closely watched, his public

movements carefully noted, and, at different times, allusions were made, from the pulpit and through the secular press, which, in his judgment, as well as that of some of his most intimate friends, were most likely designed to draw him into a public controversy. Letters, containing matter of a very objectionable character, were also addressed and sent to him, in which the writers professed to found their complaints on something which report said he had uttered at other and distant places. As a matter of course, he took no notice of these or of the other proceedings in regard to him, other than occasionally to make them subjects of conversations, in a pleasant way, among his personal and particular friends; yet they were not without their significance. They were indices to the feeling existing in the breasts of their authors, in regard to him, and they were the legitimate precursors of what followed.

Very soon, tracts and pamphlets, originating at different points and from different sources, but all opposing the polity of the M. E. Church, were industriously circulated throughout that part of the country. At first, no one seemed to know whence, or by whom, they came, or by whom they were distributed; still they were being constantly increased in numbers, and disseminated more and more widely. Many of them contained statements, in regard to the government of the Church, which were both false and slanderous — false as to the facts in the case, and slanderous as to the characters of men, both living and dead, who were concerned. One of these pamphlets, and one entitled " Questions and Answers Explanatory of the Government of the M. E. Church," was very liberally distributed, about the close of 1842, or early in 1843, and much talked of by the enemies of the Church, as a wonderfully clear and irrefutable exposition of the monarchical and tyrannical character of the government of the said Church. It is worthy of note that the distribution was most general in those sections of the country where the people were generally supposed to be less familiar with the publications of the Church, and little acquainted with its history or government, only so far as they might have learned something of the latter by its practical workings. As has been the case elsewhere, and in other times, the distributors and friends of these pamphlets, or, in other words, ministers and members of the Methodist Protestant Church — as few, if any, others were originally concerned — appeared more solicitous to show that others were wrong, than that they themselves were right — an error, this, into which many fall. Had the labor and pains which they expended in efforts to show that the M. E. Church was wrong, been spent in efforts to show they themselves were right, it would certainly have presented them in a more Christian-like and enviable attitude, although the efforts themselves had been equally fruitless. But to pull down is often easier than to build up, and human nature sometimes seeks to conceal its own weakness and errors, by earnestly calling attention to the supposed weakness and errors of others. But the course is as impolitic as it is disingenuous. Men of liberal minds and right feelings can not long retain their respect for that which seeks to commend itself more by its opposition to something else than by any intrinsic merit of its own. Fault-finding and flaw-picking are trades that may be carried on with very little capital, and usually are carried on by such as have not the ability for higher and more manly pursuits; and, in the case under notice, it was ultimately ascertained to be a much easier work for them to urge objections against others, than to answer objections made against themselves.

For some time, but little notice was taken of this pamphlet of questions and answers, until, at last, its friends became more bold and more open in its circulation and advocacy; and the preachers went so far as to speak of it publicly, and publicly to recommend it to their congregations. On one occasion, this was done by a minister of the Protestant Methodists, who not only recommended the pamphlet, but publicly pledged himself to sustain every allegation it made, if they were denied, or publicly recant what he had said in commendation of it. This bold declaration was regarded by many as a challenge to all ministers and members of the M. E. Church, and, as such, was accepted by a local preacher of that Church, who lived in the vicinity where the declaration was publicly made. After a correspondence, in which the usual preliminaries in such cases were discussed and agreed upon, it was resolved that the statements contained in the pamphlet should be publicly discussed, as to their truth, and Mr. Patton was prevailed on by his friends to act as one of the parties in the discussion. To those who were well acquainted with his general character, and particularly with his settled disinclination to such things, this course was strange, and can only be satisfactorily accounted for on the supposition that there were circumstances and influences of a peculiar character connected with the affair, which were un-known to those at a distance. There must have been some reasons other than those usually prevailing in most cases where public discussions on such questions are had, else he never would have engaged in it ; and it is altogether probable these reasons might have been found in the then existing state of the public mind generally, rather than in either the pamphlet or the individual persons who had taken upon themselves the onerous task of publicly defending its statements. Such discussions very rarely accomplish great good — never, unless carried on with great care, and with a desire to elicit truth, rather than gain a temporary victory ; and it is often very difficult for poor human nature to be perfectly open to honest convictions of truth, when pledged, before large audiences, to make good certain propositions previously announced. The desire for success — for victory — is very likely, under such circumstances, to cloud the intellect, warp the judgment, and greatly hinder the mind in its free and full investigations of truth, for truth's sake. Besides, when preparations are being made for such contests, the mind is led to look favorably on one side of the question, and unfavorably on the other. It strains itself in efforts to strengthen every argument to be ad-vanced for, and to weaken those that may be urged against, the favorite propositions ; and, just in propor-tion as these efforts are great and continued, in the same proportion is the danger of estimating the one above, and the other below, its real merits. Then, again: It is awarding rather too much to human nature, in its present state, to suppose two debatants would enter upon such a contest with an entire willingness on the part of each, that the other might prove himself in the right, and he in the wrong. Each is, no doubt, desirous to elicit the truth; but, at the same time, each, most likely, has a secret and a very strong desire that the truth should prove to be on his side, and not on the side of his opponent; and in this feeling a large proportion of the hearers, usually assembled on such occasions, concur. They all desire the truth—certainly; but they desire it should be found here, and not there—in this, and not in that; or, in other words, they greatly desire their favorite theories should be proven true, rather than those of their opponents; and this desire has often more to do in shaping their opinions than they, perhaps, are ready to admit. Men are often very willing to be convinced of their errors, but always prefer that conviction should be private, rather than public; and the most agreeable manner in which this conviction can be brought about, is by their own mental labor and research. The next is by instruction from an acknowledged friend; but to be convinced of error by one who publicly assumes, and with all his might maintains, the character of an opponent, is altogether another thing, and such a case, were it to occur, would be well worth recording and preserving among the records of man's history. Let a man be privately convinced of his errors, and especially if the conviction be the result of his own efforts, in due time he will readily and cheerfully acknowledge it publicly, and act accordingly. But the same man will be very difficult to convince of an error, and very loth, indeed, to confess it to a large audience, before which he has been debating the very questions involved; and, as the great mass of hearers, on such occasions, partake largely of the same class of feelings, public discussions, such as now alluded to, often serve more to engender pride, stubbornness and self-will, than to advance the cause of truth.

In due time, the preliminaries were all arranged, the parties ready, and the discussion was had. It was held in the month of July, 1843 — each party, no doubt, doing their best, and, in the end, as is usually the case, each party claiming the victory. The main question was, "Are certain statements contained in the aforesaid pamphlet true?" — Mr. Patton denying. Judges were chosen, and, as there were several specifications, they, with impartiality, decided some of these specifications in favor of one, and some in favor of the other; so the matter was left pretty much as it had been before, and neither party seemed altogether pleased with the proceedings, and especially with the decisions. However, very soon after this, the matter of the pamphlet and its contents passed away, and things went on much as they had done previously to its existence.

It is proper to remark in this connection, that, not long before this discussion, Mr. Patton had written a pamphlet, of 32 octavo pages, in which he closely reviewed, and severely criticized, the statements of the author of the pamphlet referred to, and, with much ability and clearness of manner, exposed its errors, and defended the discipline of the M. E. Church. This publication of his, it is believed, did much more to maintain and defend the views entertained by the M. E. Church, on the subject of ecclesiastical govern- ment, than was done by the public discussion. The pamphlet was entitled, " Minutes of the Trial and Con- viction of a Prisoner ;" and, in the preface, the author remarked that, not knowing any person, either minister or member, of the Methodist Protestant Church, in all that country, whom he was willing to charge with circulating the pamphlet reviewed, he had chosen to ascribe personality and agency to the pamphlet itself, and had arraigned it as a prisoner, which he proceeded to try and convict; and, it must be confessed, the evi- dence of guilt was clear and indisputable, and the prisoner received no more than his just deserts. As has already been intimated, the public mind was much agitated, and the Church much disturbed, by the nu- merous pamphlets, newspaper articles, sermons, lectures and addresses bearing on this subject, and, for some time previously to the debate, the excitement in the bounds of Mr. Patton's district was pretty general, and, in some particular localities, it was intense. Earnest efforts had industriously been made to disaffect the minds of Episcopal Methodists with the govern- ment of the Church to which they belonged, and to carry out a system of proselyting, by no means cred- itable to any Christian minister or Christian denom- ination. For Mr. Patton, as the chief pastor of the Church in that section of the country, to throw him- self in opposition to such movements, and do whatever he could to preserve the peace, as well as the purity, of the people of whom he had charge, was no more than natural, and no more than was both right and. proper. To have done otherwise, would have been recreant to the trust committed to his keeping. To be placed in such a situation, was by no means congenial to his feelings, but, when stern duty called, he ever sought to obey her calls, no matter what might be the sacrifice of personal ease or inclination.

While these things were going on, he was subjected to a trial, much more severe, from another quarter. His time on that district embraced a period of the most intense and bitter excitement, on questions of partisan politics, that had been witnessed in that country from the time of the famous Frankland revolution, down to the period named. It had commenced some time previous to the exciting election for President, in 1840, and, aggravated sometimes by one thing and sometimes by another, had gone on, until it reached a point where the social and religious relations of life were greatly disturbed. There were Whig and Democratic parties — Whig and Democratic papers. The hotels, the stores, and even the shops, were regarded as Whig or Democratic, and thus patronized by the parties. There was scarcely any such thing as neutrality. Almost every one — high or low, rich or poor, black or white — was arrayed on one side or the other ; and if any one, though a minister of the Gospel, refused to allow himself to be classed with either party, he was very apt to be denounced by both. It so happened that, during part of the time of Mr. Patton's presidency in that district, two of the most prominent of the party-leaders were members and preachers of the

Methodist Church. They were also editors of the
leading partisan papers — one Democratic, the other
Whig. In such a state of things as then existed, it is
not strange that feelings of a personal, as well as of a
political, character should be manifested in matters
pertaining to the Church. And this was very soon
the case. These preachers and editors were respectively charged with unministerial and unchristian conduct, arraigned before the Church, and, by the proper
authorities, tried under the charges. From first to
last, the matter agitated the Church, during several
months — indeed, during two or three years. Each of
these men had his personal, as well as his social and
political, friends, whose interest and ardor of feeling
increased as the affair progressed before the Church;
and although, in the end, one was believed to have
been fairly acquitted of having violated the law of the
Church, and the other as fairly convicted, the decision
did not satisfy the friends of the parties. The friends
of the preacher acquitted complained that proceedings
had been instituted and carried on through improper
feelings, and from improper motives; while those of
the convicted preacher roundly asserted that unfairness
had been practiced and injustice done, and boldly ac-
cused Mr. Patton of mal-administration in the exercise
of the functions of his office, as Presiding Elder. But
the subject will, perhaps, be more satisfactorily understood by inserting here some remarks made by Mr.
Patton, before the Holston Annual Conference, at its
session in 1844. When his name was called, in the
regular examination of the character of the preachers,
severally, he arose, and, after giving a tolerably full

account of the condition and prospects of the Church, in the bounds of the district of which he had been in charge, said :

" Mr. PRESIDENT : Having said thus much with regard to the work on my district, I beg the indulgence of the Chair and of the Conference to make a few remarks. It is but seldom that I take the liberty to speak of myself ; but a moderate share of self-respect, and a sense of duty to the Conference, forbid that, under existing circumstances, I should be entirely silent. You have gravely asked the question, ' Is there anything against Brother Patton?' This Conference have as gravely answered, ' *Nothing*.' There is, then, nothing against my moral, ministerial or official character, that requires investigation before this Conference. So says this moral, respectable and intelligent body. Now, sir, it is known to some in this Conference, that there is an exceeding bitter and extensive outcry, in the upper counties of East Tennessee, against my mal-feasance in office — against the corruption, partiality and intrigue of my administration. I introduce this subject here, for reasons which will appear before I have done. During the year 1843, I had charge of the Abingdon District, then including the Jonesborough Circuit. In that year, three local brethren — an elder, a deacon and a licensed preacher — were severally charged with certain offenses against the moral law, and tried by the Quarterly Meeting Conference of the circuit. The elder was tried in two cases, but not convicted in either. The deacon was acquitted, and the licensed preacher was found guilty, and silenced. The elder was, and still is, editor of a political paper.

The preacher was, and still is, editor of a paper of
of different politics. After the conviction of the
preacher, he commenced, and kept up, an attack on the
Quarterly Meeting Conference, and especially on myself, for some six or eight months, almost incessantly.
He took the stump, and made speeches, for some thirty
or forty, or more, miles around ; the object of all of
which effort was to convince the people that the Quarterly Meeting Conference was corrupt, and that I
especially, under the influence of personal friendship
for his enemies, and for partisan political purposes, had
acted partially, illegally and corruptly in the trials
which had occurred. Many hard and bitter things
have been said, much angry feeling has been aroused,
and much of it in the Church. During all this time,
no man appears in his proper place, and before this
proper tribunal, to charge and make good his charges
against me. I have challenged investigation — I have
courted investigation. But no. The tribunal of the
Church is not the place. Meanwhile, the outcry is still
kept up, and every few weeks, or months at most, furnishes an addition to the stock of charges and complaints already on hand. Why, sir, it is as current as
gold and silver, and much more so (if circulation constitutes any part of currency), that I make political
speeches—that, when I went to New York, last spring,
I went a hundred and fifty miles out of my way, to attend the great Whig convention of nomination, and,
in consequence, lost two days from the General Conference ; and, on this score, there are bitter complaints,
both in the Church and out of it, among a good and
tender-hearted sort of sinners, who greatly deplore the

corruption of the Church, and especially of the ministry. Now, sir, with the outcry of the world I can put up. To the bitter complaints of portions of the Church, I can submit, and account for it on the ground of high political prejudices and excitement, and the fact that certain political leaders regard the propagation of falsehood and slander, in reference to myself, as gaining (exactly in proportion to its prevalence) to the cause in which they are engaged. Yes, sir, I can regard as Christians and as brethren men of whom advantage has been taken, till their prejudices have been wrought up to a high pitch against me.

" I know something of the deceitfulness of the human heart, and of my liability to be deceived myself. I have, however, endeavored to weigh the subject impartially, and in the light of truth ; and, if I am not exceedingly mistaken in my own feelings and principles of action, I am prepared to say that, as a man, in reference to my private character, and as a citizen of my country, I utterly disregard all the outcry that has been raised ; and, as to personal friendships, associations and enjoyments, I am willing to take my own, but coveting an exchange with no man. But there is one view of this subject in which, I confess, I am pained. I regard my public, ministerial and official character as not my own, but as belonging to the Church ; and just in so far as my public and ministerial character form any part of the character of Methodism, in the estimation of men, just in so far whatever affects me affects Methodism, in a certain and qualified sense, which you and this Conference will readily understand. But there is one item in this affliction which is peculiarly painful, and it is one the notice of which will probably fall strangely upon the ears of the Conference; and yet it is one which, as an honest man, I can not suppress. It is this: There is an agency connected with this Conference, which has given currency to false and injurious reports, the object of which is to affect my influence as a preacher, and to arm the credulous, and such as are capable of being imposed upon, with objections to my ministerial efforts for the common good. I do not say an agency which *originated* such reports, but an agency which has given currency to them; and I can but believe it has been done without considering, in this case, the connection between cause and effect — without considering that the word, especially of a preacher, will eat as doth a canker. Again: I can not admit that this agency is extensive, although of its existence I have demonstration. I am naturally unsuspecting. I have come in conflict with but few preachers, in the entire history of my connection with preachers; and every man who knows that he is not in the category of those embraced in this agency, may feel perfectly at rest in his mind, with reference to these remarks. But when I am met with the sayings of a brother preacher, who is presumed to understand things as they are, and whose character I hold too sacred to admit of an attack from me, even in defense, it unmans me, it disarms me, and subjects me to peculiarly painful exercises of mind. But, notwithstanding this, it is my settled purpose not to complain, or allege aught against any brother, on the examination of his character; and candor requires me to say that, in my response to questions asked in the

examination of character, whether by *silence* or by answering, '*Nothing*,' I wish it distinctly understood
that no reference is had to anything which may have
been said concerning my character, motives or administration. My reasons for this purpose are : first, such
sayings are personal, and personal to myself ; second,
men claim a right to their opinions, whatever may
have been the sources of the information on which
those opinions are founded. As to the right which
one brother has to use the name of another injuriously,
that is another question, and one which the Bible and
the philosophy of morals will decide. A third reason
is found in the conclusion which I draw from the first
and second : I do not believe that any investigation
of such matters here would result in any good.

"But, sir, having made these remarks, I regard it as
both a duty and a privilege to say that, for the Holston
Conference, as such, I entertain none other than sentiments of profound respect, and feelings of ardent
attachment, with unabating confidence in its integrity
and firmness. But for my connection with the Holston
Conference, my confidence in it, my attachment to it,
and my devotion to the work embraced in its boundary,
I should have been, probably more than ten years ago,
in the West, or some other section of country. More
than one-half of my natural life has been spent in connection with the traveling ministry of the Methodist
Episcopal Church — nineteen years of that time in
connection with the Holston Conference. With it, as
a body, I have never had any difficulty, and but little
with any of its members. During that time, out of the
nineteen years, I have filled the office of Presiding

Elder fourteen years. I have been three times put out of that office—once on account of ill health, and twice, as some present will bear me witness, at my own earnest solicitation. And now in closing these remarks, I wish to say one thing more, and, for the best of reasons, I wish to say it in open Conference : I respectfully request of the Chair, that I may not be appointed to any district the ensuing year. My liability to attacks of sore throat, and my extreme susceptibility to cold, disqualify me for the kind and measure of labor that is expected of a Presiding Elder ; but, independently of these considerations, there are other and substantial reasons which justify me in making this request, and making it in this public manner. Probably some work can be found which I can do ; if not, my path will be plain."

Strong as is the language used in the foregoing, it gives but a very imperfect idea of the violence with which he had been assailed, or the vindictiveness with which he was pursued. There was a studied, combined and persistent effort to break down his influence, both as a man and a minister, and in this effort many things were said and done, which were as much at war with truth and justice as they were with gentlemanly propriety and Christian courtesy. To the attacks made, and so often repeated, through the public papers, he replied only once or twice,·and then gave merely a statement of facts, as they occurred. To the many public speeches delivered, he made no public reply at all, but preached and prayed, and attended to his religious duties, public and private, as he had been accustomed to do in times gone by, leaving his accusers and revilers pretty much to their own course ; and they, being thus left, in due time ran their race, and succeeded in nothing so well as in effecting their own downfall.

In regard to the great principles and leading questions of political economy, Mr. Patton had read and thought much, consequently had his opinions ; and these opinions differed from those entertained by some of his warmest and most endeared personal friends ; but he never allowed himself to obtrude those opinions upon others, never entered into a public—and very seldom into a private—discussion of political doctrines, political creeds, or the claims of political parties. Regarding it as his business to preach the Gospel to all, he was exceedingly careful to give no just cause of offense to any, and never allowed mere political matters to interfere with his social—much less his religious and ecclesiastical—relations and duties.

> " But, in his duty, prompt at every call,
> He watch'd and wept, he prayed and felt for all."

But these were seasons of sore trial, and spiritual conflict of an extraordinary kind. To one of his temperament, it was exceedingly annoying to be made thus the subject of so many newspaper articles, so many public addresses, and so much conversation in · more private circles ; and then to retain the quiet, forbearing and forgiving spirit of the Christian, under attacks so oft-repeated, so malignant, so unjust, and so utterly groundless, required a degree of watchfulness, self-control, and direct aid of Divine grace, that few

possess. And yet it may safely be written, he remained
a Christian, in spirit and in life, through it all, and,
like gold "tried in the fire," came out the brighter
and purer for the ordeal.

At the session of the Conference for 1843, in connection with E. F. Sevier and T. Stringfield, he was
elected a delegate to the General Conference, to be
held in May following. These delegates all attended
the General Conference, and bore their part in the
business of that memorable occasion, and conducted
themselves in a way that gave general satisfaction to
those whom they there represented. Returning from
the General Conference, and participating largely in
that intense interest everywhere aroused, in the Methodist mind, by the singular acts of a majority of that
body, Mr. Patton, at the proper time, drew up, for the
consideration and action of the Holston Conference,
a paper of singular ability, from the preamble and resolutions of which the following extract has been taken :

" Whereas the late General Conference of the M. E.
Church, at its session in New York, had action in certain cases affecting the basis of union between the
North and the South, on the subject of slavery—First,
in the case of F. A. Harding (an appellant from the
Baltimore Annual Conference), confirming his indefinite
suspension from the ministry, solely on account of a
legal connection with slavery, which is recognized and
provided for by the Discipline of the Church, said
Harding not being charged either with immorality or
a breach of the rules of the Discipline, but with a 'violation of the purpose and usage of the Baltimore Conference ;' second, in the case of Rev. J. O. Andrew,

one of the Bishops of said Church, against whose moral
or ministerial character no shadow of charge was alleged, and who it was not even pretended had 'sinned
either against Christ or against the laws of the Church,'
but was 'connected with slavery,' in a slave-holding
State, where it was not alleged that the laws admitted
of emancipation, or permitted a liberated slave to enjoy
freedom ; but, on account of such connection, it was
deemed expedient, by a majority of. the Conference, to
virtually depose him from his office, by declaring it
to be the 'sense of the General Conference that he
desist from the exercise of the functions of his office,
so long as the impediment of his connection with
slavery remains,' notwithstanding Bishop Andrew was
a member, a minister and a Bishop of the M. E.
Church, according to all the forms of law known to
the Church, and both his moral and official character
unimpeached and unimpeachable ; therefore,

" *Resolved*, by the Holston Annual Conference, in
Conference assembled, That the action of the General
Conference, in both the above-mentioned cases, was
extra-administrative, and, precisely in so far as the
subjects of such action were either punished or subjected to disabilities, said action was extra-judicial,
and violative of the disciplinary rights of ministers of
the M. E. Church.

" *Resolved*, that the rule of Discipline governing ministers of the M. E. Church, who become the owners of
slaves, was founded in wisdom, and based on the moral
code established by Christ and his apostles ; and, therefore, any departure from the principles embraced in
said rule is not only a violation of the rule itself, but

a new test of privilege in said Church, and one not sanctioned by the New Testament.

"*Resolved*, That, according to the rule governing ministers of the M. E. Church, in slave-holding States, all that is not required of them is retained by them, and therefore any act of any Church tribunal — administrative or judicial, subordinate or supreme — which asks or demands more than the rule requires, is *ex post facto*, retro-active, subversive of the basis of union between the different sections of the Church, violative of the rights of ministers in slave-holding States, and ought not to be submitted to by those who are the legally constituted guardians of the Church's interests.

"*Resolved*, That we cordially approve of the ground taken by the protest of the minority, at the late General Conference, *to wit :* That we are satisfied with the Discipline of the Church, *as it is* — neither asking, seeking or desiring any change in the rules concerning slavery ; and therefore, in the event of a separation, and an independent organization, in the Southern Conferences, the Church in the South has, according to the Discipline, and in equity, in truth and in righteousness, an indefeasible right to the patronymic name of the M. E. Church, in the United States.

"*Resolved*, That it is 'the sense' of this Conference, that it must be known to all who are conversant with the history of the late General Conference, that the action of that body, in relation to Bishop Andrew, was based, professedly, on the expediency of the measure, in view of preventing secessions in the North ; and that the action of that body, providing, so far as it had authority in the premises, for a peaceable separ-

ation of the South from the North, by geographical
lines, was based on the expediency of the measure, in
view of preventing secession in the South, carefully
guarding ministers of every grade from censure, in the
selection they might make for their membership, either
North or South ; and therefore that the charge of secession, frequently thrown out in advance, by corres-
pondents of the Christian Advocate and Journal, and
sanctioned by the senior editor of that paper, is wholly
gratuitous, and seems as though it were intended to in-
timidate, by threatening Southern members, first, with
the loss of membership in the M. E. Church, and, sec-
ondly, with disfranchisement of their rights, in relation
to Church property, within the geographical limits of
their own division.

"*Resolved*, in behalf of ourselves and the people of
our charge, That we are now what we always have
been — ministers and members of the M. E. Church,
based on the Discipline as it is. Here we plant our
feet — here we take our stand — cheerfully yielding all
which the Discipline demands of us, and fearlessly asserting our right to all which the Discipline secures to
us. And, if it be found that a majority of the legal
representatives of the Church have violated the principles of our union with the North, or disregarded the
terms of the original compact, as embodied in the
Discipline, and that violation or disregard is sanctioned
by their constituents, it becomes both our duty and our
interest to have a separate organization ; and, basing
that organization on the Discipline, we enter our solemn protest, before the Church and the world, against
the charge of secession, alleged in advance, by the

Christian Advocate and Journal; and, to sustain our protest, we appeal, in the sight of heaven and the whole Christian world, to the law and to the testimony in the case, as it is embodied in our most excellent Discipline.

" *Resolved,* That the labored efforts of the Christian Advocate and Journal, to make the impression that, in the event of separation, the Church in the South must be regarded as the advocate of slavery, and will probably sacrifice, on this very account, the friendship and confidence of the whole Christian world beside, is exceedingly disingenuous, and is based on an assumption directly at war with the candid, open and explicit avowal of the collective body of Southern representatives at the late General Conference.

" *Resolved,* That it is the 'sense' of this Conference, that Methodism takes the world as she finds it, and her legitimate work is to make all sorts of people, and all grades of society, *better;* and any changes in the civil relations of her adherents are contemplated, not as the result of her interference in such matters, but as the result of her moral operations, in refining, sanctifying and saving her adherents from those passions and dispositions which originate all misrule and all oppression.

" *Resolved,* That a pastoral ministry, in the slave-holding States, of less than one-third of the entire pastoral ministry of the M. E. Church, having, as the fruits of its own labor in the Lord, almost one-half the entire membership of the Church, furnishes the proof that Methodism *as it is,* and under the government of the Discipline as it is, has been, to say the least of it, not less successful in the South than in the North, unless it can be shown that these seals of the Southern ministry are a spurious offspring. But 'by their fruits ye shall know them,' is as sure a test of discipleship to Christ now as when first uttered.

"*Resolved*, That we deplore the necessity of separation; but, believing that necessity to exist, while we feel it our duty to refrain from any harsh judgment concerning the moral character of the causes which have produced it, we will bow submissive to the dictates of an event which is, at least, providential to us.

"*Resolved*, That we will send delegates to the contemplated convention of Southern delegates, to be held at Louisville, Ky., in May next.

"*Resolved*, That we most cheerfully accord to our brethren of the Conferences in non-slave-holding States, all they ask on the score of honesty in their purposes, and purity of design in their actions; but honesty is not argument, and purity of design is not always a correct expositor of law; and therefore, that, while we regard their action at the late General Conference, on the subject of ministerial connection with slavery, as lawless and inexpedient, we recognize them as brethren, and intend to cultivate towards them those Christian and fraternal feelings ever characteristic of the different departments of the great Wesleyan family, in all the organizations in which it has yet appeared.

"*Resolved*, That it is both our duty and high privilege devoutly to implore the blessing of the great Head of the Church upon our beloved Methodism, both North and South, and especially that he would, at this critical period in our history, superintend the deliberations and operations of the Southern Conferences, and the contemplated convention of Southern delegates, and guide them to a happy issue in laying a broad basis for the future peace of the Church, and the success and prosperity of Methodism, embracing, in its extensive range, the greatest possible sum of good to man."

The views set forth in the above were entertained, generally, by the Holston Conference, and the action taken, and the course pursued, by that body are of too recent occurrence, and too generally known, to require particular notice here. The views were just, and the action under them was such as the circumstances imperatively required. The Conference adopted, in substance, the foregoing resolutions, and acted accordingly. At that time, the Holston Conference, together with the Conferences of the South, generally, was satisfied with the Discipline of the Church, as it was, and their complaint was not of the Discipline. That protected them in the stand they had taken, but they justly complained of the action of the majority of the General Conference, by which the provisions of the Discipline had been violated, and they arbitrarily denied the protection it should have afforded them. Since that time, some changes have been made in the Discipline by the Southern General Conference, and some made, also, by that of the North, though neither party looked to such changes in their action of 1844. No complaint was then made of the Discipline, by either party, and no intimation given of any desire, on the part of either, to have it changed. The changes made, have been made under necessities which have arisen since that period, and in accordance with those principles recognized by the Church, during every period of its existence, to suit the details of plans of operations to the necessities which might, from time to time, arise. In the opinion of many, Methodism, in its peculiar developments, is a child of Providence; hence it has ever been the policy of those in charge of her interests to follow as Providence seemed to lead.

CHAPTER XIII.

LABORS AT KNOXVILLE, TENN. — THE EPISCOPALIAN, AND
THE CONTROVERSY WITH DR. ROSS AND OTHERS —
FROM 1846 TO 1850.

AT the session of the Conference held in the fall of
1845, Mr. Patton was appointed to the charge of the
First Methodist Church in the city of Knoxville, and
was also chosen by the Conference editor of a paper
proposed to be established as early as practicable, for
the maintenance and defense of the doctrines and
polity of the Methodist Church against the many and
bitter attacks then being made in the bounds of that
Conference.

The project of establishing such a paper originated
with the late T. Stringfield and the writer of these
lines.   Estimates were made, and the whole plan for
publishing matured and laid before a number of the
members of the Conference, who had met in Knoxville,
on their way to Athens, where the Conference session
was held.   By these the project and plans were approved.   They were approved also by the Conference.
A Publishing Committee was appointed ; proposals
were circulated, subscribers obtained ; and the first
number of a religious weekly paper was issued on the
5th of May, 1846, and thenceafter regularly, until the

death of the subject of these sketches. Some of the reasons which influenced the friends of this enterprise in the course they pursued may be gathered from the following extract from the Prospectus :

" The necessity for a religious periodical, suited to the mountainous and isolated position of the Holston Conference, has been long and deeply felt; and the desideratum would have been supplied, had it not been for the difficulty of sustaining such an enterprise. Several attempts to do so have been made, but they have been suffered to fail for want of adequate patronage. In a Conference having under its control eighty traveling preachers, and within its bounds some thirty-five thousand members, it is believed that not more than five hundred of our Church papers are taken. This state of things has had, and, if it continues to exist, must continue to have, a most blighting influence on the benevolent institutions and spiritual interests of the Methodist Episcopal Church, within the limits of this Conference. A most devoted, self-sacrificing, self-denying and laborious ministry have traversed the country at large, and have done much to advance the cause of Christ; but how much more efficient would be their labors if those among whom they labor and toil were the constant and attentive readers of a well-conducted religious newspaper! Would not the Missionary cause, the cause of Sunday Schools, and the interests of our colleges and academics, be greatly promoted by such a paper, if it were published in our midst? And will not our ministerial brethren, and other numerous friends, generally, unite with us in this effort to establish among us such a vehicle of useful knowledge, suited to our varied wants? They are

cordially invited to do so, and confidently expected to
engage in the work.   We have no PECUNIARY interests
to serve, and only aim to glorify God, by the promotion of his cause among our fellow-men.

"At this eventful crisis of our Church, when the
separation of the South from the North is being so extensively spoken of, it is not our object to increase,
but to allay, the excitement, maintaining the unity of
the spirit in the bonds of peace.   Touching the doctrines and discipline of our Church, we shall act on
the defensive, and repel the assaults of our assailants,
in the spirit of the Gospel.   And, while items of general news, and other intelligence herein alluded to, are
given, the Agricultural interests of the country will
not be overlooked."

The periodical was at first called "The Methodist
Episcopalian," under which title it continued to be
published for about four years.   It was then changed
to that of "The Holston Christian Advocate," and
under this title it was published a little more than
four years longer.   The change of name was made at
the suggestion of prominent and influential ministers
of the Church, and done soon after the General Conference of 1850, which had given its sanction to the
publication.

From first to last, the paper rendered the Church
and the interests of Methodism valuable service by its
able defense of the doctrines and polity of the Church,
and, by its miscellaneous matter, did no little towards
the advancement of all the true interests of society.
The more papers the Church has, the better for her, if
they are pecuniarily sustained.   They stir each other

up, provoking to good works, and, by laudable efforts on the part of each to excel, they are all made better, while each serves an interest, fills a gap, or performs a work that could be done by none of the others. So in the present case ; this paper met an emergency that, so far as human wisdom could see, would not, and could not, have been met by any other.

From the close of the session of the Conference to the time when the paper was commenced, Mr. Patton occupied himself in diligent attentions to the interests of the Church assigned him, usually preaching three times each week, visiting the families and classes of his charge, attending the prayer-meetings, and, besides this, once each week, during a part of the winter, while his health allowed, he favored the people with a lecture on some historical or biographical subject, taken from the sacred Scriptures. These lectures may properly be termed intellectual feasts, for such they really were, evincing a depth of thought, an extent of research, and accuracy of acquaintance with Biblical history, that few possess. As may be supposed, they were well attended, and listened to with unusual interest. Only the outlines were written, and, though some of these are still among the private papers he left behind, they are so meager as to be of little or no use to any one. He simply noted some leading points, facts or dates connected with the subject he proposed to discuss, and then supplied the rest from a mind well stored with both generalities and particulars. But these labors proved too much for him. His health began again perceptibly to decline, and, ere mid-winter had passed, had very sensibly failed—so much so, that what work he did was often performed in great pain and bodily suffering, and not unfrequently he was, for several days and nights in succession, closely confined to his room, if not to his bed. These frequent and severe attacks greatly affected his entire nervous system, and it was soon after a partial recovery from one of these attacks he wrote the following, which is introduced here because of its singularity, rather than of anything else :

"HALLUCINATIONS OF A SICK ROOM.—It was about 10 o'clock at night. The servant had lain down, visitors had retired, and the sound of the doctor's feet upon the staircase had scarcely died away. The candle had been extinguished at my request, and a dim and flickering blaze from the fire shed a pale and unsteady light upon the various articles of furniture in the room, and rendered them barely visible, when a sprightly young man, much below the common size, stepped in, in the character of a surgeon. His outside dress was altogether of white cambric or linen, I could not determine which. He took his seat in a pompous manner at the side of my bed, stretched out his feet towards the fire, and looked steadfastly at me. I scanned him narrowly, and found that his out dress was closely filled with surgical instruments, in a regular line from his ankles to his breast. These were shining and glittering from their places, with all the splendor of polished steel. He sat a few minutes, without saying a word, and then retired. No sooner was he gone than two other young men, surgeons, came in. They were dressed in the common, fashionable style of gentlemen, and carried their surgical instruments concealed. They

sat down, one on each side of the fire-place, and looked
at me, but said nothing; of course I said nothing.
They remained for a short time, and, like their forerunner, taking it for granted there was no employment
for them there, they also retired. They were immediately succeeded by a company of old-fashioned,
musty-looking apothecaries, with little flat hats, and
each with his marble mortar and pestle on his arm.
These took their stations at the foot of my bed, rather
on the left side, and commenced pelting and pounding
in their mortars, beating up red paint, lampblack, etc.,
to make pills. One of them took a candle, came and
pulled the cover off one side of my face, thrust his
fingers into my hair, and held the candle so close that
the light hurt my eyes. Then he, or another, went to
my feet, stripped the cover off them, took hold of them,
and felt of them with as much care as if they had been
searching for a scar or a mark. This being done, they
all marched off very quietly, with their mortars on
their arms. Immediately on their retirement, a company of little folks, with little leather hats, came in at
the front window, and pranced over the floor to the
fire-place, took a saucer off a cup of rice-water which
stood there, and commenced dipping out, and drinking,
my rice-water. While they were at that, a splendid
company of mounted dragoons came in at the same
window, and paraded in the floor with a great deal of
pomp and show, brandishing their swords, and exhibiting their pistols, in a manner calculated to strike terror
into the hearts of all who might not be assured of
their friendship and protection. The little folks took
fright at this exhibition of military grandeur, and

scampered off in great haste. I could not tell whether they made their escape through the chimney, under the door-shutter, or between the sash of the windows ; but I was amused to see how the guilty little dogs fled when they were caught stealing my rice-water. The dragoons performed some evolutions, and peacefully retired. After them came two private individuals, and seated themselves by my bed-side. One of them looked me full in the face, said nothing, but his countenance was strongly expressive of the malign passions, and I suspected that he meditated some injury. He was the illest-looking man I ever saw. The other appeared to be mild and bland ; and, although I could not see his face fully, I took him for a friend, for I could see under his hat that his countenance was exceedingly pleasant, and I believed that he came along to prevent the other from doing me any harm. Having sat awhile, they both retired, and I fell into a sweet sleep. It was not a dream. I was awake all the time, and knew it. It was simply the power of imagination, when the body was in a weak and debilitated state, and, withal, under the influence of medicine. This occurred on the night of January 13, 1846."

Had all persons taken as sensible a view of such hallucinations as did he, there would have been less of that ridiculous stuff about ghosts, hobgoblins and witches, that has so greatly disquieted the minds, and disturbed the peace, of so many.

It was also during the feeble state of health brought on by these attacks that he experienced some of those horrible mental sufferings alluded to in a previous chapter.

At the time now under notice, his family, to whom he was attached with exceeding tenderness, still remained at their home called Spring Place, in Sullivan county, Tenn. ; and his separation from them, combined with his affliction, rendered his condition exceedingly unpleasant. It is true, he was in the midst of friends who were ready and anxious to do for him all that could be done, and no man appreciated the kindly feelings and friendly acts of others more than he did ; yet his earnest love of his family, and his deep solicitude for the real welfare of his children — nearly all of whom were then of the age most needing a father's watchful eye and godly counsels — necessarily affected him ; and the admonitions given at this time, in his letters, were as touching as they were wholesome. A specimen is here given — given as found in the original, and given with the hope that it may not only lead to a juster appreciation of the man, but also be of real benefit to the pious reader. It is as follows :

S. PATTON, TO HIS ABSENT CHILDREN.

Softly, children—there are dangers
  Crowding all along your way ;
Foes unwearied—ceaseless rangers—
  Wait to lead your souls astray.
You were rear'd beneath the *awning*
  Where the holy Book of God
Shed the light of morning's dawning
  On the path your feet have trod.

Once, around the hearth *paternal*,
  You, like olive plants, did stand,
Blooming, fresh as flowrets *vernal*,

Juv'nile, joyful, happy band.
Then, again, in silent slumbers,
　'Mid the darkness of the night,
Sleep, as soft as sacred numbers,
　Lull'd till dawn of morning light.

Childish follies—childish pleasures,
　Fled on swift-winged time apace ;
Children's toys and children's treasures,
　Mem'ry links with Spring Grove Place.
Spring-house, kitchen, garden, meadow,
　Barn-yard, orchard—all around,
Show a long receding shadow
　Of days which will no more be found.

Fond caresses—infant kisses,
　Fled with days that gave them birth
And the mem'ry of them whispers
　They have pass'd away from earth.
Time, careering, marks the progress
　Of the trav'ler through life's vale,
Till his days are sad and joyless—
　Thus winds up the mournful tale.

But, though wave and mountain sever,
　Those who-drink the crystal stream
Flowing from life's ancient river,
　Find that life is not a dream ;
There's a place of mutual greeting
　In this home of shadows here,
And at that, friends will be meeting,
　Though it cost a transient tear.

Friendship is not an empty name,
　Carv'd with chisel's hammer'd stroke,

'Tis not the frosty breath of fame
  Blown in leaves of sturdy oak—
Pure silken cord, of friendship's tie,
  'Twined in paradise above,
Binding your hearts until you die,
  Must make heaven a place of love.

Meet, then, dear children, often meet—
  Meet ye at the place of prayer—
Meet ye where kindred spirits greet,
  Shrin'd in union's mantle there.
While the day of life is flying,
  Think on kindred, parents, home—
Soon we'll meet where no more dying
  Tinges life's unfading bloom.

With the opening spring, Mr. P. found his health
somewhat recruited; and, as he had been elected a
delegate to the General Conference, to be held at
Petersburgh, Va., commencing on the first of May, he
prepared matter for the first number of the Episcopalian, and set off, late in April, to attend that Conference. As was his custom always, he was there in
good time, attended the sittings regularly, and bore
his full part in the transaction of the important
business that came before the Conference. On his return, in June, he found himself literally forced into
another controversy, which, in some of its aspects, was
the most unpleasant in which he ever engaged. The
history of it may be given, summarily, as follows:

About the year 1842, the Rev. Mr. Musgrove, a
Presbyterian minister, of the city of Baltimore, or, as
he was pleased to style himself, "Bishop of the Third
Presbyterian Church, Baltimore," considered himself

insulted by the act of some unknown person, who left
at his private residence, a tract — a "controversial
tract" — on the subject of election. The act was regarded by the good "Bishop" as a "personal insult,"
and seems to have been the cause of his taking great
offense at the whole Methodist Church, and particularly
at her ministers. Immediately after having, on the
same blessed Sabbath day, informed his congregation
of what had occurred, he set about preparing an "exposition and vindication" of his "belief on the subject
of divine decrees." This "exposition and vindication,"
which appeared in pamphlet form, called forth some
writer, who reviewed and criticised its doctrines,
through the columns of one of the city papers. A
controversy sprang up, which resulted, on the part of
Bishop Musgrove, in the publication of an octavo
volume, of nearly 350 pages, filled with some of the
worst caricatures of Methodism, and some of the most
bitter things that had ever been written of Methodists,
by either open or secret foes. Though mainly a com-
pilation, it was somewhat remarkable for having collected the gall, rather than the sweetness, of all from
which it was compiled. The compiler seemed to have
drawn mainly on the writings of two distinguished
divines, of the same Church, one of whom once lived
and labored in the city of Philadelphia, and the other
in Pittsburgh, and both of whom were quite noted for
their hostility to Methodism. Although the writings
of these men had been reviewed, and their accusations
and objections answered, soon after their first appearance, they, nevertheless, subserved well the purpose
of the Baltimore Bishop, and, doubtless, as well ac-

corded with his spirit; and the objections were repeated, and the accusations reiterated, with as much apparent assurance as though nothing had ever been said or written in refutation.

Very soon after the appearance of this book, the Rev. Mr. Ross, a Presbyterian minister, in Tennessee, caught up a similar strain, and followed it in a series of set sermons, delivered at various points in East Tennessee and South-western Virginia. In these sermons, both the doctrines and polity of the Methodist Church came in for a full share of attention, and were sifted, analyzed and criticised with no mean ability, and rather extraordinary severity. Not content with this, he followed up the effort by the publication and distribution of what he denominated a " tract," which, indeed, was rather a *book* than what is usually denominated a tract, the leading object of which was to show that " the doctrine of the direct witness of the Spirit, as taught by Rev. John Wesley, was unscriptural, false, fanatical, and of mischievous tendency."

In this book, Methodism, both as to doctrines and polity, and Methodists, were handled severely. A copy was sent to Mr. Patton, by the author, under such circumstances, and accompanied with such references, that all honorable principles demanded of him an answer. Indeed, such were the circumstances, that he was compelled to reply, or be regarded as yielding the points at issue. Accordingly, soon after his return from the General Conference, he addressed himself to the task, and soon presented a review of the book, and answer to the arguments, in a 12mo. volume, of 156 pages. This was prefaced by two short essays, the first of which maintained that "The operations of the Holy Spirit upon a human heart are always direct, according to the critical definitions, as well as the popular acceptation, of that phrase;" and the second maintained that "The operations of the Holy Spirit upon a human heart are not only direct, but sensibly felt, and the fact is matter of experience."

In these essays it was argued that the moral emotions and feelings of moral obligations, inspired by Christianity, are the effects of the *direct operations* of the Holy Spirit; and most ably and conclusively was the position sustained. Then it was insisted, as a necessary corollary, that the operations of the Spirit, being direct, and these being the effects, were sensibly felt, and became matter of consciousness and experience.

The author then proceeded to a careful and critical examination of the positions and arguments of Mr. Ross, carefully stating precisely what Mr. Wesley had taught on the subject noticed, and comparing it with the teachings of the sacred Scriptures, the writings of many of the ablest and best men of the Christian Church, with the design to show the hearty concurrence of all in the advocacy of the doctrine of the direct witness of the Holy Spirit in the hearts of all true believers. How far he succeeded in this, is not the business of the biographer to determine, though it is not at all out of place to say his friends, and those, generally, who had previously subscribed to the doctrine of the direct witness of the Spirit, were well satisfied with the results of his effort; and, if his opponents were not convinced, they did not choose to send out another book. The controversy, however, did not end

with this. The Calvinistic Magazine, of which mention has been made (see page 198), had been revived,
and its pages became the media through which Mr.
Ross continued his attacks; and the columns of the
Episcopalian were freely used for replies and defense.
After the publication of Mr. Patton's book, the grounds
of the controversy were changed from points of doctrine to questions of Church polity; and, in the discussion of these, the greatest severity was manifested.
Other ministers participated. Public discussions were
held, which, in some instances, were continued during
several successive days. Other papers and periodicals
were gotten up to meet the emergency of the times.
Able ministers, on both sides, went to and fro, discussing, for hours at a time, the questions in debate; and
this course was continued until the whole country became excited to a degree rarely witnessed anywhere.
The discussion took a wide range, both as to the topics
embraced and the number of persons engaged; and,
perhaps, in no part of the whole country did the doctrines and discipline of the Methodist Church ever
pass a more severe ordeal, or were ever more zealously,
ably or successfully defended. The assailants avowed
their object to be the overthrow of Methodism, because
they regarded it as unscriptural and unsound in itself,
as a system, and looked upon all its workings as detrimental to the true interests of society, and particularly
at variance with the political institutions of the country.
Hence they claimed that duty to God, to their fellow-
men, and to their common country, required they should
oppose it with whatever of zeal and ability they could
command; and right willingly did they address them-

selves to the task. The motives of Methodist preachers, as a body, were challenged; the piety of the Methodist membership was questioned, assailed and denied, and the whole system of Methodism declared to be not only powerless for good, but positively and practically bad. In these attacks, a degree of rancor was sometimes manifested, which it is painful, even now, to contemplate.

Though first in this controversy, on the part of the Methodists, Mr. Patton soon found himself sustained, not only by the sympathies of his brethren, but also by the efficient co-operation of several ministers of no ordinary ability, and such as were well versed in polemic warfare. Foremost among these were Rev. Messrs. Brownlow and Collins, the first of whom, although he had previously "fought through many a battle sore," entered upon this struggle with all the powers of his nature, and, perhaps, spent more time and means in carrying it on than were spent by all others combined. He availed himself of both pulpit and press, traveled extensively, addressed the people by hundreds — and at some places by thousands — at a time, and, for some two years, published, mainly at his own expense, first a quarterly, then a monthly, magazine, filled, almost exclusively, with the productions of his own pen, and devoted entirely to the questions directly involved, or incidentally growing out of the issues which had been made. The other was at that time President of Emory and Henry College—a man of extensive research and sound learning, well acquainted with the doctrines, discipline and history of the Church, and bold and fearless in advocating what he

believed to be true and right. Nor was Mr. Ross
alone. Many of the most able ministers of the Church
to which he belonged co-operated with him, and at
length the Synod officially indorsed and recommended
his writings. Thus, one by one, they entered the field,
and fell into the ranks on both sides, until the engage-
ment became general; and earnest, ardent and long-
continued was the contest. But it ended at last. The
events are of too recent occurrence to justify a particular notice in a work like this; but it may be remarked,
the Methodists had no reason to regret the scrutinizing
investigations to which their doctrines, discipline and
usages had been subjected. During the continuance
of the controversy, the Church, in many places, was
blessed with extensive revivals, and her aggregate increase of membership in that Conference compared
favorably with that of other years, before or since. In
the Methodist Church at Knoxville, in the heat of the
controversy, where Mr. Patton lived, preached, wrote
and published, there was the most extensive, thorough
and powerful revival of religion that Church had experienced in all its history, up to that time; nor has
the like been witnessed there since. People were converted by scores; and there are now a number of
talented, faithful and useful ministers scattered through
the Southern Conferences, who were converted at that
meeting. The work took a deep hold upon the students of the University, who were there from various
States, and of whom many were converted, to return
home, and, under the call of the Holy One, enter the
whitening fields of ministerial labor, where, to this
day, they render efficient service. So it was in other

parts of the Conference. The work of saving souls
went on ; and it is entirely safe to affirm that, in point
of numbers, influence, zeal, and devotion to their cause,
the Methodists lost nothing. On the contrary, they
gained in all these respects ; but whether that gain
should be set down as the direct results of the controversy, or attributed to causes and influences indirectly
growing out of it, or whether they were entirely independent of the controversy, are questions that would
admit of considerable discussion.

How it was with the other party, or whether they
gained or lost, is not now a subject of inquiry.

As the editor of a religious paper, Mr. Patton succeeded with credit to himself, and acceptability to the
Church. He wrote well, although he wrote slowly ;
and to him the labor of writing was heavy. His style
was more solid than sprightly — too solid, perhaps, for
the columns of a weekly newspaper. A little more
elasticity and sprightliness would have given increased
interest to the paper. He discussed grave subjects, in
a grave manner, and seemed ever to strive to finish
what he undertook, and finish it at once. Hence his
articles partook largely of the character of the ex-
haustive — one thing commenced and finished, then
attention given to something else.

In addition to editing the paper, he had, for the
greater portion of the time, to perform the duties of
book-keeper and clerk — keeping the accounts, and
attending to the correspondence, which, with his lack
of early training, and want of familiarity with such
business, was a matter of very great labor. Others,
familiar with such work, might have performed it with

comparative ease, but he could not. He had entered a new field of labor, and found it one of incessant and wearisome toil. Scrupulously careful to have everything right, and yet constantly fearful he might, through forgetfulness or otherwise, fall under some mistake, his connection with the paper was, in some respects, among the most trying periods of his ministerial life. He could have served either as editor or clerk, and performed the duties; but, when the two were combined, they were too much for him; and to the continued mental care and anxiety which they gave him, may his early death be, in part, attributed. He possessed but little versatility, and turned himself from one kind of work to another with difficulty, though he worked on and worked ever, and so accomplished what he had undertaken; but it was at a mournful cost—loss of health, and, finally, loss of life.

The difference in ease and facility with which different men perform the same amount of work, is known to be very great; and mental, like physical, labor requires training and practice to be performed expertly. Mr. Patton could prepare a sermon more easily than he could write a lengthy editorial, and deliver a discourse with half the labor it cost him to spend an hour in close attention to a day-book and ledger. To the labor of the first he had trained himself, become familiar with it, and could perform it as readily as another; but with the last he was practically unacquainted, until after more than two score years of his natural life had passed away, his habits of thought and feeling been formed and fixed, and his mind, never very elastic, less so then than formerly. Hence the wonder is he succeeded at all ; nor would he, but for the most patient, persevering, unremitting toil. In all the perplexities, attendant on his new position, and amid all the trying scenes of the controversy through which he passed, and in which he bore so prominent a part, he never neglected the claims of religion upon his private and public life.. Few, if any, persons in the city where he lived, attended the regular services of the Church, the preaching, prayer and class-meetings, more faithfully and constantly than he. Morning and evening — fair weather or foul—he was there, if physically able, and, when there, entered into the solemnity of divine worship with the sincerity, reverence and devoutness of a true, simple-hearted Christian. In truth, the history of his spiritual life, could it be written, would be the history of a steady growth in grace, a constant ripening for heaven, though amid all the trials and temptations, the hopes and fears, the toils and sufferings, incident to the life of a private Christian, and of a faithful Christian minister.

He preached frequently, both in the city and at different points in the country contiguous, and always with that solemnity, earnestness and zeal which had so long characterized his pulpit ministrations, and was often called upon to deliver sermons on special occasions, or special subjects, about which it was thought necessary the people should be informed. A number of these were written *in extenso*, and sometimes read from the manuscript, and those not written were always delivered with the same care with which they had been prepared. In discussing controverted dogmas, he was respectful and kind, but never yielding any point, while he regarded it as true and right, or concealing what he believed should be revealed.

The paper of which he had charge having but a limited circulation, and not promptly paid for by all who received it, was often no little embarrassed in its pecuniary affairs, and, indeed, required the closest and most economical financiering to enable it to live at all. This also was a constant weight on his mind, and often depressed him greatly. He had undertaken the work more because of the earnest solicitations of his brethren than from any personal liking he had for such employment; but, having undertaken it, and, in common with others, seeing the necessity for its performance by some one, he, of course, was deeply anxious for its success; and this anxiety, accompanied by all the circumstances attending the enterprise, bore very heavily upon him.

Besides the controversy already referred to, and the side issues growing out of it, there were other questions sprung upon him, the discussion of which was, in several instances, very unpleasant, as well as protracted; so that, during the first four years of his editorial life, he was in controversy nearly, or quite, all the time. Nor yet was it of his seeking or provoking. It was thrust upon him by opposing parties, and, as is too often the case, it at last degenerated, on the part of some, into mere personalities. Foiled in argument, on the issues made by themselves, and driven from fields of their own choosing, they very unjustifiably turned their shafts against the person of him by whom they had been vanquished, and so far forgot the proprieties of all polemic discussion as to abuse and vilify him as a man. But here they were even more unsuccessful than before. His character was too well known, his reputation too well established, to be injured thus, while his whole life, public and private—his every-day walk and conversation—was a continued refutation of all their charges; and, as metals are but the better for the process of purifying, he came from all these " as gold tried in the furnace."

At the session of the Conference for 1849, delegates were chosen to the General Conference, to be held in St. Louis, in May following; and, though Mr. Patton was chosen first on the list, there were circumstances attending the election of delegates, which gave him great pain. These circumstances affected others, rather than himself, and are of too recent occurrence to justify a minute detail. They were such as had never before, to any considerable extent, existed in that body, and, it is to be devoutly hoped, may never exist again; and it may be safely affirmed that, although Mr. Patton attended every General Conference held by the undivided Church, from 1828 to 1844, and had also been a member of the Louisville Convention, in 1845, and of the General Conference, at Petersburgh, in 1846, he never attended under circumstances so embarrassing as he attended that of 1850. This is written advisedly, and with a pretty full knowledge of his feelings, which, to his intimate friends, were expressed freely.

At the Conference, he bore his part in what business there was transacted, and was permitted, early and safely, to return to the bosom of his family and the scene of his labors. The paper he had in charge was adopted by the General Conference as one of the official organs of the Church, its name changed, as already mentioned : but nothing was done, or at that time could have been done, to aid its pecuniary re-sources. The Church funds were locked up by the failure, on the part of the Northern brethren, to com-ply with the provisions of the agreement made at the time of the separation ; and this, and all other Church papers in the South, were left to live if they could, or die if they must. The adoption of the paper by the Gen-eral Conference had the effect, however, of inspiring its friends with greater confidence as to its perman-ency, and leading them to greater exertions for its support, by which means the paper was much better sustained afterwards than it had been before. Some changes were also made, about the same time, by which the cost of publication was considerably reduced, so that, on the whole, the position of the editor was every way more pleasant, from this time onward, than it had previously been. Still the labor was too much for him. Decline was marked upon the entire physical nature, and became more and more apparent, as each succeeding month and year passed. Still his work was faithfully and well done. By untiring industry and indomitable perseverance, he did it all. But it occu-pied all his time. He was always at work. Late and early, he worked on, and thus only was it that he ac-complished what he had undertaken.

CHAPER. XIV.

THE LAST YEARS OF HIS LIFE, AND HIS DEATH — FROM 1850 TO 1854.

THE action of the General Conference of 1850, in regard to the paper of which Mr. Patton had charge, had an effect on him as favorable, in some of its aspects, as on others of its friends. It seemed to have inspired him with brighter hopes and freshened zeal. Hence he addressed himself to the work of conducting it with all his powers, and prosecuted that work, as already intimated, with whatever of energy and perseverance he could command. He felt his responsibility had been greatly increased, and, with the increase of responsibility, there should, if possible, be an increase of attention, care and effort. The paper had previously been an organ of a whole Conference, and one, too, that numbered nearly one hundred traveling, and several hundred local, preachers, with some forty thousand Church members, besides tens of thousands of men, women and children, who, though not really members of the Church, were attendants upon her ministry, and, to a greater or less extent, under her influence, and looked to her for spiritual ministrations. To conduct a paper speaking to, and in some sense for, all these, involved, certainly, no ordinary degree of responsi-

bility; but, under the change referred to, it became
one of the organs of the whole Church, numbering its
thousands of ministers, its hundreds of thousands of
members, and still greater number of adherents; and,
as a matter of course, the responsibility was, in some
sense, increased. Doubtless he had previously done as
well as he could, under the circumstances that attended
him; but increased responsibilities, when properly felt
and appreciated, often serve to reveal powers that seem
to have existed in a latent state, and developed only by
by their proper excitants; so that few men really
know what they can do, until a fair trial has been
made, and that, too, under the proper surroundings.
Although the sternest duty never calls a man beyond
his ability, it always requires him to come up to the
full measure thereof, and that measure can be determined only by his surrounding relations. If these be
properly understood, and their consequent obligations
properly felt and appreciated, then an honest man will
work to the full measure of his ability. Thus it was
with the subject of these sketches. Few men ever apprehended their relations, both to God and man, more
clearly, or felt their corresponding obligations more
keenly; hence he always worked in whatever he was
called to do, to the extent of his ability; and if, in
this respect, he erred at all, it was in going beyond,
rather than stopping short of, what he was able to perform. But, like other men, he found that new positions
and new duties called forth new powers, and these
powers acquired facility in execution, in proportion as
they were exercised. The increased interest, therefore,
which his paper manifested, and the improvement which

marked it, may justly be attributed partly to a sense of increased responsibility on the part of its conductor, and partly to a facility in execution which had been gained by previous experience and practice.

The work of conducting a newspaper, like work of almost every other kind, is to be perfected only by close application, and long-continued practice ; and he who has the talent and tact suited to the undertaking, will, if he be industrious and faithful, improve himself and improve his paper, as long as he continues it. They mistake greatly, who suppose this to be a work that may be performed with facility and success by any novice who may choose to undertake, or happen to be thrust into, it. To perform it well, requires a previous apprenticeship, through a much longer time than is usually devoted to learning how to arrange the types and print the paper. Mr. Patton had now served four years, had given close attention to his work, and was acquiring greater facility, so that the second term of his service was somewhat less toilsome, and more pleasant, than the first.

Soon after, the Trustees and Faculty of Emory and Henry College, without his seeking, and without his knowledge, conferred on him the title of *Doctor of Divinity ;* and never did they confer honors on a more worthy subject. To him it was as unexpected as it had been unsought ; but he was as far from being insensible to the estimate in which he was held, and which had been manifested, in part, through this channel, as he was from being inflated and puffed up by a sounding title, which, as applied and used by many, means just nothing at all.

From this time until the fall of 1853, but little occurred to vary the scenes incident to his calling, and
less, perhaps, to lighten the labors he was called to
perform. As he had previously done, he preached as
his health would permit, and without the slightest
abatement in his own personal interest of feeling for
the prosperity of the Church and the salvation of
souls, or of the instructive, impressive and interesting
character of his sermons. His faith in Christ, and in
the truth and power of the Gospel, increased with the
increase of his years, and it may in truth be said, "he
ripened for heaven as he ripened for the grave."

In the fall of 1853, he was again, and for the last
time, chosen by his brethren of the Conference to represent them in General Conference. This General
Conference was to meet on the first day of May following, at Columbus, Georgia. He had now lived
almost fifty-seven years, thirty-five of which had been
spent in the active, laborious work of the ministry,
and, with an enfeebled constitution when he commenced
that work, it is not wonderful he was near the end of
his earthly career. The greater part of his children
were now grown—two sons and one daughter married
and settled, another daughter successfully engaged in
teaching, at a distance from home, and the remainder
of the family removed from Knoxville, and resettled
at their own "Spring Place" home, in Sullivan county,
he visiting them as opportunity served, and spending
his time in Knoxville, at the residence of his friend,
Rev. W. G. Brownlow, between whom and himself
there had existed a sincere friendship, for a quarter of
a century, and at whose office the paper was then pub-

lished. During the winter, his health was much as it had been during several previous years—no better, and not much worse.

In the month of April, after visiting his family, he set off for the seat of the General Conference, intending to turn aside by the way, and spend some time at the place where his eldest daughter had, for some time, been teaching. This he did, and, while there, made some pleasant acquaintances, and made, also, a very favorable impression on the minds of the people, as to his ability as a minister, and the excellence of his character as a Christian man. At the proper time, he proceeded to Columbus, was there at the opening of the Conference, and able to attend its sessions, from day to day, and participate in its deliberations. His interest of feeling in behalf of the Church was intense as ever, and all he did was done in view of his responsibilities to God. In the protracted proceedings of this General Conference, he was respectful and kind to all, not adhering to his own opinions because they were his, or opposing those of others on any other ground than that of the greatest good to the greatest number.

Soon after his return to Knoxville, his health sensibly declined, little by little, until, about the 20th of July, he was confined to his bed, and never arose. All the medical aid that could be procured, and all the kind attentions that could be bestowed, were not sufficient to arrest the progress of a disease which, though in stronger constitutions might have been easily managed, proved fatal to him. During his affliction, he enjoyed much of that peace and strong consolation he had so often and so earnestly recommended to others, was calm, patient and resigned ; and, on the first day of August, 1854, he "fell asleep in Jesus," and was taken to his rest on high. Though his death was lamented by the whole Church, and by thousands outside her pales, he died as dieth the good man, and, doubtless, exchanged the labors and toils, the sorrows and pains, of earth for the endless rest and joys of a better world.

From the many notices given of his death by the public prints, it is deemed altogether proper to copy the following. The first appeared in the Knoxville Whig, in its next issue after Dr. Patton's death occurred. It was written by the editor of that paper :

" Our Zion has, within a few days past, been called to mourn the extinction of one of her brightest luminaries, in the person of Rev. Samuel Patton, D. D., and his tomb has been consecrated by the tears of the sincerest affection. But the duty of Christians and the Church, in reference to departed ministers, does not terminate in sorrowing for their removal. The Head of the Church has enjoined on believers in Christ an affectionate remembrance of those heralds of salvation "who have spoken unto them the Word of God," whose faith they are exhorted to follow. In complying with this Divine injunction, a record of the lives of faithful ministers has been found of great service ; and, by the perusals of such records, the memories of saints have been refreshed, their faith strengthened, and their diligence in working out their own salvation quickened. On this account, were there no other reason, it is desirable to preserve from the gulf of oblivion 'the memory of the just.' This service will be rendered to

the Church by the approaching session of the Holston
Annual Conference of the Methodist Church, South,
which body the deceased has adorned from its first
organization, serving it in the office of the ministry
with signal success, his labors having been blessed to
the consolation and edification of thousands; and by
this brief notice of his death, many in East Tennessee
and Virginia will be reminded of various 'times of
refreshing from the presence of the Lord,' with which
they have been favored under his personal ministry.

"The Rev. Samuel Patton was born in South Carolina, and departed this life on Tuesday, August 1, 1854,
in the city of Knoxville, in the 58th year of his age. We
have known him intimately for thirty years, in all the
relations of life, and, for more than two years past, he
has boarded in our house. He was a pious and faithful
minister — no time-server, no secret tattler against his
brethren, nor envious detractor against their worth and
reputation. He was open and frank as day, free and
honest in the expression of his opinions — the very
antipodes of the sycophant, and, at the same time, the
steady opposer of the factious and discontented, and of
all private caballings against the Church of his choice.
His whole deportment, as a stationed preacher, a Presiding Elder, or as editor of the official organ of the
Church, was marked by a lively concern for the interests of the Church, and all over whom he exercised a
pastoral oversight; and, by assiduous and faithful attention to every department of his work, he was eminently
successful. His labors in the pulpit have been much
owned by the great Head of the Church, and have
proved an unspeakable blessing to the multitude who

attended his ministry. Living witnesses, not a few, can attest that the Gospel he preached was 'not in word only, but also in power, and in the Holy Ghost, and in much assurance.'

"As a minister of the Gospel, he was divinely instructed in the sacred truths of religion, and well qualified to discourse on those truths with clearness and precision. The matter of his subjects was well stored in his mind; but, as he did not confine himself, in the delivery of his discourses, to the work of preparation, he expressed his views in language suggested by the feelings and interests of the moment. His sermons were evangelical, judicious, profound, and frequently eloquent, delivered with great energy and pathos; and, while they conveyed the light of knowledge to the understanding, they found the way to the heart, and were rendered durably impressive. He was the ablest divine in the Holston Conference, and a man of the greatest variety. He fervently sought the spirituality of those who attended his ministry, and burned with a holy zeal for his Master's glory. These were the uniform, unvaried objects of his preaching, and, to promote these ends, he was prepared to sacrifice his ease, his health, and even his life.

"For the last eight years, he had been sole editor of the Holston Christian Advocate, one of the Church papers, South, and had made his home in this city. He was a strong and forcible writer, a prudent and cautious editor, and conducted his paper with great ability. He performed all the drudgery of that position, serving in the double capacity of editor and book-keeper, and, by his labors in this particular, seriously affected his health. He died of *diarrhea*, after an illness of twelve days, and so completely was his constitution undermined, that no remedies could arrest the ruinous progress of the disease.

"As a Christian, his piety was rational, genuine, deep and dignified. It commenced with a true conversion to God; and never did he recall that full surrender of himself unto the Lord which he made in early life. His profession of experimental religion was humble and grateful, unmixed with affectation or pretension. He never sought, by an ostentatious appearance of sanctity, to be thought eminently holy, but commended himself as a Christian man to all who knew him, by the exemplification of Christian principles, and by the manifestation of Christian graces. He died in great peace, stating to all who conversed with him on the subject, that all was well, and that, through the blood of sprinkling, he looked for salvation in the life to come — the sort of death the public would expect Samuel Patton to die.

"In preparing this imperfect account of the labors and death of one of the most excellent of men, we are not conscious of having concealed or extenuated any known fault or infirmity, nor of having in the least exaggerated any single virtue. That it has been written under the influence of a long and most endearing friendship, we are free to admit; but the feelings of the friend have not violated the fidelity of the biographer. A frequent and unrestrained intercourse with him for years warrants our asserting that he was all we have said of him, and even more."

The other is from the St. Louis Christian Advocate,

of August 17, in which the editor, after a review of his past labors, remarked as follows :

"With this running sketch as to the scene of his labor, we must be permitted to allude to his character.

"1st. *As a man.* He was a man of medium stature ; rather slender, perhaps ; of delicate health and feeble constitution. Our acquaintance with him was intimate, and only lacked a few months of extending through a period of thirty long years. It was often to us a matter of astonishment how, in his feeble health and severe bodily sufferings, he could perform the mental and physical labor which he did. But he was a man of one work. A zeal for God, and an ardent love of his cause, urged him on. But for this — had he been less pious, and less devoted to the Church — he had desisted from traveling many, many years ago. Often, when our heart has desponded, and we were tempted to think the lot of a Methodist preacher a hard one, have we looked at him, heard the stirring pathos of his sermons and exhortations, taken courage, and gone on.

"His mind was naturally far above the ordinary grade, and had been well cultivated. What his early advantages were, we can not say now ; but we know that his scientific attainments were by no means inconsiderable. To classical learning he made little or no pretensions. His heart was warm, his affection for his brethren strong, consequently he was always ready to do them any service in his power. He had a particularly tender regard for the feelings of others ; and, in his intercourse with his fellow-men, few men were ever more invariably influenced by the law of kindness ; yet, in matters of duty, he was prompt, firm and unyielding.

No matter how painful, if it were a duty, he did it, without fear or favor. We have known him to be severely tried, and never yet knew him to shrink from the discharge of duty ; and, as a Presiding Elder, and the President of Quarterly, and sometimes, in the absence of a Bishop, of Annual, Conferences, he often had trying and painful duties to perform. Much, indeed, might be said in commendation of the manner in which he demeaned himself in all the relations of civil, social and domestic life, but we forbear, and allude to him,

"2d. *As a Christian.* The Word of God was the 'man of his counsel.' By this rule he endeavored to walk and live. His piety was deep, fervent and consistent. He was not given to outbursts of feeling, on one hand, nor murmurings and complainings, on the other, though sometimes greatly dejected. His feeble health, and the occasional partial prostration of his nervous system, subjected him, particularly in later life, to seasons of great despondency. This, perhaps, was only known to his most intimate friends, but such was frequently the case. In the deep and silent watches of the night have we joined our humble petitions with his earnest strugglings for relief from such despondency.

"He was a man of much prayer. At home, on his district, by the way, wherever he was, prayer — deep, earnest, fervent prayer—characterized him. We have known him, for instance, at camp-meetings, while one preacher after another occupied the pulpit, to spend his time in the preachers' tent, remaining on his knees, wrestling with God for his blessings on the preachers and people ; and, in the dead hour of night, he would often rise, to entreat God's blessing on him, his family, the people of his charge, and the whole family of man.

"He was remarkable for his uniformity, as well as consistency. What he seemed at one time, he seemed at all times. His peculiar trials and temptations he kept, for the most part, entirely to himself. He was no 'croaker,' but took a calm, serious and dispassionate survey of what was around him. He noticed closely the 'signs of the times,' in the Church, and always sought to put the best construction possible on every change that might threaten to affect her interests. He lived for God, for his Church, and the interests of his fellow-men.

"3d. *As a minister*, he ranked far above mediocrity. Few men were more thoroughly acquainted with the doctrines of the Bible, or exhibited them from the pulpit more readily or correctly. His manner of delivery was solemn and impressive — particularly so ; and, perhaps, none ever heard anything like lightness or frivolity in his public ministrations, or anything foreign from the distinctive mission of a minister of Christ. It has rarely been our privilege to listen to a public speaker who seemed to have less difficulty in expressing his thoughts, or with whom there was so little redundancy of words. He rarely, if ever, used notes or manuscripts in the pulpit, and yet so thoroughly had he studied, and so fully mastered, the subjects which he discussed, that it seemed as if he were reading an elaborated and carefully written discourse. His theme announced, he commenced at once, right there and then, and, without circumlocution, without tautology, without repetition, pressed through, often holding hundreds, and sometimes thousands, as if chained to the spot, though few men had less of the arts and so-called graces of studied oratory. Plain, pointed and perfectly natural in all he did, he, perhaps, exhibited as little mere mannerism as any man to be found; yet there was in his sermons such a remarkable correctness of style, that even the devotee of *belles lettres* would rarely find anything to which he could object. We have scarce, if ever, known a man who, in the pulpit, so invariably used good language, without ever seeming to make it an object of special study. Not only was it grammatically correct, in the common acceptation of that term, but those nice distinctions between words, so often overlooked, or not understood, by the mass of modern speakers and writers, seemed all familiar to him, as if by intuition, so that one was rarely, if ever, used for another.

"But the best of all, and that which makes his memory most dear, was, he always preached 'Jesus and the resurrection.' The plain, simple story of the cross, with him, was first, last—all the time. In reference to the political and commercial affairs of the nation he kept himself informed; but, *as a preacher*, he meddled not with the one or the other, nor turned aside from his legitimate work of preaching the Gospel, as far as in him lay, to every creature.

"In all his public ministrations, it was manifest that he deeply felt the solemn responsibility which rested upon him. He felt the force of the truths which he uttered, and often his persuasive appeals to dying sinners were almost resistless. But we must forbear. To allude to him

" *As a writer*, is scarcely necessary. In this respect, he was 'known and read' of thousands. Besides his writings as editor of a religious paper, he was the author of several small works which seemed called for by the exigencies of the times in which they were written.

" We feel it due alike to the living and dead, that, in this connection, we make a remark or two farther. Within the recollection of the present writer, the Methodist Church in East Tennessee and Western Virginia has passed through two separate seasons of fierce and bitter controversy. In point of time, these were over twenty years apart. Her doctrines, her institutions and her usages were most bitterly assailed by the ablest ministers of a sister denomination. A number of those ministers were men of learning, of talent and influence. Their attack on Methodism was so fierce and bitter, that they seemed to have determined on a war of extermination. They were met; and, if they were satisfied with the result, sure the Methodists had no reason to complain. Rev. Thomas Stringfield, almost single handed and alone, met them in their first crusade, and Samuel Patton in their second. To the labors of these two men does Methodism in that country owe more than to any other two that were ever there. In both instances, the controversies were carried on through the press, and, in the first contest, was very unequal, at least in point of numbers. It was carried on principally by Rev. Messrs. Gallaher, Ross, and Dr. Nelson, on one part, and Rev. T. Stringfield, on the other. The first were stationary, and wrote at their leisure; the latter was not only single-handed, but, during the most of the time, was in charge of a large district, doing the work of a Presiding Elder, and, at the same time, contending against this heavy, and apparently fearful, odds; yet he contended to "the bitter end" — contended until two of his opponents thought proper to abandon the field, and remove West, and the third retired to more private life. In this struggle for the very existence, in that country, of the Church of his choice, Mr. Stringfield spent not only his time and mental labor, but hundreds, and perhaps thousands, of his worldly means, for which he will never, in this world, be recompensed. Yet, by these labors and sacrifices, he gave an impulse to Methodism, the result of which may be distinctly traced all along her history there, from that day to the present. In the second great controversy, the now lamented Samuel Patton was leader; and, though he labored under far less disadvantages, and had more assistance, than the former, he was sorely beset, but acquitted himself, and sustained his cause, nobly.

"One of these men has gone to his reward. The other we may see no more in the flesh; but, though far removed now from the scene of these transactions, we have felt it due to bear the above testimony, and have spoken that *we do know*."

ANNALS

OF THE

HOLSTON CONFERENCE.

———∘∘⊰∞⊱∘∘———

FIRST SESSION.

Held at Knoxville, commencing November 27th, 1824—Bishop Roberts, President; John Tevis, Secretary.

Numbers in Society—Whites, 13,443 ; colored, 1,491. Traveling Preachers, 41.

ADMITTED ON TRIAL—William T. Senter, David Fleming, John S. Henly, Branch H. Merrimon, M. E. Kerr, P. Cumming, L. Jones, Robt. J. Wilson, G. McDaniel.

ADMITTED INTO FULL CONNECTION—J. R. Rhoton, I. Lewis. J. R. Smith, William C. Cumming, James Y. Crawford, Francis A. Owen, Edward T. Peery.

LOCATED—Lewis S. Marshall.

STATIONS OF THE PREACHERS.

ABINGDON DISTRICT—*David Adams, P. E.* Lee Circuit, A. Still, B. H. Merrimon. Clinch, Jno. Craig, Jno. S. Henly, Tazewell, E. T. Peery. Giles, John Kelly, P. Cumming. New River, J. R. Rhoton, William C. Cumming. Ashe, Jas.

293

D. Harris. Abingdon, William Patton, I. Lewis. Blountville, James G. H. Speer, Creed Fulton. Holston, J. Daughtry, David Fleming:

KNOXVILLE DISTRICT—*Thomas Stringfield, P. E.* Knox
Circuit, George Horne, E. F. Sevier. Powell's Valley, J. R.
Smith. Cumberland Mountain, James Y. Crawford. Kings-
ton, L. Jones. Washington, Jno. Bowman, G. McDaniel.
Sequatchee, Jno. Bradfield. Tellico, A. Overall, Robert Kirk-
patrick. Hiwassee, William T. Senter. Upper Cherokee
Mission to be supplied.

FRENCH BROAD DISTRICT—*Jesse Cunnyngham, P. F.* Car-
ter's Valley, Wm. P. Kendrick, M. E. Kerr. Hawkins, Jacob
Hearn. Green, W. S. Manson, F. A. Owen. Newport, Jas.
Cumming, Robt. J. Wilson. French Broad, D. B. Cumming.
Black Mountain, I. Easterly. Little River, George Ekin.
Maryville, Thomas J. Brown.

John Tevis, transferred to the Kentucky Conference.

SECOND SESSION.

Held at Jonesborough, Tenn., commencing Oct. 20th, 1825—
Bishops Roberts and Soule, Presidents; Thomas Stringfield,
Secretary.

Numbers in Society—Whites, 14,988 ; colored, 1,485.
Traveling Preachers, 51.

ADMITTED ON TRIAL—Wm. Ketron, T. K. Catlett, C. Easterly, Jno. Trotter, U. Keener, H. Johnson, Jacob McDaniel,
H. Williams, J. W. Paddelford.

ADMITTED INTO FULL CONNECTION—Jas. D. Harris, R. Kirkpatrick, E. F. Sevier, C. Fulton, I. Easterly.

LOCATED—Sam'l Harwell, Jno. Bradfield, F. A. Owen, A.
Still, W. P. Kendrick.

STATIONS OF THE PREACHERS.

ABINGDON DISTRICT—*S. Patton*, P. E. Lee, Thomas J. Brown. Hawkins, G. McDaniel. Clinch, Jno. Bowman, H. Johnson. Tazewell, J. B. Daughtry. Giles, Thos. Rice, Wm. Ketron. New River, E. T. Peery, Jno. S. Henly. Ashe, R. Kirkpatrick. Abingdon, W. Patton, U. Keener. Blountville, Geo. Horne, D. Fleming.

FRENCH BROAD DISTRICT—*Thomas Stringfield*, P. E. Carter's Valley, W. S. Manson, W. T. Senter. Jonesborough, I. Lewis, Wm. Cumming, D. Adams, sup. Green, Jno. Kelly, Jos. W. Paddelford. Newport, J. R. Rhoton, P. Cumming. French Broad, D. B. Cumming. Black Mountain, A. Overall, Jno. Trotter. Franklin, James D. Harris. Sulphur Springs, Jas. Cumming, C. Easterly. Little River, J. Cunnyngham.

KNOXVILLE DISTRICT—*John Heninger*, P. E. Knox, J. Y. Crawford, J. Hearn. Maryville, E. F. Sevier. Tellico, L. Jones, H. Williams. Hiwassee, J. R. Smith, Moses E. Kerr. Washington, I. Easterly. Sequatchee, J. McDaniel. Cumberland Mountain, B. H. Merrimon. Kingston, C. Fulton, T K. Catlett. Powell's Valley, Jno. Craig.

Geo. Ekin, without an appointment this year.

THIRD SESSION.

Held at Abingdon, Va., commencing Nov. 2d, 1826—Bishop Soule, President; ———, Secretary.

Numbers in Society—Whites, 15,347 ; colored, 1,620.

Traveling Preachers, 54.

ADMITTED ON TRIAL—W. G. Brownlow, H. Powell, A. Murphy, J. L. Straly, O. F. Johnson, Wm. Bowers, R. Birdwell.

ADMITTED INTO FULL CONNECTION—B. H. Merrimon, G. McDaniel, J. S. Henly, W. T. Senter, P. Cumming, Moses E. Kerr, D. Fleming, L. Jones.

LOCATED—J. R. Smith, J. Cunnyngham, J. Hearn, George Horne, A. Overall.

STATIONS OF THE PREACHERS.

ABINGDON DISTRICT—*Sam'l Patton, P. E.* Abingdon Station, George Atkin. Clinch, E. T. Peery, O. F. Johnson. Tazewell, T. Rice, H. Johnson. Giles, I. Lewis, R. Birdwell. New River, J. Bunker, W. Ketron. Ashe, D. Fleming. Abingdon Circuit, J. B. Daughtry, T. K. Catlett. Blountville, W. Patton.

FRENCH BROAD DISTRICT—*T. Stringfield, P. E.* Sulphur Springs, U. Keener, J. Paddelford. Green, E. T. Sevier, Wm. R. Kendrick. Jonesborough, Jno. Craig, Geo. Ekin, sup. Carter's Valley, J. Y. Crawford, J. R. Rhoton, sup. Hawkins, Jno. Trotter. Lee, A. Murphy, H. Williams. Powell's Valley, R. Kirkpatrick. Claiborne, C. Easterly.

KNOXVILLE DISTRICT—*Jno. Heninger, P. E.* Knox, Jas. Cumming, W. T. Senter. Maryville, C. Fulton. Tellico, B. H. Merrimon, J. McDaniel. Hiwassee, J. Kelly, J. L. Straley. Washington, J. D. Harris. Sequatchee, I. Easterly. Kingston, T. J. Brown.

ASHEVILLE DISTRICT—*Wm. S. Munson, P. E.* Little River, L. Jones. Franklin, P. Cumming, H. Powell. Rayburn, M. E. Kerr. Green River, Jno. S. Henly. Black Mountain, G. McDaniel, W. G. Brownlow. French Broad, W. Cumming, D. B. Cumming, sup. Newport, John Bowman, sup., W. Bowers.

FOURTH SESSION.

Held at Knoxville, Tenn., commencing Nov. 1st, 1827—Bishop Roberts, President ; E. F. Sevier, Secretary.

Numbers in Society—Whites, 17,375—colored, 1,864.

Traveling Preachers, 58.

ADMITTED ON TRIAL—E. P. Childress, John Grant, John

Baringer, R. Gannaway, A. C. Taylor, W. H. Shannon, Oliver C. Miller, J. R. Sensibaugh, Daniel Carter, S. W. Earnest, Joseph Haskew.

ADMITTED INTO FULL CONNECTION—W. Ketron, C. Easterly, U. Keener, Jacob McDaniel, J. W. Paddelford, T. K. Catlett, John Trotter, H. Johnson, H. Williams.

LOCATED—W. T. Senter, D. B. Cumming, J. R. Rhoton, D. Adams, J. W. Paddelford.

STATIONS OF THE PREACHERS.

ABINGDON DISTRICT—*E. F. Sevier, P. E.* Abingdon Station, Sam'l Patton. Abingdon Circuit, C. Fulton, A. C. Taylor. Blountville, U. Keener, O. F. Johnson. Hawkins, H. Williams, J. J. Burum. Lee, A. Murphy, J. Haskew. Lebanon, W. C. Cumming, S. W. Earnest. Tazewell, T. K. Catlett, H. Johnson. Giles, Josiah B. Daughtry, E. P. Childress. New River, G. McDaniel, R. Gannaway. Jefferson, J. McDaniel.

FRENCH BROAD DISTRICT—*T. Wilkerson, P. E.* Sulphur Springs, J. F. Bunker, W. H. Shannon. Green, J. Y. Crawford, J. R. Sensibaugh. Jonesborough, W. Patton, T. Rice. Carter's Valley, George Ekin, R. Birdwell. Rutledge, R. Kirkpatrick.

KNOXVILLE DISTRICT—*John Heninger, P. E.* Knoxville Station, I. Lewis. Knox Circuit, W. P. Kendrick. Tellico, James Witten, B. H. Merrimon. Hiwassee, E. Pierson, John Grant. Washington, C. Easterly. Sequatchee, I. Easterly, D. Carter. Kingston, John Craig, J. L. Straly. Powell's Valley, T. J. Brown, John Baringer.

ASHEVILLE DISTRICT—*W. S. Manson, P. E.* Maryville, Jas. Cumming. Franklin, D. Fleming, P. Cumming. Pickens, J. S. Henly, H. Powell. French Broad, M. E. Kerr,

W. G. Brownlow. Black Mountain, W. Ketron, O. C Miller.
Newport, Lewis Jones. Little River, J. D. Harris.

Thos. Stringfield, Conference Agent.

E. T. Peery, John Kelly, and J. Trotter, transferred to Missouri Conference.

FIFTH SESSION.

*Held at Jonesborough, commencing Nov. 13th, 1828—Bishop
Soule, President; E. F. Sevier, Secretary.*

Numbers in Society—Whites, 17,952 ; colored, 2,012.

Traveling Preachers, 63.

ADMITTED ON TRIAL—Wm. B. Wright, E. Perkins, William
Eakin, John Weems, Ashley Wynn, Moses F. Rainwater,
Asbury Brooks.

ADMITTED INTO FULL CONNECTION—William G. Brownlow,
Abram Murphy, Oscar F. Johnson, John J. Burum, Henry
Powell, Jacob L. Straly, Russell Birdwell.

LOCATED—William P. Kendrick, Paxton Cumming, Henry
Williams, Isaac Easterly, Hugh Johnson.

STATIONS OF THE PREACHERS.

ABINGDON DISTRICT—*Samuel Patton, P. E.* Abingdon
Station, A. C. Taylor. Abingdon Circuit, I. Lewis, J. Baringer. Blountville, George Ekin. Lebanon, J. B. Daughtry, Moses F. Rainwater. Tazewell, Jesse Lee, John J.
Burum. Giles, Thomas Rice, Wm B. Wright. New River,
William C. Cumming, Robertson Gannaway. Jefferson, Jacob
L. Straly.

GREENVILLE DISTRICT—*E. F. Sevier, P. E.* Lee, R. Kirkpatrick, E. Perkins. Powell's Valley, Thomas J. Brown, Daniel Carter. Knox, John Craig, O. F. Johnson. Rutledge, G.
McDaniel. Carter's Valley, D. Fleming, Russell Birdwell.

Greene, James Y.. Crawford, Wm. H. Shannon. Jonesborough, William Patton, John Bowman, sup. Mount Sterling, C. Easterly.

WASHINGTON DISTRICT—*John Heninger, P. E.* Maryville, George Horne. Tellico, Creed Fulton, John Weems. Athens, E. Pierson. Sweet Water, J. Witten, J. Haskew. Spring Creek, Jacob McDaniel. Washington, William G. Brownlow. Sequatchee, James D. Harris, S. W. Earnest. Kingston, John S. Henly, J. Grant.

ASHEVILLE DISTRICT—*W. S. Manson, P. E.* Franklin, U. Keener, O. C. Miller. Pickens,. M. E. Kerr. Greenville, William Ketron. French Broad, Branch H. Merrimon, Asbury Brooks. Black Mountain, Henry Powell, Joseph R. Sensibaugh. Newport, L. Jones, William Eakin. Little River, A. Murphy, A. Wynn. Sulphur Springs, James Cumming, E. P. Childress, T. Wilkinson, sup.

Thomas K. Catlett, Conference Agent for the Seminary.

Thomas Stringfield, without an appointment, at his own request.

Jesse F. Bunker, without an appointment this year.

SIXTH SESSION.

Held at Abingdon, Va., Dec. 24th, 1829—Bishop Soule, President; E. F. Sevier, Secretary.

Numbers in Society—Whites, 18,270 ; colored, 2,182.

Traveling Preachers, 64.

ADMITTED ON TRIAL—John Steele, Arnold Patton, D. R. M'Anally, Jacob Nutty, George Ekin, Jr., Rufus M. Stevens, William Bower, Anthony Bewley, Harvey Cumming, A. Woodfin, William P. McConnell.

ADMITTED INTO FULL CONNECTION—E. P. Childress, John Baringer, A. C. Taylor, O. C. Miller, Daniel Carter, Joseph

Haskew, John Grant, R. Gannaway, Joseph R. Sensibaugh,
Stephen W. Earnest.

LOCATED—John J. Burum, E. Pierson, Robert Kirkpatrick,
Thomas J. Brown, George Horne, Jesse F. Bunker, A. C.
Taylor, C. Fulton.

STATIONS OF THE PREACHERS.

ABINGDON DISTRICT—*E. F. Sevier, P. E.* Abingdon Sta-
tion, Thomas Wilkerson, sup. Abingdon Circuit, George Ekin,
Hugh Johnson. Jefferson, Thomas Rice. New River, John
Craig, A. Brooks. Giles, J. D. Harris, William Bower.
Tazewell, William C. Cumming. Lebanon, David Fleming.

GREENVILLE DISTRICT—*S. Patton, P. E.* Scott, Christian
Easterly. Blountville, James Y. Crawford. Mount Sterling,
Henry Powell. Jonesborough, J. L. Straly, E. Perkins.
Green, William Patton, Jacob Nutty, William H. Shan-
non. Carter's Valley, Branch H. Merrimon, Arnold Patton.
Lee, Jacob McDaniel, William P. McConnell.

KNOXVILLE DISTRICT—*J. Cumming, P. E.* KNOX, J. B.
Daughtry, Harvey Cumming, Isaac Lewis, sup. Maryville,
James Witten. Little River, Edmund P. Childress, William
Eakin. Newport, S. W. Earnest, A. Woodfin. Sulphur
Springs, Lewis Jones, John Steele. Rutledge, Jesse Lee.
Powell's Valley, R. Birdwell, George Ekin, Jr.

WASHINGTON DISTRICT—*Thomas K. Catlett, P. E.* Kings-
ton, O. F. Johnson, D. R. M'Anally. Washington, John S.
Henly. Sequatchee, A. Murphy, R. M. Stevens. Spring
Creek, Daniel Carter. Athens, William G. Brownlow.
Tellico, John Grant. Sweet Water, Joseph Haskew, William
B. Wright.

ASHEVILLE DISTRICT—*William S. Manson, P. E.* Franklin,
John Baringer. Pickens, Moses F. Rainwater. Tugulo,
O. C. Miller. Greenville, M. E. Kerr. Black Mountain, G.

McDaniel. French Broad, U. Keener, A. Bewley. Pigeon, A. Wynn.

Thomas Stringfield and John Heninger, Conference Agents for the Seminary.

W. Ketron, J. R. Sensibaugh, transferred to Missouri Conference.

SEVENTH SESSION.

Held at Ebenezer, Green County, Tenn, commencing Nov. 4th, 1830—Bishops McKendree and Soule, Presidents; E. F. Sevier, Secretary.

Numbers in Society—Whites, 19,160 ; colored, 2,362.

Traveling Preachers, 60.

ADMITTED ON TRIAL—W. Gilmore, R. B. Rogers, John Pryor.

ADMITTED INTO FULL CONNECTION—W. B. Wright, W. Eakin, A. Brooks, E. Perkins, A. Wynn.

LOCATED—John Grant, B. H. Merrimon, O. F. Johnson, G. McDaniel, J. Lee, U. Keener.

STATIONS OF THE PREACHERS.

ABINGDON DISTRICT—*E. F. Sevier, P. E.* Abingdon Station, W. Patton. Abingdon Circuit, George Ekin, D. R. M'Anally. Jefferson, W. B. Wright. Grayson, Thomas Rice. Wythe, J. B. Daughtry, Hugh Johnson. East River, Moses E. Kerr, George Ekin, Jr. Lebanon, Christian Easterly.

GREENVILLE DISTRICT—*Samuel Patton, P. E.* Scott, Henry Powell. Blountville, James Y. Crawford. Mount Sterling, E. Perkins. Jonesborough, John Baringer, R. Gannaway. Green, David Fleming, A. Patton. Carter's Valley, William C. Cumming, A. Brooks. Lee, John Craig.

KNOXVILLE DISTRICT—*J. Cumming, P. E.* Knox, A. Murphy, J. Nutty, Thomas Wilkerson, sup. Maryville, Russell

Birdwell. Little River, Joseph R. Sensibaugh, I. Lewis, sup. Newport, A. Wynn. Dandridge, Lewis Jones, H. Cumming. Rutledge, Thomas J. Brown. Clinton, Moses F. Rainwater. Tazewell, Stephen W. Earnest.

WASHINGTON DISTRICT—*John Heninger, P. E.* Kingston, James Witten. Washington, J. McDaniel. Sequatchee, O. C. Miller, William Gilmore. Athens, Joseph Haskew, R. M. Stevens. Tellico, W. G. Brownlow, J. Pryor. Sweet Water, E. P. Childress.

ASHEVILLE DISTRICT—*T. K. Catlett, P. E.* Franklin, John S. Henly. Dickens, W. S. Manson, sup., A. Bewley. Tugulo, William Bower. Greenville, A. Woodfin. Black Mountain, J. L. Straly, R. B. Rogers. French Broad, D. Carter. Pigeon, W. Eakin.

J. D. Harris travels with Bishop McKendree this year.

Thomas Stringfield, agent for Holston Seminary.

EIGHTH SESSION.

Held at Athens, Tenn., commencing Nov. 10th, 1831—Bishop Hedding, President ; E. F. Sevier, Secretary.

Numbers in Society—Whites, 19,257 ; colored, 2,319.

Traveling Preachers, 56.

ADMITTED ON TRIAL—E. Still, H. Ingram, William Harle, N. Harrison.

ADMITTED INTO FULL CONNECTION—A. Patton, J. Nutty, R. M. Stevens, A. Bewley, A. Woodfin, D. R. M'Anally, W. Bower, H. Cumming, Moses F. Rainwater.

LOCATED—Moses F. Rainwater, A. Wynn, C. Easterly, H. Powell, J. L. Straly, E. F. Sevier.

STATIONS OF THE PREACHERS.

ABINGDON DISTRICT—*Thomas K. Catlett, P. E.* Abingdon Station, John Baringer. Abingdon Circuit, W. C. Cumming,

A. Woodfin. Jefferson, Jacob Nutty. Graysou, Jacob McDaniel. Wythe, George Ekin, William Harle. East River, Moses E. Kerr, William Gilmore. Lebanon, Joseph R. Sensibaugh.

GREENVILLE DISTRICT—*Samuel Patton, P. E.* Scott, E. Perkins. Blountville, J. B. Daughtry. Mount Sterling, Hugh Johnson. Jonesborough, R. Gannaway, Harvey Cumming. Green, A. Murphy, E. Still. Carter's Valley, L. Jones, J. S. Healy, sup. Lee, Arnold Patton, H. Ingram.

KNOXVILLE DISTRICT—*J. Cumming, P. E.* Knox, David Fleming, R. Birdwell. Maryville, John Pryor, I. Lewis, sup. Little River, A. Bewley. Newport, Thomas Rice. Dandridge, W. S. Manson. Rutledge, James Y. Crawford. Tazewell, to be supplied. Clinton, William Bower.

WASHINGTON DISTRICT—*John Heninger, P. E.* Kingston, M. Stevens. Washington, O. C. Miller. Sequatchee, John R. Craig. Athens, Joseph Haskew, R. B. Rogers. Tellico, William B. Wright. Sweet Water, James Witten.

ASHEVILLE DISTRICT—*W. Patton, P. E.* Franklin, William G. Brownlow. Pickens, S. W. Earnest. Tugulo, A. Brooks. Greenville, D. Carter. Black Mountain, N. Harrison, E. P. Childress. French Broad, David R. M'Anally. Waynesville, William Eakin.

James D. Harris travels with Bishop McKendree.

Thomas J. Brown, removed to Indiana, in good standing.

Thomas Stringfield, Ag't for Holston Conference Seminary.

NINTH SESSION.

Held at Evansham (Wytheville), Va., commencing Nov. 15th, 1832—Bishop Emory, President; Thomas Stringfield and D. R. M'Anally, Secretaries.

Numbers in Society—Whites, 20,798 ; colored, 2,316.

Traveling Preachers, 61.

ADMITTED ON TRIAL—M. C. Hawk, C. K. Lewis, J. L. Sensibaugh, W. Burgess.

ADMITTED INTO FULL CONNECTION—John Pryor, W. Gilmore.

LOCATED—Isaac Lewis, A. Murphy, W. B. Wright, M. E. Kerr, John S. Henly, R. Birdwell.

STATIONS OF THE PREACHERS.

ABINGDON DISTRICT—*T. K. Catlett, P. E.* Abingdon Station, Joseph Haskew. Abingdon Circuit, W. C. Cumming, D. T. Fulton.* Jefferson, A Bewley. Grayson, E. Still. Wythe, D. Adams. Evansham, J. Baringer. East River, D. Carter, H. Johnson. Lebanon, T. Rice.

GREENVILLE DISTRICT—*S. Patton, P. E.* Scott, J. McDaniel. Blountville, R. Gannaway. Mount Sterling, J. L. Sensibaugh. Jonesborough, L. Jones, H. Ingram. Green, J. B. Daughtry, George Ekin. Carter's Valley, J. Crawford, C. K. Lewis. Lee, J. Pryor, A. N. Ross.

KNOXVILLE DISTRICT—*J. Cumming, P. E.* Knox Circuit, J. Nutty, W. Harle. Knoxville, D. Fleming. Maryville, A. Patton. Sevierville, J. D. Harris. Newport, William Eakin. Dandridge, D. B. Cumming, J. Craig. Rutledge, W. S. Manson. Tazewell, A. Woodfin. Clinton, W. Burgess.

WASHINGTON DISTRICT—*John Henninger, P. E.* Kingston, R. M. Stevens, W. H. Rogers.* Washington, R. B. Rogers. Jasper, E. P. Childress. Pikeville, W. Bower. Athens, D. R. M'Anally, H. Cumming, sup. Tellico, O. C. Miller. Sweet Water, E. Perkins, J. Witten, sup.

ASHEVILLE DISTRICT—*W. Patton, P. E.* Franklin, S. W. Earnest. Pickens, M. C. Hawk. Tugulo, W. G. Brownlow. Greenville, W. Gilmore. Catawba, A. Brooks. Reems Creek,

---

* Owing to a defect in the published Minutes, it does not appear when these two persons were received on trial, though it is pretty clear they were received at this session.

I. Falls. French Broad, Joseph R. Sensibaugh. Waynesville, N. Harrison.

A. Still, T. Stringfield, and L. S. Marshall, Agents for the Holston Academy.

TENTH SESSION.

Held at Kingsport, Tenn., commencing Oct. 16th, 1833—Bishop Roberts, President; L. S. Marshall, Secretary.

Numbers in Society—Whites, 22,349 ; colored, 2,593. Traveling Preachers, 62.

ADMITTED ON TRIAL—W. B. Murphy, T. Sullens, W. B. Winton, B. McC. Roberts, William Spann.

ADMITTED INTO FULL CONNECTION—H. Ingram, E. Still.

LOCATED—J. Nutty, W. Eakin.

STATIONS OF THE PREACHERS.

ABINGDON DISTRICT—*T. K. Catlett, P. E.* Abingdon Station, J. Pryor. Abingdon Circuit, J. Haskew, R. Gannaway. Jefferson, E. Still. Grayson, W. Gilmore. Evansham, D. R. M'Anally. Wythe, J. Baringer. East River, H. Johnson, H. Ingram. Lebanon, T. Rice. Elizabethton, D. T. Fulton, J. Bowman, sup.

GREENVILLE DISTRICT—*L. S. Marshall, P. E.* Kingsport and Jonesborough, S. Patton. Blountville Circuit, W. C. Cumming. Scott, I. Falls, W. B. Murphy. Lee, A. Brooks, T. Sullens. Clinch River Mission, C. K. Lewis. Carter's Valley, James Y. Crawford. Green, O. C. Miller, S. W. Earnest. Jonesborough, A. Patton, W. B. Winton.

KNOXVILLE DISTRICT—*W. Patton, P. E.* Knoxville Station, D. Adams. Knoxville Circuit, Thomas Stringfield, J. L. Sensibaugh. Maryville, D. Fleming. Sevierville, L. Jones. Newport, J. McDaniel. Dandridge, W. G. Brownlow. New-

market, W. S. Manson. Rutledge, A. Still. Tazewell, W,
Burgess. Clinton, J. Craig.

WASHINGTON DISTRICT—*J. Heninger, P. E.* Kingston, A.
Bewley. Washington, E. P. Childress.. Pikeville, George
Ekin. Jasper, J. D. Harris. Athens, R. M. Stevens, M. C.
Hawk. Tellico, E. Perkins, J. Witten, sup. Sweet Water,
R. B. Rogers.

ASHEVILLE DISTRICT—*J. B. Daughtry, P. E.* Franklin, J.
R. Sensibaugh. Pickens, B. McC. Roberts. Tugulo, A. N.
Ross. Greenville, William Spann. Catawba, W. Bower.
Reems Creek, D. Carter. French Broad, D. B. Cumming, W.
H. Rogers. Waynesville, A. Woodfin.

J. Cumming, Agent for Holston Seminary.

ELEVENTH SESSION.

*Held at Knoxville, Tenn., commencing Oct. 8th, 1834—John
Heninger, President ; L. S. Marshall, Secretary.*

Numbers in Society—Whites, 21,559 ; colored, 2,478.
Traveling Preachers, 63.

[NOTE.—*The printed Minutes of this year ·do not show
who were admitted on trial, into full connection, or who
located.*]

STATIONS OF THE PREACHERS.

ABINGDON DISTRICT—*Thomas K. Catlett, P. E.* Abingdon
Station, D. R. M'Anally. Abingdon Circuit, James Y. Craw-
ford, H. Balch. Jefferson, to be supplied. Grayson, Daniel
Payne. Wythe, Arnold Patton. Giles, W. B. Winton, W.
C. Graves. Lebanon, one to be supplied, H. Johnson. Evans-
ham, I. Falls.

GREENVILLE DISTRICT—*L. S. Marshall, P. E.* Jonesborough and Kingsport, Samuel Patton. Blountville Circuit, Thomas Rice. Scott, William G. Brownlow. Lee, William Gilmore, W. B. Murphy. Clinch River Mission, to be supplied. Carter's Valley, O. C. Miller. Green, James Cumming, A. Woodfin. Jonesborough, D. Adams; O. F. Cunnyngham. Rogersville and Greenville Station, J. Baringer. Elizabethton Circuit, B. McC. Roberts.

KNOXVILLE DISTRICT—*William Patton, P. E.* Knoxville Station, John Pryor. Knoxville Circuit, to be supplied. Maryville, D. Fleming. Sevierville, Lewis Jones. Newport, D. Carter. Newmarket, A. Still, R. B. Rogers. Rutledge, John Craig. Tazewell, Wm. H. Rogers. Clinton, A. Brooks.

WASHINGTON DISTRICT—*Thomas Stringfield, P. E.* and superintendent of the Cherokee Mission. Kingston Circuit, Madison C. Hawk, J. McDaniel, sup. Washington Circuit, T. Sullens, J. Heninger, sup. Pikeville, C. Stump. Jasper, W. Burgess. Athens, George Ekin, William Hicks. Cherokee Mission, D. B. Cumming, D. T. Fulton, D. Ring. Sweet Water, W. Bower. Tellico, A. N. Ross, J. Bowman, sup.

ASHEVILLE DISTRICT—*J. B. Daughtry, P. E.* Franklin, H. Ingram. Pickens, J. R. Sensibaugh. Greenville, S. W. Earnest. Catawba, W. Spann. Reems Creek, C. K. Lewis. French Broad, J. Haskew, J. L. Sensibaugh. Waynesville, R. W. Patty. Hiwassee Mission, E. Still.

Creed Fulton, Agent for Holston Seminary.

Jesse Lee, without an appointment, in view of a mission to Liberia.

Thomas Wilkerson, James Dixon, and Harvey Cumming, superannuated.

TWELFTH SESSION.

Held at Abingdon, Va., Oct. 7th, 1835—Bishop Andrew, President; L. S. Marshall, Secretary.

Numbers in Society—Whites, 21,191 ; colored, 2,189 ; Indians, 521.

Traveling Preachers, 70.

ADMITTED ON TRIAL—George W. Baker, Wm. Bruce, E. K. Hutsell, Henry S. Koontz, John Gaston, Wm. M. Rush, John S. Weaver, John Boston, A. Campbell, A. B. Broyles.

ADMITTED INTO FULL CONNECTION—T. Sullens, W. B. Winton, B. McC. Roberts, William Burgess, J. Fields.

LOCATED—S. W. Earnest, Jesse Lee, D. Adams, O. C. Miller, John Baringer, William Bower.

STATIONS OF THE PREACHERS.

ABINGDON DISTRICT—*S. Patton, P. E.* Abingdon Station, Thomas Stringfield. Abingdon Circuit, L. Jones. Marion, R. Gannaway. Jefferson, A. Woodfin. Grayson, R. B. Rogers. Wythe, W. B. Winton, H. S. Koontz. Giles, H. Johnson, one to be supplied. Lebanon, J. McDaniel, G. W. Baker. Bluestone, A. Patton.

GREENVILLE DISTRICT—*L. S. Marshall, P. E.* Jonesborough and Kingsport, T. K. Catlett. Blountville, T. Rice. Scott, A. Brooks. Lee, D. T. Fulton. Clinch River Mission, to be supplied. Carter's Valley, W. Burgess, J. Gaston. Green, D. Carter, J. L. Sensibaugh. Jonesborough Circuit, J. M. Kelly, W. Bruce. Elizabethton, W. G. Brownlow.

KNOXVILLE DISTRICT—*W. Patton, P. E.* Knoxville, J. Pryor. Knox, R. M. Stevens. Maryville, D. R. M'Anally. Sevierville, A. Still. Newport, W. C. Graves. Newmarket, D. Fleming, John S. Weaver. Rutledge, J. Y. Crawford. Tazewell, W. Gilmore. Clinton, R. W. Patty.

WASHINGTON DISTRICT—*John Heninger, P. E.* Kingston, D. Ring, J. Craig, sup. Washington, T. Sullens. Pikeville, W. Hicks. Jasper, G. Ekin. Tellico, J. Cumming, H. Balch. Sweet Water, H. Ingram. Athens, I. Falls, E. K. Hutsell.

ASHEVILLE DISTRICT—*J. B. Daughtry, P. E.* - Franklin, J.
Bowman, sup., W. M. Rush. Pickens, W. H. Rogers, A. B.
Broyles. Greenville, D. Payne. Catawba, J. R. Sensibaugh. Reems Creek, C. K. Lewis. French Broad, J. Haskew, W. Spann. Waynesville, O. F. Cunningham.

NEWTOWN DISTRICT—*D. B. Cumming, P. E.* Chatanooga
Mission, C. Stump. Springplace Mission, M. E. Hawk.
Newtown Mission, A. N. Ross. Ellija Mission, E. Still.
Hiwassee Mission, B. McC. Roberts. Valleytown Mission, A.
Campbell. Coontown Mission, J. F. Boot. Othcalooga Mis-
sion, J. Boston, J. Fields, interpreter.

W. B. Murphy, transferred to Kentucky Conference.

T. Fields, transferred to Alabama Conference.

C. Fulton, Agent for Holston Seminary.

THIRTEENTH SESSION.

*Held at Reems Creek, N. C., commencing Oct. 12th, 1836—
Bishop Andrew, President ; L. S. Marshall, Secretary.*

Numbers in Society—Whites, 20,158 ; colored, 1,997 ;
Indians, 752.

Traveling Preachers, 70.

ADMITTED ON TRIAL—G. F. Page, S. A. Miller, L. Wilson, A.
N. Harris, J. L. Fowler, G. W. Alexander, C. Campbell.

ADMITTED INTO FULL CONNECTION—O. F. Cunningham, W.
Hicks, W. C. Graves, C. Stump, H. W. Balch, R. W. Patty,
J. L. Sensibaugh.

LOCATED—R. B. Rogers, A. Woodfin, J. L. Sensibaugh,
J. Y. Crawford, J. Pryor, W. G. Brownlow.

STATIONS OF THE PREACHERS.

EVANSHAM DISTRICT—*D. Fleming, P. E.* Evansham, W.
B. Winton, J. Bowman, sup. Jeffersonville, A. Patton.

Parisburg, W. Gilmore, J. McDaniel. Marion, T. Rice. Grayson, D. T. Fulton. Jefferson, J. S. Weaver. Tug Fork Mission, to be supplied.

ABINGDON DISTRICT—*W. Patton, P. E.* Abingdon Station, C. Campbell. Abingdon Circuit, J. Haskew. Lebanon, R. Gannaway. Estelville, H. Johnson, J. Gaston. Blountville, R. M. Stevens. Jonesboro, D. R. M'Anally, J. L. Fowler. Elizabethton, J. R. Sensibaugh.

GREENVILLE DISTRICT—*Samuel Patton, P. E.* Green, D. Carter, A. B. Broyles. Rogersville, W. Burgess. Clinch River, W. Hicks. Jonesville, to be supplied. New Market, B. McC. Roberts. Dandridge, O. F. Cunningham. Newport, I. Falls.

KNOXVILLE DISTRICT—*L. S. Marshall, P. E.* Knoxville, T. Sullens. Knox, George Horne. Maryville, L. Jones. Sevierville, E. K. Hutsell. Tazewell, R. W. Patty. Clinton, W. C. Graves. Buffalo Mission, to be supplied.

WASHINGTON DISTRICT—*J. B. Daughtry, P. E.* Kingston, Lewis Carter. Pikeville, H. W. Balch. Washington, A. N. Ross. Jasper, G. W. Alexander. Athens, H. Ingram. Madisonville, G. Ekin. Sweet Water, M. C. Hawk, G. W. Finnell.

NEWTOWN DISTRICT—*D. B. Cumming, P. E.* Cleveland, C. K. Lewis. Chattanooga, W. H. Rogers. Coontown, Turtle Fields. Springplace, E. Still. Othcalooga, J. F. Boot. Ellija, W. M. Rush. Blairsville, D. Payne. Valleytown, A. Campbell ; one interpreter to be supplied.

ASHEVILLE DISTRICT—*T. K. Catlett, P. E.* Franklin, G. W. Baker. Pickens, C. Stump. Greenville, D. Ring. Catawba, D. Hilliard. Reems Creek, A. N. Harris. Asheville, G. F. Page, L. Wilson. Waynesville, W. Bruce.

C. Fulton, Agent for Emory and Henry College.

J. M. Kelly, Agent for Holston Seminary.

A. Still, transferred to Missouri Conference.

T. Stringfield, transferred to Tennessee Conference.

FOURTEENTH SESSION.

Held at Madisonville, Tenn., October 18, 1837—*Bishop Morris, President ; L. S. Marshall, Secretary.*

Numbers in Society — Whites, 20,238 ; colored, 2,129 ; Indians, 480.

Traveling Preachers, 74.

ADMITTED ON TRIAL—George W. Stafford, Mitchell Martin, Francis M. Fanning, J. M. Crismond, W. C. Reynolds, R. Reneau, W. L. Turner, Thomas Witten, H. Tartar, Wcelooker (Cherokee), C. D. Smith, Thomas K. Harmon.

ADMITTED INTO FULL CONNECTION—George W. Baker, W. Bruce, E. K. Hutsell, John Gaston, W. M. Rush, A. B. Broyles, J. S. Weaver, A. Campbell.

LOCATED—J. Haskew, J. R. Sensibaugh, Hiram Ingram, Thomas Rice, A. N. Ross, B. McC. Roberts.

STATIONS OF THE PREACHERS.

EVANSHAM DISTRICT—*D. Fleming, P. E.* Jeffersonville, D. T. Fulton. Evansham, T. Sullens, T. Witten. Parisburg, J. S. Weaver, M. Martin. Marion, C. Campbell. Grayson, T. K. Harmon. Jefferson, G. W. Stafford. Tug Fork Mission, to be supplied.

C. Fulton, Agent for Emory and Henry College.

ABINGDON DISTRICT—*A. Patton, P. E.* Abingdon Station, W. B. Winton. Abingdon Circuit, O. F. Cunningham. Lebanon, William Bower. Estelville, H. Johnson. Blountville, R. M. Stevens. Jonesborough, R. Reneau. Elizabethton, W. H. Rogers.

G. F. Page, Agent for Emory and Henry College.

GREENVILLE DISTRICT—*T. K. Catlett, P. E.* Green, R. W. Patty, J. Bowman, sup. Rogersville, R. Gannaway.

Clinch River Mission, C. Stump. Jonesville, W. C. Reynolds, New Market, W. Hicks. Dandridge, George Horne. Newport, George W. Baker.

Samuel Patton, Agent for Holston Seminary.

KNOXVILLE DISTRICT—*L. S. Marshall, P. E.* Knoxville, J. M. Kelly. Knox, L. Jones. Maryville, D. B. Carter. Sevierville, A. N. Harris. Tazewell, W. Bruce. Clinton, G. Ekin. Buffalo Mission, J. L. Fowler, W. L. Turner.

WASHINGTON DISTRICT—*John Heninger, P. E.* Washington Circuit, E. Still. Kingston, W. Burgess. Pikeville, to be supplied. Jasper, F. M. Fanning. Athens, L. Carter, John M. Crismond. Madisonville, M. C. Hawk. Philadelphia, I. Falls. Decatur, J. McDaniel.

NEWTOWN DISTRICT—*D. B. Cumming, P. E.* Cleveland, William M. Rush, H. Tartar. Lafayette, Daniel Payne, C. D. Smith. Coontown Mission, John F. Boot, A. Campbell. Springplace, Charles K. Lewis. Othcalooga Mission, Weelooker (Cherokee). Ellija Mission, W. Gillmore. Blairsville Mission, J. Gaston. Valleytown Mission, L. Coffee.

J. Daughtry, Agent for Preacher's Aid Society.

ASHEVILLE DISTRICT—*D. R. M'Anally, P. E.* Franklin, L. Wilson. Pickens Mission, W. C. Graves. Greenville, E. K. Hutsell. Reems Creek, D. Hilliard, G. W. Alexander Asheville, D. Ring, A. B. Broyles. Waynesville, S. A. Miller.

William Patton, transferred to Missouri Conference.

Rufus M. Stevens, transferred to Missouri Conference, after laboring nine months on his circuit.

Turtle Fields, transferred to Arkansas Conference.

H. W. Balch, left without an appointment, by order of Conference.

FIFTEENTH SESSION.

Held at Wytheville, Va., November 14, 1838—Bishop Andrew, President; L. S. Marshall, Secretary.

Numbers in Society — Whites, 20,513 ; colored, 1,820 ; Indians, 440.

Traveling Preachers, 68.

ADMITTED ON TRIAL—Jesse Childers, Benjamin F. Wells, Jesse C. Derrick, A. H. Mathes, William Hickey, C. Collins.

ADMITTED INTO FULL CONNECTION—G. F. Page, S. A. Miller, L. Wilson, A. N. Harris, G. W. Alexander, C. Campbell.

LOCATED—T. D. Fulton, E. Still, W. Bruce, L. Jones, W. Burgess, M. C. Hawk, L. S. Marshall.

STATIONS OF THE PREACHERS.

EVANSHAM DISTRICT—*D. Fleming, P. E.* Evansham, W. B. Winton ; one to be supplied. Parisburg, W. H. Rogers, J. Childers. Jeffersonville, J. S. Weaver. Marion, G. Ekin. Grayson, S. A. Miller. Jefferson, to be supplied. Tug Fork Mission, to be supplied.

ABINGDON DISTRICT—*A. Patton, P. E.* Abingdon, Rufus M. Stevens, G. F. Page. Lebanon, C. D. Smith. Estelville, M. Martin. Blountville, H. Johnson. Jonesborough, R. W. Patty, B. F. Wells. Elizabethton, G. W. Alexander. Guess' River Mission, to be supplied.

Emory and Henry College, C. Collins, President ; C. Fulton and T. Sullens, Agents.

GREENVILLE DISTRICT— *T. K. Catlett, P. E.* Green, R. Reneau, John Bowman, sup. Rogersville, R. Gannaway. Clinch River Mission, W. C. Reynolds. Jonesville, J. M. Crismond. New Market, L. Wilson. Dandridge, D. B. Carter. Newport, W. Hickey.

Holston College, A. H. Mathes. Samuel Patton, Agent.

KNOXVILLE DISTRICT—*J. Cumming, P. E.* Knoxville, J. Baringer. Knox, W. C. Graves. Maryville, W. M. Rush. Sevierville, W. S. Manson. Tazewell, C. Stump. Clinton, W. Gilmore. Buffalo Mission, J. L. Fowler, J. C. Derrick.

WASHINGTON DISTRICT—*J. Heninger, P. E.* Washington, William Bower. Kingston, T. Trower. Pikeville, T. K. Harmon. Jasper, J. Gaston. Athens, J. M. Kelly. Decatur, F. M. Fanning. Madisonville, C. Campbell. Philadelphia, I. Falls, T. Witten.

NEWTOWN DISTRICT—*J. B. Daughtry, P. E.* Cleveland, O. F. Cunningham. Lafayette, A. N. Harris. Springplace Mission, Daniel Payne. Ellija Mission, A. B. Broyles. Blairsville Mission, J. McDaniel, H. Tartar.

ASHEVILLE DISTRICT—*D. R. M'Anally, P. E.* Franklin, W. Hicks. Pickens Mission, G. W. Baker. Greenville, D. Hilliard. Reems Creek, D. Ring, W. L. Turner. Asheville, E. K. Hutsell; one to be supplied. Waynesville, A. Pickens.

Thomas Wilkerson, transferred to Tennessee Conference.

D. B. Cumming, John F. Boot, A. Campbell, Weelooker, transferred to Arkansas Conference.

H. Balch, suspended from his ministry for one year.

SIXTEENTH SESSION.

Held at Greenville, Tenn., October 30, 1839.—T. K. Catlett, President; D. R. M'Anally, Secretary.

Numbers in Society—Whites, 23,859; colored, 1,832. Traveling Preachers, 69.

ADMITTED ON TRIAL—J. D. Gibson, D. White, R. G. Ketron, J. Atkins, A. M. Goodykoontz. E. F. Sevier, re-admitted.

ADMITTED INTO FULL CONNECTION—M. Martin, T. K. Harmon, F. M. Fanning, J. M. Crismond, W. L. Turner, H. Tartar, C. D. Smith, R. Reneau (an Elder).

LOCATED—D. Hilliard, J. B. Corn, H. Balch, O. F. Cunningham, T. Trower.

STATIONS OF THE PREACHERS.

WYTHEVILLE DISTRICT—*D. Fleming, P. E.* Wytheville Circuit, G. Ekin, J. Childers. Parisburg Circuit, G. W. Alexander, A. M. Goodykooutz. Jeffersonville Circuit, W. H. Rogers. Marion Circuit, R. Gannaway. Grayson, G. W. Baker. Jefferson Circuit, H. Tartar. Tug Fork Mission, to be supplied.

ABINGDON DISTRICT—*Samuel Patton, P. E.* Abingdon Circuit, J. M. Kelly, J. D. Gibson. Lebanon, G. F. Page. Blountville, H. Johnson. Jonesborough, R. W. Patty, S. A. Miller. Elizabethton, T. K. Harmon. Estelville Circuit and Guess' River Mission, W. Gilmore ; one to be supplied.

C. Collins, President of Emory and Henry College. E. F. Sevier and T. Sullens, Agents.

GREENVILLE DISTRICT—*T. K. Catlett, P. E.* Green Circuit, R. Rengau; J. Atkins. Rogersville, J. S. Weaver. New Market, D. B. Carter. Dandridge, W. S. Manson. Newport, F M. Fanning. Jonesville, L. Wilson. Clinch River Mission, to be supplied.

A. H. Mathes, President Holston College. C. D. Smith, R. M. Stevens, Agents.

KNOXVILLE DISTRICT—*C. Fulton, P. E.* Knoxville Circuit, J. Baringer, J. M. Crismond. Maryville, W. C. Graves. Sevierville, W. Hickey. Tazewell, W. C. Reynolds. Clinton, A. B. Broyles. Buffalo Mission, W. L. Turner.

George Horne, Agent for Preachers' Aid Society.

WASHINGTON DISTRICT—*J. Cumming, P. E.* Athens Circuit, A. N. Harris, John Bowman, sup. Madisonville, Ira Falls. Philadelphia, C. Campbell. Kingston, J. Gaston. Washington, W. Bower. Pikeville, J. C. Derrick. Jasper Circuit and Dade Mission, T. Witten ; one to be supplied.

NEWTOWN DISTRICT—*J. B. Daughtry, P. E.* Cleveland Circuit, M. Martin ; one to be supplied. Lafayette, W. Hicks, D. White. Springplace, C. K. Lewis. Ellija Mission, J. McDaniel. Blairsville, R. G. Ketron, C. Stump.

ASHEVILLE DISTRICT—*D. R. M'Anally, P. E.* Asheville

Circuit, W. M. Rush. Franklin, D. Payne. Greenville Circuit and Pickens Mission, D. Ring, B. F. Wells. Reems Creek, E. K. Hutsell. Waynesville, A. Pickens.

SEVENTEENTH SESSION.

Held at Lafayette, Ga., Nov. 11, 1840—Bishop Morris, President; E. F. Sevier, Secretary.

Numbers in Society—Whites, 26,206 ; colored, 2,420.
Traveling Preachers, 72.

ADMITTED ON TRIAL—T. K. Munsey, E. E. Wiley, A. C. Mitchell, Alexander Haren.

ADMITTED INTO FULL CONNECTION—Jesse Childers, W. H. Hickey, Jesse C. Derrick, Benjamin F. Wells, Charles Collins, Thomas Witten.

LOCATED — W. C. Graves, W. Bower, J. McDaniel, A. Brooks.

STATIONS OF THE PREACHERS.

WYTHEVILLE DISTRICT—*T. K. Catlett, P. E.* Wytheville Circuit, C. D. Smith, J. Atkins. Parisburg, John M. Crismond. Jeffersonville, W. H. Rogers. Marion, R. Gannaway. Grayson, Jesse Childers. Jefferson, D. Payne. Tug Fork Mission, to be supplied.

ABINGDON DISTRICT—*S. Patton, P. E.* Abingdon Circuit, J. S. Weaver, Thomas Wilkerson, sup. Lebanon, O. F. Cunningham, Blountville, G. Ekin. Jonesborough, W. Gilmore, John D. Gibson. Elizabethton, W. L. Turner. Estelville, T. K. Harmon: Guess' River Mission, to be supplied.

Emory and Henry College, Charles Collins and E. E. Wiley, Professors. T. Sullens, E. F. Sevier and J. Grant, Agents.

GREENVILLE DISTRICT—*D. Fleming, P. E.* Green Circuit, G. F. Page ; one to be supplied. Rogersville, W. B. Winton,

T. K. Munsey. New Market, W. S. Manson. Dandridge, D. B. Carter. Newport, George W. Alexander. Jonesville, John Gaston. Clinch River Mission, Hiram Tartar.

Holston Seminary, A. H. Mathes, Principal. Rufus M. Stevens, Agent.

KNOXVILLE DISTRICT—*Creed Fulton, P. E.* Knoxville Station, John M. Kelly. Knoxville Circuit, E. K. Hutsell. Maryville, A. N. Harris. Sevierville, J. Cumming. Tazewell, W. B. Murphy. Clinton, George W. Baker. Buffalo Mission, J. C. Derrick ; one to be supplied.

George Horne, Agent for Preachers' Aid Society.

ATHENS DISTRICT—*T. Stringfield, P. E.* Athens Circuit, R. W. Patty, A. C. Mitchell. Madisonville, Ira Falls. Philadelphia, C. Campbell. Kingston, W. M. Rush, J. Bowman, sup. Washington, L. Wilson. Pikeville, A. B. Broyles. Jasper, A. M. Goodykoontz. Dade Mission, D. White.

LAFAYETTE DISTRICT—*J. B. Daughtry, P. E.* Cleveland, W. Hicks. Lafayette, R. Reneau, T. Witten. Springplace, W. H. Hickey. Ellija Mission, J. B. Corn. Blairsville Mission, S. A. Miller. Murphy Mission, R. G. Ketron.

ASHEVILLE DISTRICT—*D. R. M'Anally, P. E.* Asheville Circuit, F. M. Fanning. Franklin, Andrew Pickens. Reems Creek, C. Stump. Waynesville, B. F. Wells. Greenville, to be supplied. Pickens Mission, A. Haren. Luftah Mission, D. Ring.

EIGHTEENTH SESSION.

Held at Rogersville, Tenn., October 6, 1841—S. Patton, President ; E. F. Sevier, Secretary.

Numbers in Society—Whites, 27,950 ; colored, 2,832 ; Indians, 80.

Traveling Preachers,

ADMITTED ON TRIAL—W. T. Harlow, R. Steele, J. L. Fowler, M. Southard, W. T. Jones. W. C. Graves, re-admitted.

ADMITTED INTO FULL CONNECTION—J. D. Gibson, D. White, J. Atkins, R. G. Ketron, A. M. Goodykoontz, A. H. Mathes.

LOCATED—J. Gaston, W. M. Rush, J. C. Derrick, A. Pickens, W. Gilmore, J. Grant.

STATIONS OF THE PREACHERS.

WYTHEVILLE DISTRICT—*T. K. Callett, P. E.* Wytheville, J. Atkins, C. Campbell. Parisburg, A. N. Harris. Tazewell, R. Gannaway. Marion, J. M. Crismond. Grayson, A. B. Broyles. Jefferson, C. Stump. Sandy River Mission, to be supplied.

ABINGDON DISTRICT—*S. Patton, P. E.* Abingdon Station, J. M. Kelly. Abingdon Circuit, W. B. Winton. Lebanon, to be supplied. Blountville, G. Ekin ; one to be supplied. Jonesborough, C. D. Smith, W. Hicks. Elizabethton, to be supplied. Estelville, D. Payne. Guess' River Mission, R. G. Ketron.

Emory and Henry College, C. Collins. President ; E. E. Wiley and W. T. Harlow, Professors ; J. D. Gibson, Agent.

GREENVILLE DISTRICT—*D. Fleming, P. E.* Green, G. F. Page. Rogersville, O. F. Cunningham, T. Witten. New Market, W. S. Manson: Dandridge, W. H. Rogers. Newport, W. L. Turner. Jonesville, R. Steele. Clinch River Mission, to be supplied.

Holston Seminary, A. H. Mathes, President ; D. B. Carter, Agent.

KNOXVILLE DISTRICT—*C. Fulton, P. E.* Knoxville Station, T. Sullens. Knoxville Circuit, R. M. Stevens. Maryville, T. K. Harmon, J. Bowman, sup. Sevierville, W. B. Murphy. Claiborne, E. K. Hutsell. Clinton, J. L. Fowler. Buffalo Mission, to be supplied.

George Horne, Agent for Preachers' Aid Society.

ATHENS DISTRICT—*T. Stringfield, P. E.* Athens, R. W.

Patty. Madisonville, W. C. Graves. Philadelphia, B. F.
Wells. Kingston, Ira Falls. Washington Circuit and Dade
Mission, G. W. Alexander, H. Tartar. Pikeville and Jasper,
G. W. Baker, A. C. Mitchell.

LAFAYETTE DISTRICT—*J. B. Daughtry, P. E.* Cleveland,
L. Wilson, C. K. Lewis. Lafayette, R. Reneau, M. Southard.
Springplace, W. H. Hickey. Ellija, W. T. Jones. Blairsville
Mission, A. Haren. Murphy Mission, A. M. Goodykoontz.
Benton Mission, J. B. Corn.

ASHEVILLE DISTRICT—*E. F. Sevier, P. E.* Asheville, D.
R. M'Anally. Franklin, J. Childress. Burnsville, J. S.
Weaver. Waynesville, D. White. Greenville and Pickens,
S. A. Miller, T. K. Munsey. Hendersonville, F. M. Fanning.
Echota, D. Ring ; one to be supplied.

NINETEENTH SESSION.

Held at Knoxville, Tenn., Oct. 5, 1842—Bishop Waugh, President ; E. F. Sevier, Secretary.

Numbers in Society—Whites, 35,466 ; colored, 3,805.
Traveling Preachers, 65.

ADMITTED ON TRIAL—Robert H. Palmer, A. W. Howard,
J. S. Burnett. Re-admitted, A. N. Ross.

ADMITTED INTO FULL CONNECTION—T. K. Munsey, A. C.
Mitchell, A. Haren.

LOCATED—C. K. Lewis, D. White, D. B. Carter, F. M.
Fanning, George W. Baker.

STATIONS OF THE PREACHERS.

WYTHEVILLE DISTRICT—*T. K. Catlett, P. E.* Wytheville,
J. M. Crismond ; one to be supplied. Parisburg, C. Campbell.
Tazewell, George Ekin. Marion, A. N. Harris. Grayson,
C. Stump. Jefferson, to be supplied. Lebanon, to be supplied.

ABINGDON DISTRICT—*S. Patton, P. E.* Abingdon Station, James Atkins. Abingdon Circuit, W. B. Winton. Estelville, to be supplied. Blountville, O. F. Cunningham, A. W. Howard. Jonesborough, J. M. Kelly, R. H. Palmer. Elizabethton, D. Payne. Jonesville and Guess' River Mission, W. L. Turner, H. Tartar.

Emory and Henry College, C. Collins, President; E. E. Wiley, Professor ; C. D. Smith, Agent.

GREENVILLE DISTRICT—*D. Fleming, P. E.* Green, John D. Gibson, R. Gannaway. Rogersville, G. F. Page. Clinch, to be supplied. Claiborne, R. Steele. New Market, W. Hicks. Dandridge, W. H. Rogers. Sevierville, to be supplied. Newport, E. K. Hutsell.

Holston College, A. H. Mathes, President; George Horne, Agent.

KNOXVILLE DISTRICT—*Creed Fulton, P. E.* Knoxville, T. Sullens. Knox, R. M. Stevens. Maryville, L. Wilson. Madisonville, W. C. Graves. Athens, J. B. Daughtry, A. Haren. Clinton, R. W. Patty. Buffalo Mission, to be supplied. Philadelphia, B. F. Wells. Kingston, I. Falls, T. Witten.

Knoxville Female Academy, J. E. Douglas.

LAFAYETTE DISTRICT—*T. Stringfield, P. E.* Cleveland, R. Reneau. Lafayette, W. H. Hickey ; one to be supplied. Benton, A. M. Goodykoontz. Murphy, J. Childers. Springplace, A. N. Ross. Ellija, M. Southard. Pikeville, George W. Alexander, J. S. Burnett. Washington, T. K. Munsey, A. C. Mitchell.

ASHEVILLE DISTRICT—*E. F. Sevier, P. E.* Asheville, J. S. Weaver. Waynesville, R. G. Ketron. Franklin, to be supplied. Greenville, to be supplied. Pickens, A. B. Broyles. Hendersonville, D. R. M'Anally. Burnsville, S. A. Miller. Echota Indian Mission, D. Ring.

W. T. Harlow, transferred to Providence Conference.

J. B. Corn, transferred to North Carolina Conference.

TWENTIETH SESSION.

Held at Abingdon, Va., Oct. 4, 1843 — Bishop Morris, President; E. F. Sevier, Secretary.

Numbers in Society — Whites, 36,252 ; colored, 4,001 ; Indians, 169.

Traveling Preachers, 73.

ADMITTED ON TRIAL—C. W. Charlton, E. W. Dunbar, W. C. Daily, Aaron Shell, J. R. Bellamy, A. Williams, A. Gass, W. G. E. Cunnyngham, James M. Marshall, S. H. Cooper, D. Crenshaw, J. C. Pendergrast, Milton Rowley.

ADMITTED INTO FULL CONNECTION—E. E. Wiley.

LOCATED—A. C. Mitchell, George Horne, John S. Weaver, T. K. Harmon.

STATIONS OF THE PREACHERS.

WYTHEVILLE DISTRICT—*T. K. Catlett, P. E.* Wytheville Circuit, W. Hicks, C. W. Charlton. Newbern, W. C. Daily. Parisburg, C. Campbell. Princeton, to be supplied. Marion, J. Haskew. Grayson, D. Ring. Jefferson, C. Stump.

ABINGDON DISTRICT—*D. Fleming, P. E.* Abingdon, G. W. Alexander. Abingdon Circuit, J. M. Crismond. Tazewell, to be supplied. Lebanon, D. Payne. Estelville, W. G. E. Cunnyngham. Guess' River Mission, E. W. Dunbar. Taylorsville, A. Shell. Blountville, R. Gannaway.

ROGERSVILLE DISTRICT—*Samuel Patton, P. E.* Kingsport, to be supplied. Rogersville, G. Ekin. New Market, I. Falls. Rutledge, A. W. Howard. Claiborne, W. L. Turner. Jonesville, to be supplied. Clinch Mission, J. C. Pendergrast.

GREENVILLE DISTRICT—*C. Fulton, P. E.* Elizabethton, A. N. Harris. Jonesborough, W. B. Winton. Rheatown, to be supplied. Green, G. F. Page. Newport, R. G. Ketron. Dandridge, E. K. Hutsell.

KNOXVILLE DISTRICT—*Thomas Stringfield, P. E.* Knoxville, J. Atkins. Knoxville Circuit, L. Wilson. Jacksborough, J. M. Marshall. Clinton, J. Baringer. Buffalo Mission, to be supplied. Kingston, W. C. Graves. Maryville, R. M. Stevens. Sevierville, A. Gass.

ATHENS DISTRICT—*O. F. Cunningham, P. E.* Athens Station, J. M. Kelly. Athens Circuit, J. B. Daughtry, T. Witten. Decatur, S. H. Cooper. Jasper, M. Southard. Pikeville, S. A. Miller. Washington, A. Williams. Philadelphia, to be supplied. Tellico, to be supplied. Madisonville, D. B. Carter.

LAFAYETTE DISTRICT— *T. Sullens, P. E.* Cleveland, R. Reneau. Lafayette, W. H. Hickey. Benton, A. Haren. Murphy, H. Tartar. Blairsville, to be supplied. Ellija, to be supplied. Springplace, D. Crenshaw. Summerville, A. N. Ross. Chattanooga, T. K. Munsey. Newtown, to be supplied.

ASHEVILLE DISTRICT—*E. F. Sevier, P. E.* Asheville, M. Rowley. Hendersonville, A. B. Broyles. Waynesville, J. R. Bellamy; one to be supplied. Franklin, B. F. Wells. Pickens, J. S. Burnett. Greenville, F. M. Fanning. Burnsville, A. M. Goodykoontz.

Emory and Henry College, Charles Collins, President; E. E. Wiley, Professor; C. D. Smith, Agent.

Holston College, A. H. Mathes, President; W. H. Rogers, Agent.

East Tennessee Female Institute, D. R. M'Anally, President.

Joseph E. Douglas, transferred to Tennessee Conference.

TWENTY-FIRST SESSION

Held at Reems Creek, N. C., October 9, 1844 — Bishop Janes, President; E. F. Sevier, Secretary.

Numbers in Society—[Not answered in the Minutes.]
Traveling Preachers, 77.

ADMITTED ON TRIAL—A. F. Cox, J. S. Edwards, E. W. Chanceaulme, Samuel Lotspiech, J. G. Swisher, W. Robeson, A. F. Shannon, Benjamin Morgan, William Sturges, W. Ingle, W. R. Long, S. D. Adams, Martin C. Robinson, John W. Thompson, A. D. Shields.

ADMITTED INTO FULL CONNECTION—A. W. Howard, J. S. Burnett, M. Southard.

LOCATED—R. G. Ketron, T. Witten, A. Haren, W. L. Turner, B. F. Wells, C. Stump, D. Ring.

STATIONS OF THE PREACHERS.

WYTHEVILLE DISTRICT—*W. Hicks, P. E.* Wytheville, C. D. Smith ; one to be supplied. Newbern, R. Gannaway. Parisburg, W. C. Daily ; one to be supplied. Princeton, B. Morgan. Tazewell, C. Campbell. Marion, J. M. Crismond. Grayson, C. W. Charlton. Jefferson, A. Shell.

ABINGDON DISTRICT—*D. Fleming, P. E.* Abingdon, Samuel Patton. Abingdon Circuit, J. Haskew. Lebanon, W. Ingle. Estelville, S. H. Cooper. Guess' River Mission, to be supplied. Blountville, W. H. Rogers ; one to be supplied. Jonesborough, G. W. Alexander, A. N. Harris, sup. Elizabethton Circuit and Johnson Mission, E. W. Chanceaulme, W. R. Long.

Emory and Henry College, C. Collins, President ; E. E. Wiley, Professor ; T. K. Catlett, Agent.

ROGERSVILLE DISTRICT—*Creed Fulton, P. E.* Kingsport, A. M. Goodykoontz. Rogersville, A. W. Howard, H. Johnson, sup. Clinch Mission, W. Sturges. Jonesville, J. C. Pendergrast. Rutledge, A. Gass. New Market, L. Wilson. Greenville, R. W. Patty, sup. ; one to be supplied. Rheatown, M. Southard ; one to be supplied.

Holston College, A. H. Mathes, President ; T. Stringfield, Agent.

KNOXVILLE DISTRICT—*T. Sullens, P. E.* Knoxville, James

Atkins. Knox Circuit, John Baringer. Maryville, George Ekin. Little River, W. Robeson. Dandridge, David Adams. Claiborne, S. Pope. Clinton, M. C. Robinson. Jacksborough, to be supplied. Strait Fork Mission, to be supplied.

East Tennessee Female Institute, D. R. M'Anally, President.

CUMBERLAND MISSION DISTRICT — *R. M. Stevens, P. E.* Washington, Samuel A. Miller. Jasper, J. L. Sensibaugh. Pikeville, J. M. Kelly. Sulphur Springs, to be supplied. Kingston, W. C. Graves. Montgomery Mission, H. Tartar. Jamestown Mission, to be supplied. Roane, J. G. Swisher.

ATHENS DISTRICT — *O. F. Cunningham, P. E.* Athens Station, T. K. Munsey. Athens Circuit, A. Williams. Tellico Mission, E. D. Shields. Madisonville, D. B. Carter. Philadelphia, A. B. Broyles. Decatur, J. W. Thompson. Chattanooga, W. G. E. Cunnyngham. Cleveland, S. W. Earnest, A. F. Cox. Benton, J. S. Edwards.

ASHEVILLE DISTRICT — *E. F. Sevier, P. E.* Asheville Circuit, J. S. Burnett. Burnsville, E. K. Hutsell, sup., S. D. Adams. Hendersonville, J. R. Bellamy. Waynesville and Echota Mission, A. F. Shannon; one to be supplied. Franklin, F. M. Fanning. Sevierville, Samuel Lotspiech. Newport, G. F. Page.

D. Payne, transferred to Texas Conference.

R. Reneau, transferred to Georgia Conference.

TWENTY-SECOND SESSION.

Held at Athens, Tenn., October 8, 1845 — Bishop Andrew, President; C. D. Smith, Secretary.

Numbers in Society — Whites, 34,446; colored, 3,975; Indians, 155.

Traveling Preachers, —.

ADMITTED ON TRIAL — George K. Snapp, William D. Snapp,

R. M. Hickey, John Alley, Robert A. Young, Carroll Long,
J. B. Lawson, R. M. Whaley, Robert W. Pickens, John H.
H. Young, J. W. Miller, W. Milburn.

ADMITTED INTO FULL CONNECTION—C. W. Charlton, W. C.
Daily, James R. Bellamy, A. Williams, A. Gass, W. G. E.
Cunnyngham, S. H. Cooper, J. C. Pendergrast.

LOCATED—H. Johnson, G. F. Page, A. N. Harris, S. Pope.

STATIONS OF THE PREACHERS.

WYTHEVILLE DISTRICT—*W. Hicks, P. E.* Wytheville Circuit,
D. Fleming, R. M. Whaley. Newbern, John M. Kelly.
Parisburg, J. Crismond, J. H. H. Young. Tazewell, C.
Campbell, R. M. Hickey. Marion, Miles Foy, J. B. Lawson.
Grayson, A. Williams. Jefferson, A. Shell.

ABINGDON DISTRICT—*E. F. Sevier, P. E.* Abingdon Station, J. S. Burnett. Abingdon Circuit, George Ekin. Lebanon, S. H. Cooper. Estelville, A. F. Shannon. Guess'
River Mission, W. Sturges. Blountville Circuit, J. D. Gibson.
Jonesborough, F. M. Fanning, A. C. Hunter. Elizabethton
and Johnson Mission, G. K. Snapp, R. W. Pickens.

Emory and Henry College, C. Collins, President; E. E.
Wiley, Professor ; T. K. Catlett, Agent.

ROGERSVILLE DISTRICT—*O. F. Cunningham, P. E.* Kings-
port Circuit, W. Milburn. Rogersville, R. W. Patty. Clinch
River Mission, S. A. Miller. Jonesville Circuit, W. Ingle.
Rutledge, M. Southard. New Market, D. Adams. Green-
ville, T. K. Munsey, C. Long. Rheatown, G. W. Alexander,
W. D. Snapp.

Holston College, A. H. Mathes, President ; T. Stringfield,
Agent.

KNOXVILLE DISTRICT—*T. Sullens, P. E.* Knoxville Station,
Samuel Patton. Knoxville Circuit, J. Baringer. Maryville,
S. B. Harwell. Little River, Andrew Gass. Dandridge, R.

A. Young. Clinton, A. M. Goodykoontz. Claiborne, J. C. Pendergrast, J. Alley. Jacksborough and Strait Fork Mission, M. C. Robinson, J. L. Fowler.

East Tennessee Female Institute, D. R. M'Anally, President.

CUMBERLAND DISTRICT—*R. M. Stevens, P. E.* Washington Circuit, J. G. Swisher. Jasper, J. R. Bellamy. Pikeville, Wm. Robeson. Sulphur Springs Mission, W. R. Long. Kingston Circuit, W. G. E. Cunnyngham. Montgomery and Jamestown Mission, J. L. Sensibaugh. Roane, H. Tartar.

ATHENS DISTRICT—*J. Atkins, P. E.* Athens Station, C. D. Smith. Athens Circuit, D. B. Carter, J. W. Miller. Madisonville and Tellico, A. F. Cox ; one to be supplied. Philadelphia Circuit, W. C. Graves. Chattanooga, Wm. C. Daily. Cleveland, S. W. Earnest. Benton, J. Gaston.

ASHEVILLE DISTRICT—*J. Haskew, P. E.* Burnsville Circuit, B. F. Wells, C. Godby. Asheville, C. W. Charlton, E. W. Chanceaulme. Hendersonville, U. Keener. Waynesville and Echota Mission, A. B. Broyles, J. W. Thompson. Franklin Circuit, R. Gannaway. Newport, S. D. Adams. Sevierville, J. S. Edwards.

W. H. Rogers, Sunday School Agent.

C. Fulton, left without an appointment.

A. W. Howard, left without an appointment.

TWENTY-THIRD SESSION.

Held at Wytheville, Va., October, 21, 1846—Bishop Capers, President; C. D. Smith, Secretary.

Numbers in Society—Whites, 38,932 ; colored, 4,083 ; Indians, 108.

Traveling Preachers, 94.

ADMITTED ON TRIAL—W. M. Kerr, W. Jones, L. W. Crouch, R. D. Wells, W. H. Bates, J. A. Ragan, James N. S. Huffaker, W. W. Neal, W. T. Dowell.

Admitted into Full Connection—A. F. Cox, J. G. Swisher, Wm. Robeson, M. C. Robinson, W. R. Long, John W. Thompson, A. F. Shannon, S. D. Adams, James S. Edwards, W. Ingle, W. Sturges, A. Shell.

Located—Benjamin F. Wells, J. Gaston, John D. Gibson.

STATIONS OF THE PREACHERS.

Wytheville District—*Wm. Hicks, P. E.* Wytheville, T. K. Munsey. Newbern, J. W. Miller. Parisburg, W. Robeson, E. W. Chanceaulme. Tazewell, S. A. Miller, J. A. Ragan. Marion, T. K. Catlett. Grayson, J. M. Crismond. Jefferson, R. M. Whaley. New River Mission, J. B. Lawson.

Abingdon District—*E. F. Sevier, P. E.* Abingdon Station, T. Sullens. Abingdon Circuit, J. S. Burnett, R. D. Wells. Lebanon, W. Ingle. Blountville, G. Ekin, A. C. Hunter. Jonesborough, F. M. Fanning, J. N. S. Huffaker. Elizabethton, S. H. Cooper. Estelville and Guess' River Mission, George K. Snapp, A. Shell. Johnson Mission, A. B. Broyles.

Emory and Henry College, C. Collins, President; E. E. Wiley, Professor ; C. Fulton, Agent.

Rogersville District—*O. F. Cunnyngham, P. E.* Kingsport, W. Milburn. Jonesville, C. Long. Rogersville, C. D. Smith ; one to be supplied. New Market, D. Adams, John Alley. Greenville, G. W. Alexander ; one to be supplied. Rheatown, C. Campbell, W. Jones. Clinch Mission, J. L. Sensibaugh, H. Tartar.

Holston College, A. H. Mathes.

Knoxville District—*R. M. Stevens, P. E.* Knoxville Station, Miles Foy. Knoxville Circuit, Charles W. Charlton, R. M. Hickey. Maryville, S. B. Harwell. Little River, A. F. Cox. Dandridge, J. C. Pendergrast. Clinton, A. Williams. Claiborne, John Baringer, W. D. Snapp. Jacksborough, R. W. Patty. Strait Fork Mission, John H. H. Young.

~ East Tennessee Female Institute, D. R. M'Anally, President.

Thomas Stringfield, Agent for American Bible Society.

W. H. Rogers, Agent of the Conference for the promotion of Sunday Schools.

S. Patton, Editor of the Methodist Episcopalian.

CUMBERLAND DISTRICT—*D. Fleming*, *P. E.* Kingston, J. R. Bellamy. Washington, J. G. Swisher. Pikeville, A. M. Goodykoontz. Jasper, M. C. Robinson. Spencer Mission, W. Sturges. Cumberland Mission, J. S. Edwards. Montgomery Mission, W. R. Long. Roane Mission, J. L. Fowler.

ATHENS DISTRICT—*James Atkins*, *P. E.* Athens Station, W. G. E. Cunnyngham. Athens Circuit, L. Wilson, W. T. Dowell. Philadelphia, W. C. Graves, L. W. Crouch. Chattanooga, W. C. Daily. Cleveland, J. M. Kelly, W. W. Neal. Benton Mission, S. W. Earnest. Madison and Tellico Mission, A. F. Shannon, W. H. Bates.

ASHEVILLE DISTRICT—*Joseph Haskew*, *P. E.* Burnsville, M. Southard. Catawba, C. Godby. Henderson, U. Keener. Asheville, S. D. Adams, W. M. Kerr. Franklin, R. Gannaway. Newport, D. B. Carter. Sevierville, A. Gass. Waynesville and Echota Mission, John W. Thompson, R. W. Pickens.

TWENTY-FOURTH SESSION.

Held at Jonesborough, Tenn., Oct. 20, 1847 — Bishop Andrew, President; C. D. Smith, Secretary.

Numbers in Society — Whites, 34,678 ; colored, 3,957 ; Indians, 132.

Traveling Preachers, 96.

ADMITTED ON TRIAL—J. H. Bruner, J. M. McTeer, J. T. Smith, J. H. Peck, George W. Renfro, C. W. Bewley, S. D. Gaines, R. A. Claughton, E. E. Gillenwaters.

ADMITTED INTO FULL CONNECTION—George K. Snapp, W. D. Snapp, R. M. Hickey, John Alley, C. Long, A. C. Hunter, E. W. Chanceaulme, W. Milburn, J. B. Lawson, R. M. Whaley, R. W. Pickens, J. W. Miller, C. Godby.

LOCATED—M. Southard, S. A. Miller, A. B. Broyles, J. L. Seusibaugh.

STATIONS OF THE PREACHERS.

WYTHEVILLE DISTRICT—*William Hicks, P. E.* Wytheville Circuit, T. K. Catlett. Newbern, W. C. Daily. Parisburg, J. W. Miller, W. Jones. Tazewell and Sandy Mission, E. W. Chanceaulme. Princeton Circuit and New River, W. Sturges, R. A. Claughton. Marion, R. Gannaway, George K. Snapp. Grayson, J. M. Crismond. Jefferson, J. B. Lawson.

ABINGDON DISTRICT—*E. F. Sevier, P. E.* Abingdon Station, T. Sullens. Abingdon Circuit, P. Anderson, J. H. Bruner. Lebanon, W. Ingle. Blountville, M. Foy, J. N. S. Huffaker. Jonesborough Station, J. S. Burnett. Jonesborough Circuit, D. B. Carter, J. M. McTeer. Estelville and Guess' River Mission, S. D. Gaines; one to be supplied. Elizabethton and Johnson, W. Milburn; one to be supplied.

Emory and Henry College, C. Collins, President; E. E. Wiley, Professor.

ROGERSVILLE DISTRICT—*C. D. Smith, P. E.* Kingsport, J. M. Kelly. Jonesville, J. R. Bellamy. Rogersville, F. M. Fanning. Claiborne, A. M. Goodykoontz, G. W. Renfro. Greenville, C. Campbell. Rheatown, G. Ekin, A. Shell. Clinch Mission, W. T. Dowell, H. Tartar.

Holston College, C. Fulton, President and Agent.

KNOXVILLE DISTRICT—*R. M. Stevens, P. E.* Knoxville, W. G. E. Cunnyngham. Knoxville Circuit, D. Adams, J. Thompson. Maryville, R. W. Patty, E. E. Gillenwaters. Little River, R. D. Wells. Dandridge, C. W. Charlton.

New Market, C. W. Bewley, W. W. Neal. Clinton, J. G. Swisher. Jacksborough and Strait Fork Mission, A. F. Cox, J. Smith.

East Tennessee Female Institute, D. R. M'Anally, President. Methodist Episcopalian, S. Patton, Editor.

CUMBERLAND DISTRICT—*D. Fleming, P. E.* Kingston, J. C. Pendergrast. Washington, R. M. Hickey. Pikeville, J. S. Edwards. Jasper, J. Alley. Spencer Mission, W. R. Long. Cumberland, C. Long. Montgomery, C. Godby. Jamestown, R. W. Pickens.

ATHENS DISTRICT—*J. Atkins, P. E.* Athens Station, G. W. Alexander. Athens Circuit, A. F. Shannon. Philadelphia, S. B. Harwell. Decatur, L. Wilson. Chattanooga, W. D. Snapp. Cleveland, W. Robeson, J. H. Peck. Benton, L. W. Crouch. Ocoee Mission, S. W. Earnest. Madisonville Circuit and Tellico Mission, S. H. Cooper, J. A. Ragan.

ASHEVILLE DISTRICT—*J. Haskew, P. E.* Asheville Circuit, M. C. Robinson, R. M. Whaley. Burnsville, A. C. Hunter. Catawba, A. Williams. Hendersonville, W. M. Kerr. Franklin, J. Baringer. Newport, A. Gass. Sevierville, W. H. Bates. Waynesville Circuit and Echota Mission, U. Keener; one to be supplied.

A. H. Mathes, transferred to Missouri Conference.

T. Stringfield, Agent for American Bible Society.

W. H. Rogers, Sunday School Agent.

S. D. Adams, left without an appointment, on account of health.

TWENTY-FIFTH SESSION.

Held at Knoxville, Tenn., October 11, 1848 — Bishop Payne, President; C. D. Smith, Secretary.

Numbers in Society — Whites, 35,456; colored, 3,817; Indians, 150.

Traveling Preachers, 94.

ADMITTED ON TRIAL—A. G. Worley, H. Wilson, W. H. Kelly, J. H. Hogue.

ADMITTED INTO FULL CONNECTION—J. N. S. Huffaker, J. A. Ragan, W. F. Dowell, W. M. Kerr, W. W. Neal, W. H. Bates, L. W. Crouch, R. D. Wells.

LOCATED—S. W. Earnest, J. B. Daughtry, J. B. Lawson.

STATIONS OF THE PREACHERS.

WYTHEVILLE DISTRICT—*W. B. Winton, P. E.* Wytheville Circuit, W. Robeson, A. G. Worley. Newbern, P. Anderson. Parisburg, W. W. Neal, J. W. Miller, sup. Jeffersonville, R. A. Claughton. Princeton Circuit and New River Mission, W. H. Kelly ; one to be supplied. Marion, George Ekin, J. T. Smith. Grayson, L. C. Waters. Jefferson, J. H. Hogue. Hillsville, W. Sturges. Sandy Mission, to be supplied.

ABINGDON DISTRICT—*T. K. Catlett, P. E.* Abingdon Station, L. Wilson. Abingdon Circuit, W. Hicks, J. H. Peck. Lebanon, J. M. Crismond. Blountville, W. Ingle, E. E. Gillenwaters. Jonesborough Station, W. M. Kerr. Jonesborough Circuit, M. Foy, G. K. Snapp, sup. Estelville, J. Y. Crawford. Elizabethton Circuit and Johnson Mission, W. Milburn, A. Shell. Guess' River Mission, H. Tartar.

Emory and Henry College, C. Collins, President; E. E. Wiley, Professor.

ROGERSVILLE DISTRICT—*C. D. Smith, P. E.* Greenville and Rogersville Station, J. M. Kelly. Kingsport, D. B. Carter. Jonesville, to be supplied. Rogersville Circuit, F. M. Fanning. Tazewell, W. G. E. Cunnyngham. Powell's Valley, J. M. McTeer. Greenville, C. Campbell. Rheatown, W. C. Daily. Clinch Mission, W. R. Long.

KNOXVILLE DISTRICT—*R. M. Stevens, P. E.* Knoxville

Station, E. F. Sevier. Knoxville Circuit, R. W. Patty, J. N. S. Huffaker. Maryville, T. K. Munsey. Little River, W. H. Bates, J. Cumming, sup. Dandridge, R. M. Whaley. New. Market, C. W. Charlton. Clinton, J. G. Swisher. Jacksborough Circuit and Strait Fork Mission, J. R. Bellamy.

East Tennessee Female Institute, D. R. McAnally, President.

Methodist Episcopalian, S. Patton, Editor.

Strawberry Plains High School, C. Fulton, Superintendent.

Knoxville and Muddy Creek Colored Mission, J. Baringer.

CUMBERLAND DISTRICT—*D. Fleming, P. E.* Kingston, C. Long. Washington, J. W. Thompson. Pikeville, M. C. Robinson. Jasper, C. Godby. Spencer Mission, J. S. Edwards. Cumberland Mission, R. W. Pickens. Montgomery Mission, W. T. Dowell. Jamestown, to be supplied.

ATHENS DISTRICT—*J. Atkins, P. E.* Athens, R. M. Hickey, J. H. Bruner. Philadelphia, S. B. Harwell. Decatur, A. F. Shannon. Chattanooga and Hiwassee Mission, J. C. Pendergrast; one to be supplied. Cleveland, G. W. Alexander, H. Wilson. Benton Circuit and Ocoee Mission, L. W. Crouch. Madisonville Circuit and Tellico Mission, W. H. Rogers, George W. Renfro.

ASHEVILLE DISTRICT—*J. Haskew, P. E.* Asheville Station, J. S. Burnett. Asheville Circuit, A. Williams. Burnsville, W. Jones. Hendersonville, A. M. Goodykoontz. Catawba, A. F. Cox. Franklin, J. A. Ragan. Newport, A. Gass. Sevierville, A. C. Hunter. Waynesville Circuit and Echota Mission, U. Keener; one to be supplied.

T. Stringfield, Agent for American Bible Society.

T. Sullens, W. D. Snapp, R. D. Wells, left without appointments, on account of ill health.

E. W. Chanceaulme, left without an appointment.

S. H. Cooper, transferred to Georgia Conference.

TWENTY-SIXTH SESSION

*Held at Cleveland, Tenn., Oct. 11, 1849—Bishop Andrew, Pres.;
E. F. Sevier and W. G. E. Cunnyngham, Secretaries.*

Numbers in Society—Whites, 35,057; colored, 3,525;
Indians, 158.

Traveling Preachers, 95.

ADMITTED ON TRIAL—E. H. King, N. C. Edmonson, W. F.
Parker, John C. Hyden, J. M. Varnell, W. W. Hargraves,
R. M. Moore, W. J. Witcher, R. A. Giddens.

ADMITTED INTO FULL CONNECTION—John H. Bruner, J. M.
McTéer, J. T. Smith, R. A. Claughton, G. W. Renfro, E. E.
Gillenwaters, W. Jones.

LOCATED—W. Sturges, J. W. Thompson, J. S. Burnett, A.
Gass, John Alley, W. D. Snapp.

STATIONS OF THE PREACHERS

WYTHEVILLE DISTRICT—*W. B. Winton, P. E.* Wythe-
ville Circuit, C. Long, E. H. King. Newbern, E. W. Chan-
ceaulme. Parisburg, A. Williams. Princeton Mission, L. C.
Waters. New River Mission, H. Tartar. Hillsville, W. H.
Kelly. Grayson, A. M. Goodykoontz. Jefferson, R. A.
Claughton.

ABINGDON DISTRICT—*T. K. Catlett, P. E.* Abingdon Sta-
tion, W. G. E. Cunnyngham. Abingdon Circuit, G. W.
Alexander. Lebanon, J. S. Edwards. Jeffersonville, J. M.
Crismond. Johnson and Watauga Mission, to be supplied.
Estelville, R. W. Pickens. Guess' River Mission, W. Jones.
Blountville, W. Milburn, George Ekin. Marion, J. H. Bruner.

Emory and Henry College, Charles Collins, President; E.
E. Wiley, Professor.

GREENVILLE DISTRICT—*C. D. Smith, P. E.* Greenville

Circuit, M. Foy. Jonesborough, W. Robeson. Jonesborough Circuit, C. Campbell, R. M. Moore. Elizabethton, W. T. Dowell. Rheatown, D. R. Carter, George K. Snapp. New Market, R. M. Whaley. Newport, A. F. Cox.

Holston College, P. Anderson, President.

Strawberry Plains High School, C. Fulton, President.

ROGERSVILLE DISTRICT—*J. Haskew, P. E.* Rogersville, W. Ingle. Kingsport, W. W. Neal. Jonesville, J. Y. Crawford. Powell's Valley, W. R. Long. Tazewell, J. M. Kelly. Sneedsville, J. T. Smith. Clinch Mission, J. C. Hyden.

KNOXVILLE DISTRICT—*James Atkins, P. E.* Knoxville, C. W. Charlton. Knoxville Circuit, R. W. Patty. Clinton, J. N. S. Huffaker. Jacksborough Circuit and Strait Fork Mission, J. R. Bellamy. Maryville, T. K. Munsey. Little River, J. G. Swisher. Sevierville, N. C. Edmonson. Dandridge, R. M. Hickey. Knoxville and Muddy Creek Colored Mission, J. Cumming.

Samuel Patton, Editor Methodist Episcopalian.

D. R. M'Anally, President of E. T. Female Institute.

CUMBERLAND DISTRICT—*R. M. Stevens, P. E.* Kingston, W. H. Bates. Washington, C. Godby. Jasper, J. M. McTeer. Pikeville, J. A. Ragan. Montgomery Mission, W. J. Witcher. Jamestown, to be supplied. Cumberland Mission, J. M. Varnell. Spencer Mission, to be supplied.

ATHENS DISTRICT—*D. Fleming, P. E.* Athens, J. C. Pendergrast, J. W. Miller. Philadelphia, E. E. Gillenwaters. Decatur, L. W. Crouch. Chattanooga, M. C. Robinson. Hiwassee, R. L. Giddens. Cleveland, W. C. Daily, W. F. Parker. Benton, G. W. Renfro. Madisonville and Tellico Mission, to be supplied.

ASHEVILLE DISTRICT—*W. Hicks, P. E.* Asheville, W. M. Kerr. Asheville Circuit, W. H. Rogers. Burnsville, H. Wilson. Hendersonville, F. M. Fanning. Catawba, U.

Keener. Franklin, A. F. Shannon. Waynesville, A. G. Worley. Echota Mission, A. Hunter.

T. Stringfield, Bible Agent.

W. C. Graves, Sunday School Agent.

E. F. Sevier, T. Sullens, L. Wilson, J. H. Peck, left without an appointment, on account of ill health.

S. B. Harwell, permitted to rest.

TWENTY-SEVENTH SESSION.

Held at Abingdon, Va., October 2, 1850 — Bishop Capers, President; D. R. M'Anally, Secretary.

Numbers in Society — Whites, 35,882; colored, 3,542; Indians, 140.

Traveling Preachers, 95.

ADMITTED ON TRIAL—J. D. Baldwin, J. Cox, D. P. Hunt, R. N. Price, D. Sullens, E. Wexler, L. C. White.

ADMITTED INTO FULL CONNECTION—W, H. Kelly, A. G. Worley.

LOCATED—P. Anderson, W. T. Dowell, M. C. Robinson, R. D. Wells. R. M. Whaley.

STATIONS OF THE PREACHERS.

WYTHEVILLE DISTRICT—*W. B. Winton, P. E.* Wytheville Circuit, C. Long, E. W. Chanceaulme. Newbern, George W. Renfro. Parisburg, C. W. Charlton. Princeton Circuit and New River Mission, L. C. Waters; one to be supplied. Hillsville, R. W. Pickens. Grayson, E. W. King. Jefferson, W. H. Kelly.

ABINGDON DISTRICT—*T. K. Catlett, P. E.* Abingdon, W. G. E. Cunnyngham. Abingdon Circuit, John M. Crismond Lebanon, George K. Snapp. Jeffersonville, L. W. Crouch.

Sandy River Mission, D. P. Hunt. Johnson Circuit, W. R. Long. Watauga Mission, to be supplied. Blountville, George Ekin, W. W. Neal. Marion, Miles Foy, W. Jones.

Emory and Henry College, C. Collins, President; E. E. Wiley, Professor.

GREENVILLE DISTRICT—*T. Stringfield, P. E.* Greenville Circuit, W. C. Graves. Jonesborough, W. Robeson. Jonesborough Circuit, W. M. Kerr. Elizabethton, A. G. Worley. Rheatown, D. B. Carter. New Market, R. W. Patty. Newport, John Cox.

ROGERSVILLE DISTRICT—*J. Haskew, P. E.* Rogersville, W. Ingle. Estelville, W. Milburn. Guess' River Mission, W. F. Parker. Kingsport, R. M. Hickey. Jonesville, A. Williams. Powell's Valley, to be supplied. Tazewell, J. M. Kelly. Pattonsville, L. C. White. Clinch Mission, J. D. Baldwin.

KNOXVILLE DISTRICT—*J. Atkins, P. E.* Knoxville, T. Sullens. Knox Circuit, J. H. Bruner. Muddy Creek, A. F. Shannon. Clinton, J. R. Bellamy. Jacksborough, E. E. Gillenwaters. Huntsville Mission, to be supplied. Maryville, W. H. Rogers. Little River, J. G. Swisher. Sevierville, H. Wilson. Dandridge, W. H. Bates.

C. Fulton, President of Strawberry Plains High School.

D. R. M'Anally, President of East Tennessee Female Institute, and will assist Brother Sullens.

E. F. Sevier, left without an appointment, on account of ill health.

CUMBERLAND DISTRICT—*R. M. Stevens, P. E.* Kingston, J. M. McTeer. Washington, J. N. S. Huffaker. Jasper, N. C. Edmonson. Pikeville, W. J. Witcher. Montgomery Mission, J. C. Hyden. Jamestown Mission, to be supplied. Cumberland, J. T. Smith. Spencer Mission, H. Tartar.

S. B. Harwell, left without an appointment, on account of ill health.

ATHENS DISTRICT—*D. Fleming, P. E.* Athens, J. W.

Miller. Philadelphia, C. Godby. Decatur, R. A. Giddens.
Chattanooga, J. C. Pendergrast. Cleveland, W. C. Daily.
Charleston, A. F. Cox. Benton Circuit and Ocoee Mission,
W. W. Haymes. Madisonville and Tellico Mission, A. M.
Goodykoontz, J. M. Varnell.

A. C. Hunter, left without an appointment, on account of
ill health.

ASHEVILLE DISTRICT—*W. Hicks, P. E.*, and Superintendent
of Indian Mission. Asheville, G. W. Alexander. Asheville
Circuit, J. A. Ragan, R. N. Price. Burnsville, D. Sullens.
Hendersonville, F. M. Fanning. Catawba, J. S. Edwards.
Franklin, R. A. Claughton. Waynesville, E. Wexler; one to
be supplied. Indian Mission, U. Keener.

TWENTY-EIGHTH SESSION.

*Held at Athens, Tenn., October 1, 1851—Bishop Andrew,
President; D. R. M'Anally, Secretary.*

Numbers in Society — Whites, 37,129; colored, 3,817;
Indians, 151.

Traveling Preachers, 93.

ADMITTED ON TRIAL—George Stewart, W. W. Smith, John
Boring, G. W. Roark, R. H. Guthrie, S. Phillips, Ch.
Mitchell, W. Boring, E. Rowley, J. R. Long.

ADMITTED INTO FULL CONNECTION—W. F. Parker, J. M.
Varnell, E. W. King, W. J. Witcher, W. C. Edmonson, R.
A. Giddens, J. C. Hyden.

LOCATED—W. H. Kelly, A. C. Hunter, W. Jones, M. Foy.

STATIONS OF THE PREACHERS.

WYTHEVILLE DISTRICT—*W. B. Winton, P. E.* Wytheville
Circuit, W. M. Kerr. Newbern, C. Long. Parisburg, G.
Stewart; one to be supplied. Princeton and Flat Top Mission,

J. S. Edwards. Hillsville, W. J. Witcher. Grayson, L. W. Crouch. Jefferson, L. C. Waters. Marion, W. F. Parker.

ABINGDON DISTRICT—*J. Haskew, P. E.* Abingdon, R. M. Hickey. Abingdon Circuit, W. Robeson. Saltville, to be supplied. Jeffersonville, E. Wexler. Lebanon, W. Boring. Blountville, D. B. Carter. Taylorsville, J. T. Smith. Watauga Mission, to be supplied. Sandy River Mission, C. Mitchell.

Emory and Henry College, Charles Collins, President; E. E. Wiley, Professor; C. Fulton, Agent.

GREENVILLE DISTRICT—*E. F. Scvier, P. E.* Greenville, W. C. Graves. Jonesborough, E. E. Gillenwaters. Jonesborough Circuit, G. W. Alexander. Elizabethton, J. McTeer. Rheatown, F. M. Fanning. Russellville, R. W. Patty. Newport, John Cox.

ROGERSVILLE DISTRICT—*T. K. Catlett, P. E.* Rogersville, J. M. Crismond. Estelville, W. Milburn. Guess' River, H. Wilson. Kingsport, W. Ingle. Jonesville, J. D. Baldwin. Powell's Valley, G. K. Snapp. Tazewell, C. Godby. Pattonville, W. W. Smith. Clinch, L. C. White.

KNOXVILLE DISTRICT—*J. Atkins, P. E.* Knoxville, J. C. Pendergrast. Knox Circuit, T. Stringfield. Dandridge, J. H. Bruner. Maryville, W. H. Rogers. Little River, A. Gass. Sevierville, J. M. Varnell. Muddy Creek, A. G. Worley. Clinton, A. F. Cox. Jacksborough, A. F. Shannon. Huntsville Mission, H. Tartar.

Samuel Patton, Editor of the Holston Christian Advocate. Strawberry Plains High School, C. D. Smith, Agent.

CUMBERLAND DISTRICT—*R. M. Stevens, P. E.* Kingston, A. Williams. Washington, J. B. Lawson. Pikeville, J. N. S. Huffaker. Jasper, W. C. Edmonson. Spencer, G. W. Roark. Cumberland Mission, D. Hunt. Jamestown Mission, John Boring. Montgomery Mission, to be supplied.

ATHENS DISTRICT—*D. Fleming, P. E.* Athens, W. C. Daily. Cleveland, A. M. Goodykoontz. Charleston, R. A.

Giddens. Chattanooga, W. H. Bates. Harrison, R. Guthrie, Philadelphia, J. G. Swisher. Madisonville, W. W. Neal. Decatur, to be supplied. Benton Circuit and Ocoee, E. W. King. Tellico Mission, to be supplied.

ASHEVILLE DISTRICT— *W. Hicks, P. E.* Asheville, D. Sullens. Asheville Circuit, G. W. Renfro. Hendersonville, E. W. Chanceanlme. Catawba, S. Phillips. Burnsville, R. N. Price. Waynesville, J. C. Hyden. Franklin, J. A. Ragan. Marshall Mission, to be supplied. Echota Mission, U. Keener, J. R. Long.

E. Rowley, President of Western Carolina Female College.

W. G. E. Cunnyngham, Missionary to China.

D. R. M'Anally, transferred to St. Louis Conference, and appointed Editor of St. Louis Christian Advocate.

J. R. Bellamy, transferred to Eastern Texas Conference.

George Ekin, R. W. Pickens, T. Sullens, S. B. Harwell, J. M. Kelly, left without appointments, in consequence of feeble health.

TWENTY-NINTH SESSION.

Held at Asheville, N. C., September 29, 1852—*Bishop Capers, President; C. D. Smith and G. W. Alexander, Secretaries.*

Numbers in Society—Whites, 37,962 ; colored, 3,881 ; Indians, 176.

Traveling Preachers, 97.

ADMITTED ON TRIAL—W. Ballinger, J. W. Belt, J. R. Burchfield, O. B. Callahan, R. K. Coen, John W. Dickey, A. C. Ely, J. H. Green, John D. F. Jennings, J. B. Little, J. Reed, George H. Wells, H. West, B. F. White.

ADMITTED INTO FULL CONNECTION—J. D. Baldwin, D. P. Hunt, R. N. Price, D. Sullens, E. Wexler.

LOCATED—C. Collins, C. Fulton, S. B. Harwell, J. B. Lawson, W. R. Long, G. K. Snapp.

STATIONS OF THE PREACHERS.

WYTHEVILLE DISTRICT—*G. W. Alexander, P. E.* Wytheville Circuit, W. M. Kerr, J. R. Burchfield. Newbern, C. Long. Parisburg, J. S. Edwards, R. M. Coen. Princeton Circuit and Flat Top Mission, C. Mitchell. Jeffersonville, George Stewart, Sandy River Mission, to be supplied. Hillsville, G. W. Roark. Grayson, J. B. Little. Jefferson, L. C. Waters. Marion, A. Williams.

ABINGDON DISTRICT—*J. Haskew, P. E.* Abingdon, J. N. S. Huffaker. Abingdon Circuit, W. Robeson. Saltville, J. D. F. Jennings. Lebanon, J. M. Crismond. Estelville, A. G. Worley. Guess' River, J. M. Varnell. Blountville, D. B. Carter, J. W. Belt. Elizabethton, W. Ingle. Taylorsville, W. W. Smith. Watauga Mission, to be supplied.

E. E. Wiley, appointed to Henry and Emory College.

ROGERSVILLE DISTRICT—*T. K. Catlett, P. E.* Rogersville Circuit, W. C. Graves. Rogersville, W. H. Bates. Kingsport, C. Campbell. Jonesville, W. Boring. Tazewell, J. M. Kelly. Tazewell Circuit, J. D. Baldwin. Sneedsville, O. B. Callahan; one to be supplied. Morristown, A. F. Cox, J. H. Green. Greenville, W. Milburn, W. Ballinger. Rheatown, F. M. Fanning, A. C. Ely. Jonesborough, D. Sullens. Jonesborough Circuit, J. McTeer, G. H. Wells.

KNOXVILLE DISTRICT—*J. Atkins, P. E.* Knoxville, E. E. Gillenwaters, C. D. Smith, sup. Knox Circuit, George Ekin. Dandridge, R. W. Patty. Newport, J. H. Bruner. Sevierville, J. T. Smith. Little River Circuit and Smoky Mountain Mission, W. T. Dowell. Maryville, W. W. Neal. Muddy Creek, W. H. Rogers. Clinton, A. Gass. Jacksborough Circuit and Huntsville Mission, L. W. Crouch, A. F. Shannon.

Samuel Patton, Editor of Holston Christian Advocate.

T. Stringfield, Agent for Strawberry Plains High School.

CUMBERLAND DISTRICT—*R. M. Stevens, P. E.* Kingston, C. Godby. Washington, W. J. Witcher. Pikeville, J. Boring. Jasper, R. N. Price. Spencer Mission, J. Reed. Cumberland Mission, to be supplied. Jamestown Mission, D. P. Hunt. Montgomery Mission, H. West.

ATHENS DISTRICT—*D. Fleming, P. E.* Athens, W. C. Daily. Cleveland, A. M. Goodykoontz. Charleston, R. H. Guthrie. Chattanooga, R. M. Hickey. Harrison, to be supplied. Philadelphia, J. G. Swisher. Madisonville, G. W. Renfro. Decatur, E. W. King. Benton Circuit and Ocoee Mission, R. A. Giddens. Tellico Mission, John W. Dickey.

T. Sullens, Agent for Sunday Schools.

ASHEVILLE DISTRICT—*W. Hicks, P. E.* Asheville, E. W. Chanceaulme. Asheville Circuit, W. F. Parker; one to be supplied. Hendersonville, E. C. Wexler, H. Tartar. Catawba, W. H. Kelly. Burnsville, S. Phillips. Waynesville, B. H. White. Tuccaseige, J. R. Long. Franklin, J. C. Hyden. Marshall Mission, to be supplied. Echota Indian Mission, U. Keener.

J. A. Ragan, Agent for Holston Conference Female College, at Asheville, N. C.

J. C. Pendergrast, transferred to the Pacific Conference.

THIRTIETH SESSION.

Held at Wytheville, Va., October 12, 1853—Bishop Paine, President; W. C. Graves, Secretary.

Numbers in Society — Whites, 38,573; colored, 3,885; Indians, 187.

Traveling Preachers, 99.

ADMITTED ON TRIAL—G. Taylor, W. H. Keene, P. Reed, J. A. Williamson, R. Washburn, H. A. Guthrie, M. P. Swain, T. M. Dula, W. K. Foster, W. K. Cross.

ADMITTED INTO FULL CONNECTION—John Boring, W. Boring, R. H. Guthrie, J. R. Long, C. Mitchell, S. Phillips.

LOCATED—E. W. Chanceaulme, J. A. Ragan.

STATIONS OF THE PREACHERS.

WYTHEVILLE DISTRICT—*G. W. Alexander, P. E.* Wytheville Circuit, F. M. Fanning ; one to be supplied. Newbern, A. G. Worley. Parisburg, W. H. Kelly. Princeton, W. K. Foster. Jeffersonville, A. F. Cox. Sandy River Mission, to be supplied. Hillsville, J. W. Williamson. Grayson, J. S. Edwards. Jefferson, C. Mitchell. Marion, C. Long.

ABINGDON DISTRICT—*J. Haskew, P. E.* Abingdon Station, E. C. Wexler. Abingdon Circuit, J. M. McTeer. Saltville, J. W. Dickey. Lebanon, A. F. Shannon. Estelville, S. Phillips. Guestville, James W. Belt. Blountville, W. Robeson. Elizabethton, W. Ingle. Taylorsville, W. K. Cross. Watauga, W. W. Smith.

Emory and Henry College, E. E. Wiley, President.

ROGERSVILLE DISTRICT—*W. Hicks, P. E.* Rogersville Station, R. M. Hickey. Rogersville Circuit, W. C. Graves. Kingsport, D. B. Carter. Jonesville, to be supplied. Tazewell Station, R. N. Price, W. Ballinger. Sneedville, D. P. Hunt. Morristown, to be supplied. Greenville, W. Milburn ; one to be supplied. Rheatown, W. Boring. Jonesborough, C. Campbell. Jonesborough Circuit, J. M. Crismond ; one to be supplied.

KNOXVILLE DISTRICT—*T. K. Catlett, P. E.* Knoxville Station, W. M. Kerr. East Knoxville, J. N. S. Huffaker. Knox Circuit, W. F. Parker, G. Taylor. Dandridge Station, E. W. King. Dandridge Circuit, A. Gass. Newport, L. C. Waters. Sevierville, W. H. Keene. Little River, W. T. Dowell. Maryville, W. W. Neal ; one to be supplied. Clinton, J. H. Green. Jacksborough, J. B. Little. Huntsville Mission, J. Reed.

S. Patton, Editor of the Holston Christian Advocate.

D. Sullens, Strawberry Plains College.

CUMBERLAND DISTRICT—*D. Fleming, P. E.* Kingston Circuit, J. Boring. Washington, W. H. Guthrie. Pikeville, B. F. White. Jasper, J. R. Long. Spencer Mission, H. West. Cumberland Mission, O. B. Callahan. Jamestown Mission, H. A. Guthrie. Montgomery Mission, R. K. Coen.

ATHENS DISTRICT—*T. K. Munsey, P. E.* Athens Station, W. Witcher. Athens Circuit, A. M. Goodykoontz. Cleveland, W. C. Daily. Charleston, to be supplied. Chattanooga, W. H. Bates. Harrison, to be supplied. Philadelphia, W. H. Rogers. Loudon Station, C. Godby. Madisonville, J. G. Swisher. Decatur, P. Reed. Benton Circuit and Ocoee Mission, J. Burchfield. Tellico Mission, T. M. Dula.

J. H. Bruner, Hiwassee College.

ASHEVILLE DISTRICT—*R. W. Patty, P. E.* Asheville Station, E. E. Gillenwaters, and Agent for Holston Conference Female College. Asheville Circuit, J. D. Baldwin, M. P. Swain. Hendersonville, J. D. F. Jennings. Catawba, J. C. Hyden. Burnsville, L. W. Crouch. Waynesville, J. M. Varnell. Webster, R. Washburn. Franklin, J. T. Smith. Echota Indian Mission, U. Keener.

W. G. E. Cunnyngham, Missionary to China.

T. Sullens, Agent for Emory and Henry College

J. Atkins, Agent for American Bible Society.

A. Williams, transferred to St. Louis Conference.

George Roark, left without an appointment.

INDEX

www.ingramcontent.com/pod-product-compliance
Lightning Source LLC
Chambersburg PA
CBHW071831270326
41929CB00013B/1956